RECLAIMING THE URBAN FAMILY

Dr. Willie Richardson

RECLAIMING THE URBAN FAMILY

How to Mobilize the Church as a Family Training Center

ZondervanPublishingHouse
Grand Rapids, Michigan

A Division of HarperCollinsPublishers

Reclaiming the Urban Family
Copyright © 1996 by Willie Richardson

Requests for information should be addressed to:

ZondervanPublishingHouse
Grand Rapids, Michigan 49530

Library of Congress Cataloging-in-Publication Data

Richardson, Willie, 1939–
    Reclaiming the urban family : how to mobilize the church as a family training
center / Willie Richardson.
       p.   cm.
    Includes bibliographical references.
    ISBN: 0-310-20008-3 (softcover)
    1. Church work with families. 2. Family. 3. Marriage. I. Title.
BV4438.R53 1996
259'.1—dc20   95-40708
                                                      CIP

Edited by Gerard H. Terpstra
Interior design by Sue Koppenol

Printed in the United States of America

02 /❖ DH/ 10

To my wife, Patricia, and our children,
who allowed me, with loving support,
to spend many hours in my "cave"
to write this book

CONTENTS

ACKNOWLEDGMENTS

I am especially grateful to the following people:

Stanley Gundry for consistently prompting me over the years to write for Zondervan Publishing House.

Ed van der Maas, senior editor, for his patience with me in my underestimating how long it would take to complete this project.

Anita L. Patterson and Tracey M. Claxton, my secretaries, who not only typed the manuscript and corrected errors but also coordinated my schedule and assisted me administratively so I could write and pastor the church at the same time.

Deandrea L. Ford and Carol L. Hughes for serving as researchers.

Bill Krispin and Roxann Covington, who critiqued this book and made suggestions for clarifying its ministry.

Sheila R. Staley and the pastors of Resources for Better Families, who are co-laborers with me in church family ministry.

Dr. Lee June and Matt Parker for their continual encouragement to me as a writer.

The leaders and congregation of Christian Stronghold Baptist Church for their prayers and support.

INTRODUCTION

The great challenge of the church today is to save families. In some cases, although we have been effective in the soul-saving of families, the families were destroyed because they did not know how to be a Christian family. As pastors, we have to lead our churches and mobilize our congregations to get involved in saving and building families. This book is divided into four parts so that we can take a look at ways to establish or improve ministry to families and make the church a training center for outreach, prevention, enrichment, and problem solving.

PART 1: THE SPIRITUAL CHALLENGE

Only Christ-centered families can enjoy and be fulfilled by God's biblical direction for the home. Living out salvation at home is essential. The manifestation of the Holy Spirit must be apparent in the life of every member of a family. The pastor's family is looked at as a model family, though such families do not like the role. If nothing else, except out of self-defense, we pastors must learn how to be better spouses and parents.

PART 2: THE TRAINING OF SINGLE CHRISTIANS

I am totally convinced that what happens during the life of a single adult and during courtship has more to do with the success of a marriage than what happens after people take marriage vows. The lifestyle of a single Christian must be understood and pursued over against an unconverted nonbeliever's single lifestyle. Courtship must be guided by biblical principles rather than by passion alone. Selecting a lifelong partner should be done with unrushed deliberation, and not just on the basis of physical love and at the speed of fast food.

PART 3: TRAINING FAMILIES FINANCIALLY

Part of the preparation for marriage is reaching financial stability before marriage. How single people will make it financially after marriage should not be a guess or taken for granted, for some marriages dissolve quickly, simply over financial problems.

There are a great number of married people with financial problems. Many of these problems can be resolved with training and knowledge. Every Christian needs to learn not only that money is a resource, but also that we as creatures of God are a resource. God has given us gifts, and we have acquired some abilities that can be transferred into income.

PART 4: TRAINING IN FAMILY RELATIONSHIPS

We can help single-parent families have stable Christian homes that produce children who are reared with the goal to establish two-parent households for themselves. A deeper commitment must be made by married people to stay together in marriage "for better or for worse." The knowledge of God's biblical roles for husbands, wives, and children strengthens a family and cuts down on the confusion that plagues many of today's families. We have to train couples in communication and understanding. This deepens the love between them. Training couples in problem solving cuts down on a pastor's workload. As churches learn to be family training centers, communities will know where to turn for help, because they will see the results in the church families—families that are filled with the love of Christ.

APPENDICES: RESOURCES FOR FAMILY MINISTRY

The last section of the book is a resource guide to people and organizations that will be helpful in formulating family ministry.

Part 1

THE SPIRITUAL CHALLENGE

Chapter 1

THE NEED OF SALVATION IN THE FAMILY

REAL CHRISTIAN FAMILIES

This country is simply spinning its wheels in the mud of futility because we are excluding the God of the Bible from issues of morality and family. I believe that too often even the church does not take seriously the great ally we have in God concerning family matters. God created and defines the family by what He instituted. First, He instituted marriage when He created Adam and Eve, then He completed the family when He did not create Cain and Abel, but instead created within Adam and Eve the capacity to reproduce other human beings. The family unit consisted of the husband, the wife, and their offspring (Gen. 2:19–24; 4:1–2). Charles Sell explains the biblical view of the family:

> Biblical scholars tend to agree that the basic form of family created by God is the nuclear family, which gives the highest priority to the husband-wife relationship. Elements of Genesis 2:24 make it clear that a husband and wife's first loyalty are to each other and not to any extended family relationship. That the man is said to leave his father and mother to be united to his wife suggests he replaces one commitment with another. The fact that husband and wife become one flesh supports the priority of the nuclear pair. That Adam says of his

wife, "This is now bone of my bones and flesh of my flesh" is especially significant. The Hebrew words for bone and flesh are frequently used to describe extended family relationships (Genesis 29:14; Judges 9:2; 2 Samuel 5:1; 2 Samuel 19:12–13; 1 Chronicles 11:1). That the same terms are used to describe both the marriage (conjugal) relationship and blood (consanguineous) relationships shows that blood ties are not superior to the marital union. It is true that in Old Testament times, for political and economic reasons whole groups of families joined together to make a unit. A major political unit, tribes, were made up of extended kin. Yet, the nuclear family identity was pronounced within these groupings and there is nothing to suggest that any extended family arrangement was part of God's creative order. This is especially significant for Christians in societies where non-Christian traditions dictate that the parent-adult child relationship should have priority over the husband-wife union. It also has crucial practical application to Christians whenever parents interfere or compete with their son's or daughter's marriage.[1]

America is a world power and a leader among affluent nations, yet it is full of hurting families. We are constantly reminded by television talk shows and social and behavioral scientists of the overwhelming number of dysfunctional families. Compared to pre-1972, there is the statistical fact of high divorce rates year after year.

In recent elections, some politicians have made the family a political issue. They cry that we must protect our family values, which are seen as continually eroding. There is even confusion and debate as to what constitutes a family. There is a direct correlation between the ever-decreasing age of children involved in violent crimes and their family situations.

What the world needs is more real Christian families. We have a great number of so-called Christian families, but the problem is that too many are not real Christian families.

Christ has no impact on these so-called Christian families. Many of the family members are not converted, regenerated, or born again. They can be church members, but often they are not saved. Too often we assume that because someone joins the church, he or she is or has become a Christian. We have had hundreds of people ready to join our church by Christian experience only to discover that although they had been baptized earlier in their lives, they do not know Christ as their personal Savior and Lord. I don't believe the church has been called to simply marry people, but to establish Christian homes. Without salvation in Christ, a person or a family is not truly Christian.

Why is there a need of salvation in the family? Without salvation, there is no spirituality. When people are saved, it means they are converted. They have been regenerated by God, the Holy Spirit. It is not enough to have a family as church members. All of them—the husband, the wife, and their children—must give their lives by faith to Jesus Christ. The church must not assume that they have done so; those in leadership must be sure that people are truly believers in Christ.

A couple came to me for counseling from another church in the city because they were having marital problems. In the first session, I asked them if they had received Jesus Christ as their personal Savior. They answered yes. They had been church members since they were children. I asked them to explain to me what receiving Jesus Christ as their personal Savior meant. I listened as they both expressed themselves. They said all the right things, but I still had doubts because the church to which they belonged did not have a reputation of having sound doctrine. Nevertheless, I agreed to counsel them because they had their pastor's permission to come to me. In the first few counseling sessions, we sorted through and defined what the problems were and agreed on some assignments for both of them based on God's role for husbands and wives as revealed in the Bible. It was clear after a few attempts that they could not carry out the assignments. I honestly believe they wanted to do what the Bible said, but they did not have the power. I pointed this out to them, using 1 Corinthians 2:6–16 and Ephesians 2:1–10. Then step by step I showed them the plan of salvation in the Bible. I asked them if they were willing to pray a prayer of salvation, receiving Jesus into their hearts as Lord and Savior. They said yes, and I led them in prayer. At the end of the prayer, they both began to cry vehemently and fell into each other's arms and continued to cry. After a few minutes, they regained their composure. From that session on, it was clear that this couple had been converted. The Holy Spirit empowered them to live the Christian life.

WITHOUT SALVATION THERE IS NO SPIRITUALITY

When people are not saved, at best they have a limited human love that is self-focused, self-seeking, and selfish. It is the kind of love that goes into a marriage with expectations that the spouse should meet their every need with little consideration for the other person's needs. It is a love that is based on selfish fantasy. Human love in marriage is motivated by the question "What am I getting out of this?" It is a love that loses its motivation when love is not returned according to a person's selfish desires.

RECLAIMING THE URBAN FAMILY

Time and time again I have heard married people say, "I want a divorce. I fell in love, but I no longer love my spouse." The cue here is that they "fell in love." Their love was based on emotionalism rather than commitment. Many young men and older men during mid-life have said to their wives, "I don't want to be married anymore," and they leave their wives and children. Wives have taken a lover because, they say, he meets their emotional needs. These situations I have described here are of professing Christians!

When people don't have salvation in Jesus Christ, they lead godless lives controlled by a sin nature. It does not make any difference how often they attend church because the only experience is a religious experience. When there is godlessness, there is no real Christian character, for to be a Christian is to be Christlike. You can't be Christlike if you do not have Christ. Their lives are controlled by a sin nature that gives way to indulging in evil desires, being insensitive, and being separated from the life of God (Eph. 4:17–19).

The Bible has very clear directions for the family, but unconverted church members can hear the Word of God but have no authority of God's will in their life. God's will for a wife means nothing. God's will for a husband means nothing. There is no motivation to obey the Word of God.

The minute a person receives Jesus Christ, we must help him or her to grow spiritually. We cannot leave new converts on their own. They still have a distorted view of what is right and wrong. They used to walk according to the course of this world, and they may still believe that their personal individual rights are the priority of life. That's why you can hear a Christian husband say, "This is the money I have earned" to his home-making wife. A Christian wife may say, "I cannot stay home from work and be with my young children. I don't want to ask my husband for anything. I want my own money." These people must become spiritual. They must think biblically. These people need God's wisdom.

Some families are full of trouble because they are devoid of wisdom. Bad decision after bad decision is made based on the wisdom of the world. Some would rather separate or get a divorce than get help to work through their marital problems. They do not understand biblical forgiveness.

SPIRITUAL GROWTH IS ESSENTIAL FOR DEVELOPING A CHRISTIAN FAMILY

When a person accepts Christ as Lord and Savior and is converted, there is a radical change in his or her life. The movement and speed of this change depends on the church's ministry and the convert's commitment

18

to that ministry. A new convert who is committed is teachable and eager to learn. Jesus is his life—his reason for living. Christ is the one he lives to please—no longer himself. He wants to know God's will for his life as revealed in the Bible. God's Word is the authority in his life for Christian living. The committed person is continually growing and becoming more Christlike. The fruit of the Spirit can be seen in his life (Gal. 5:22–25).

The person who is converted and growing spiritually has a capacity to love that is similar to the way God loves. God's love practiced in the family is what makes a wholesome family. Behavioral scientists tell us that people who experience love are healthier than people who do not. It is just as important to love as it is to be loved. A spiritual person is a loving person.

A spiritual person can forgive in much the same way as God does. Without God's willingness to forgive us, we cannot remain in fellowship with Him. So it is in a marriage. If husbands and wives refuse to forgive each other, they cannot stay in fellowship. They cannot be friends. They cannot grow into a deep, mature companionship.

If married people can grow in God's love (agape love, unconditional love for one another), nothing can break up that marriage. Not only will there be permanency in the marriage, but it will also be a fulfilling and joyous marriage. God is the very essence of love. Those born of God have His love in their bosom. We must help them grow spiritually to reach their love potential in Christ.

THE GOAL OF SPIRITUAL GROWTH

The goal of spiritual growth is to be like Jesus Christ. "The man who says, 'I know him,' but does not do what he commands is a liar, and the truth is not in him. But if anyone obeys his word, God's love is truly made complete in him. This is how we know we are in him. Whoever claims to live in him must walk as Jesus did" (1 John 2:4–6). This is not asking too much. We are not simply speaking of church members, but people who have received salvation in Christ, people who are indwelt by God, the Holy Spirit, who have the mind of Christ and have the very nature of Christ. They have the potential to "grow up in Christ."

We want to help Christians develop the fruit of the Spirit in their lives. The fruit of the Spirit is a description of Jesus Christ and is essential in a marriage and family that will honor and glorify God. The fruit of the Spirit can be measured in a Christian family. We can know if we are making progress. The nine parts of the fruit of the Spirit can be seen in action in a spiritual Christian family.

Love

Love is what motivates the expression of the other parts of the fruit of the Spirit, as seen in 1 Corinthians 13. Love is seen when a man who is frustrated with his wife or with life does not physically abuse her or their children. He can never justify hitting her, even if she gets angry and frustrated and hits him. Love will cause him to restrain her by holding her, not beating her. The love of God causes a man to be a man, not an uncontrollable abuser misguiding his sons by his model as a husband.

Love will cause a woman not to be rude or disrespectful regardless of the time of month, pregnancy, or change of life. She will know that such behavior does not honor or edify the man she loves. A woman who has a disrespectful attitude toward her husband is not a good example for her daughters.

Love will cause sisters and brothers growing up together to stand with one another, minimizing sibling rivalry or nullifying it altogether. These children will protect and be loyal to each other.

God's love in a family prepares and matures children for marriage because they see a model of not being selfish or self-seeking and not keeping a record of wrong done against them when they see how Mom and Dad forgive each other, demanding they do the same.

Joy

Married couples need to learn to accept the fact that it is not possible for their mate to keep them happy, for joy comes from within, out of the indwelling Spirit. Learning this will rid us of a tremendous amount of pressure and unachievable expectations. Too many people come to marriage believing that a mate can make up for the misery they experienced both in growing up and in leading a dissatisfying single life. Joy comes from God. Only saved people have this joy. This is another reason that salvation is needed in a family.

God's joy will give you a sense of humor. My wife has made the statement that she married a serious man who later turned into a comedian. The truth of the matter is that I received Christ the year before we were married. Before this time, I knew nothing but misery. My mom and dad had divorced after having seven children. I grew up in North Philadelphia in poverty. At night we fought cat-sized sewer rats in our kitchen and bedroom with broom handles or a length of pipe, too afraid to go to sleep. I had to fight my way to school and back home again because of gang activity in my neighborhood. I was more terrorized by brutal policemen who assumed every young African-American male was a criminal. This kind of lifestyle does not lend itself to developing a sense of humor. I used to practice in front of a mirror how to look mean so I could survive. I had a terrible self-image and no confidence.

I immediately experienced the joy of the Spirit when I received Christ. I enjoy being a Christian. God has helped me to laugh at myself and accept my limits and mistakes.

The joy of the Lord causes families to have fun together—to laugh and play together. This joy causes children to grow up with warm memories of their past. Marriage and family are too serious without the joy of the Lord.

Peace

Many fights that take place between husbands and wives happen because the individual is not experiencing peace from within. There is personal turmoil going on, and it spills out onto other innocent family members. Sometimes this is true because the husband, the wife, or the children are not saved. However, if we as Christians have unconfessed sin in our lives, that too will kill our peace within. Harboring bitterness over disappointment in a mate can be destructive and counterproductive to having a good Christian marriage.

When we receive Christ as Lord and Savior, we receive His peace and peace with God. The family should be experiencing peace because of God's peace in us, generated by the Holy Spirit. Family members must be taught and trained to be active peacemakers in the home.

Patience

Without patience, marriage can never be developed into what God wants it to be. Christian parents can never come close to emulating their heavenly Father by parenting their children without patience. It is common to hear the news media report the death of an infant caused by a parent who had lost patience because the baby wouldn't stop crying. That parent lacked patience.

Some husbands withdraw from their wives because women are very different from men in certain ways. Those men do not have patience. Many wives have climbed a ladder or painted the house, taking on their husbands' responsibilities because they do not exercise patience. God would have taken our lives a long time ago except for His long-suffering with us. God knows what it takes to put up with us. So, by His Spirit He gives us the ability to be long-suffering with each other. The patience to suffer in a marriage is a supernatural skill that affords a marriage the time needed to grow, change, mature, and become a blessing.

Kindness

Over and over again I hear wives complaining that their husbands are not nice. Yet single women are tricked and fooled into marrying men who were nice during the courtship but turned into Attila the Hun after marriage. Husbands complain that their wives were so sweet during courtship but after marriage they constantly ride a witch's broom. The kindness that comes from God, the Holy Spirit, causes married people to be tolerant of each other. Kindness causes us to be tactful in correcting or discussing difficult matters with our mates. The kindness of the Spirit causes husbands to be nice and wives to be sweet.

Goodness

Goodness will cause married people to follow Jesus' example (1 Peter 2:23) when they have been insulted by their mate. Married people, exercising goodness, will not retaliate in kind, but entrust themselves to God who will judge justly. A good man will not yell at his wife, nor a good mother at her children. A Christian who practices goodness is a pleasant person whom family members love being around and can't wait to return home to see. A good person reaches out to meet the needs of family members without being asked. A Christian husband who practices goodness is not a rigid leader of his family but is flexible in considering the views and opinions of his family members. He puts himself in their place and tries to imagine what it would be like being under his leadership, which is imperfect and full of flaws.

Faithfulness

The church needs married people who are faithful to God and to one another. Many marriages of church members have ended as a result of unfaithfulness. Most married people have little idea what they committed to when they pledged their wedding vows. Part of the problem is that some of us pastors did not go over the vows with the couple before the wedding day, helping them to understand their meaning. Another problem is that too many married people do not practice their marriage faithfulness and commitment to God and their spouse.

The lack of faithfulness to God is proved by the fact that many married people do not exercise Christianity at home. We have a counseling center that ministers not only to our church members, but also to Christians and non-Christians throughout the Philadelphia area. Again and again, we have discovered Christian couples who sing together in their church choir, but are out of fellowship—not sleeping together, refusing a sexual relationship. Some Christians will gladly serve people at church but are not motivated to serve their own spouses.

A spiritual, growing Christian will be faithful to his or her spouse.

Gentleness

This part of the gift of the Spirit will enable a man to be a gentleman and a woman to be a lady. Gentleness yields a harvest of humility and sensitivity. Gentleness manifests itself in a considerate husband who will help his wife who works all day as a homemaker or is employed outside the home. He will help her with cooking, housekeeping, and caring for the children. Gentleness will cause a husband to care for his wife the way he cares for his own body.

Gentleness will cause a Christian wife to have a calming, peaceful influence over her husband as defined by the Greek words used for "a gentle and quiet spirit" in 1 Peter 3:4, causing him no disturbance.

Self-Control

A growing, spiritual Christian has self-control. Self-control enables a person to apply wisdom in difficult marital situations. We all have the problem of the flesh. Sometimes neither spouse is in the best of moods or dispositions. Irritability can be dominant at crucial times. As if this is not bad enough, the evil one, Satan, insinuates himself into a marriage and family, and we give the Devil a foothold in our homes. Self-control allows wisdom to tell us "this is not the time to say anything." Self-control will empower us to bind a bad temper and "take low"—humble ourselves, suffering injustice or ill treatment from a spouse temporarily and allowing for imperfections in a mate.

Self-control will enable a man to adjust to not having sex when his wife is tired, ill, emotionally out of it, or has her period. It is difficult to be submissive to God and others sometimes. Self-control will allow a wife to submit to her husband's leadership when she believes she is smarter, when she knows he is wrong and she is right. She will be able to trust and submit both to God and to her husband. She might be able to give a word of encouragement to her defeated husband when time later proves she was right and he was wrong.

I have used only two verses from the Bible to demonstrate the impact of spirituality on marriage and the family. Another way of defining being spiritual is Christlikeness. Christian husbands and wives need to be more Christlike in their relationships.

BOOKS FOR FURTHER KNOWLEDGE AND USE IN FAMILY MINISTRY

Blackaby, Henry T., and Claude V. King. *Experiencing God*. Nashville: Broadman & Holman, 1994.

Bridges, Jerry. *The Pursuit of Holiness*. Colorado Springs: NavPress, 1978.

Crabb, Larry. *Finding God*. Grand Rapids: Zondervan, 1993.

Eims, Leroy. *The Basic Ingredients for Spiritual Growth*. Wheaton: Victor, 1992.

Loritts, Crawford W. *A Passionate Commitment*. San Bernardino: Here's Life, 1989.

Chapter 2

THE CHURCH AS A FAMILY TRAINING CENTER

What institution will come forward and have a positive impact on families and their problems? Some of our lawmakers have attempted to address the problem by enacting legislation designed to penalize parents of delinquent children with fines and jail sentences. It was thought that this would cause parents to hold their children more accountable. Some teenagers have been tried in our courts as adults to demonstrate society's outrage against the crimes they have committed; however, it does not appear that these are effective deterrents for our wayward youth.

Who are the people who will come forward and have a positive impact on families and their problems? Family counselors, psychologists, psychiatrists, therapists, and divorce lawyers are professionals who often get involved after the damage has been done—after hatred and bitterness have solidified. Sometimes they can help, but too often they cannot.

I am sorry to say that most of the time, we as pastors get involved long after the problem has begun. How many times have we received a phone call from a distraught wife, husband, or child wanting to see us right away because they "can't go on like this any longer"? Because they have heard our sermons about faith in God and His miraculous powers, they expect us to transform their chaotic family life with merely a prayer or two pastoral counseling sessions. It is not fair to expect any professional to deal quickly with some of the problems that have continued from one generation to the next, dominated by ignorance, family trauma, frustration, and, most of all, lack of direction.

THE CHURCH SHOULD BE A FAMILY TRAINING CENTER

The Bible says, "Unless the LORD builds the house, its builders labor in vain" (Ps. 127:1). Some Christians and non-Christians have tried to build their families without God. The shame of this is that many young Christians get married with the idea that marrying another Christian will automatically bring marital bliss. They are told to be sure they are not "unequally yoked with unbelievers" (2 Cor. 6:14). While this is good instruction, couples must investigate each other further. Some couples are surprised to find that after six months of marriage to a seemingly "spiritual" person, their marriage is in deep trouble.

The church should be a family training center. Most people do not know how to let God build their family. They don't know how to include God in their family as the third partner of a marriage. There are many reasons why the church should and can be a family training center. I will give just a few:

1. The church represents God in the world. It is the visible demonstration of the living God.
2. God is the creator of marriage and family. Marriage was designed to glorify God and bless families. Man and the Devil invented divorce. God created the first couple and married them, and they stayed together until death. Divorce, the destructive force in a family, helps give birth to dysfunctional people.
3. The church has been commissioned to reach the world for Christ. The world is a place of spiritual wickedness where individuals and families are lost, groping in an attempt to find their way. The church, through Christ, offers not only eternal salvation, but also abundant life here on earth for families.
4. The church has received agape love (God's love) to dispense to others in need. The world does not know how to love with agape love because that kind of love is supernatural. Only those who are indwelt, empowered, and filled by God, the Holy Spirit, can produce the fruit of the Spirit. Every family needs to experience the mani-

festation of love, joy, peace, gentleness, patience, self-control, faithfulness, kindness, and goodness.

5. The body of Christ has been given gifts to edify its members and produce spiritual growth and maturity. Families need these spiritual strengths.

6. The church is the embassy that houses Christ's ambassadors, who must specialize in the ministry and the word of reconciliation. Just think how many divorced couples could have benefited from ambassadors skilled in conflict resolution.

7. The church is the light of the world—ever illuminating, ever advancing and showing the way. The church is salt in a rotten world. Thus, the church must show families the way and preserve them as it leads.

8. The church is involved with people from birth. Week after week, the news of a baby born into a family brings joy to other members of the church. We pray for the baby and mother during the time of pregnancy and minister to children and teenagers through such activities as the Sunday school and youth ministry. We have an opportunity to instill family values in children while they are growing up, instead of trying to accomplish it a few weeks before marriage.

THE FAMILY SHOULD NOT BE LEFT ON ITS OWN WITHOUT HELP

Why are married people left on their own to learn by trial and error, searching aimlessly to find marital fulfillment, when God has direction and instruction? Hasn't marriage been around long enough to profit from the church's ministries during this time of unprecedented technical genius and advancement?

Before becoming a pastor, I was a mechanical-design engineer. Our group worked on mathematical problems for days before we could draw one blueprint. Sometimes, after we were well into designing, we ran into difficult and complex problems that took ten determined people, sitting in a conference room for hours or days, to come up with an answer. These were very complex and difficult problems that, when resolved, would result in a product.

As a husband, father, pastor, and family counselor, dealing with marriages can be more complicated than anything I ever faced in engineering. I find myself doing the same thing at our weekly counselors' meetings that I did in engineering. Our senior counselors bring difficult cases to the table, and we do what is called "flattening the case out." This means we will not identify the counselees or give any information that might disclose their identity, such as place of employment or church affiliation. Sometimes they are members of the church that I pastor, but I cannot identify them when I hear the case. What we are attempting to do around the table is to come up with God-given answers to complex and difficult marital and family problems.

Modern-day living and new evils that accompany it make it much more difficult to have a stable family today. Preparation for the job market can change so radically that freshmen choose a promising field of work, but by the time they graduate four years later, jobs have dissipated because of new technology. Of course, it is even worse for those who have no formal training beyond high school to establish themselves financially for marriage.

In our urban areas, drugs have had a devastating effect on hundreds of families. Drugs have brought crime, sickness, fear, and death, sometimes causing family members to sleep with their valuables, fearing that another family member will steal them. Spouses or parents struggle with the agonizing decision of whether or not they should put a loved one out in the street. Such living conditions and tensions have led some family members to drinking in order to find relief.

This lack of communication and understanding among family members can be the unraveling of what may be thought to be a good relationship. There is an art of listening that is rarely considered important by a disgruntled spouse. The church has built great theological seminaries to see that its clergy have been trained in homiletics, in pastoring, and in congregational relationships in practical theology, yet the church seems to expect its married couples to know how to communicate with each other without any training, simply because they are Christians.

Why is the accountant failing in family finances? Why is the doctor failing at the healing process after fighting with his or her spouse? Why are the faucets at the plumber's house dripping and driving the spouse mad? Why is the judge who sits on the bench downtown unwilling to be reconciled with his or her spouse? Why are there so many grown children from affluent Christian families now bitter because they were given material things while growing up in a good church, but now feel deprived of parental love? Could there be spiritual reasons and solutions for these situations? The answer is yes, because the church specializes in spiritual understanding and can help hurting families.

HOW CAN THE CHURCH BECOME A FAMILY TRAINING CENTER?

We must reach single and married people who are in the world without Christ. I do not believe the answer for better marriages and families is *simply* leading a person to salvation in the Lord Jesus Christ. This has to be followed by discipleship. Discipleship goals should include helping a couple achieve a higher level of marital love, spirituality, and unity.

Without salvation in Christ, marriage can never be what God intended. As a matter of fact, we may discover, as we minister to professing Christian couples, that they have never really been converted. At this point, we can help a couple to move beyond a religious experience to a vibrant personal relationship with Jesus Christ. It takes three people to produce the kind of marriage God wants—a husband, a wife, and the Lord Jesus Christ.

If couples are genuine Christians, they have the basic foundation to build a marriage and family. Such couples repented of their sins and now have a heightened sensitivity to what is right and wrong. They have placed their faith in the Lord Jesus Christ and are on the road to learning how to live a Christ-centered rather than a self-centered life. They are now indwelt by the Holy Spirit and have the power to walk in obedience to God and His Word.

Reaching and Preparing Single People for Marriage

Single men, in particular, must be evangelized and brought into the church. There is a shortage of single men in too many of our churches. We must teach single women not to date or marry unsaved men. However, because single women generally outnumber men in most churches by very wide margins, their level of frustration about finding a husband is elevated.

Christian singles must be trained in order to know the differences between Christian courtship and the world's ideas on courtship, which most often are the beginnings of a failed marriage. Just because one has become a Christian doesn't mean one automatically knows what to do on a date. It may be noble to do the Christian thing by marrying because the woman has become pregnant, but it may be a disastrous decision for a lifelong commitment. Wouldn't it be better if the woman had not become pregnant in the first place? Pregnancy can be avoided by limiting the levels of intimacy and affection early in the relationship.

Engaged couples should go through extensive marriage training, not just a few weeks of premarital counseling. Some professionals attend colleges and universities for four, six, eight, and even ten years to become qualified for occupations that are less demanding than marriage. I am not advocating that engaged couples stay in training for years; however, it does take more than a few weeks if we are taking into consideration the preparation for setting up a home without going into deep debt, which is one of the top causes of the disintegration of marriages.

Certainly, premarital counseling is included in the training process. There must be an analytical examination of the strengths and weaknesses of the couple, resulting in a forecast of potential problems. These potential problems must be addressed in two ways:

First, plan how to resolve and overcome problems.

Second, if the problems look insurmountable, the couple should consider not getting married. It is better to break an engagement than to break up a marriage.

Single Parents

Single-parent families constitute over half of our African-American families and the number is continually growing in all ethnic groups. The majority of single-parent families are headed by women. However, because of the impact of drug addiction and the fact that some women are declaring their independence, even from their children, there is also an increase in single-parent homes headed by men.

There are unique problems plaguing single-parent homes, and some of these homes need more help than others. Where there is a strong Christian extended family, some of the issues are absorbed into the larger family system. There is a distinction between the poor unemployed mother and the working single parent. Where a strong extended family does not exist, the church must provide a single-parent support system. The youth ministry can also serve as a "surrogate" parent, building character and training the children in how to help sustain their parents who have the awesome responsibility of raising children alone.

Training Married Couples

Sometimes it is extremely difficult if not almost impossible to counsel a married couple who for years have experienced conflict, humiliation, rejection, bitterness, and hatred. Some couples have had marital misery for so long that they can't even begin to imagine that anything else is possible. However, we must build hope. "Old dogs" can learn new ways of living.

Teaching Children and Teenagers About Marriage

I often ask, "Why do we wait until children are grown before the church ministers to them concerning marriage and family?" Some of the great heroes of the faith were teenagers. David was sixteen when he killed Goliath; Esther was a teenage queen; Shadrach, Meshach, and Abednego were teenagers when they were cast into the fiery furnace; Mary, the mother of Jesus, was nineteen when she gave birth to Jesus; and Jesus was twelve when He engaged in dialogue with the elders.

Most of us wait too long to give our children mature responsibilities or to teach them to do serious thinking. While the children are growing up, they must learn what marriage involves from their parents and the church, while they can still see it firsthand and ask questions. A father who has learned from and adjusted to the emotional differences of his wife and daughter should also be teaching his son. A mother who has learned and adjusted to the weaknesses of her husband's ego should be able to teach her daughter what to expect from men and how to interact with them. A child growing up in a single-parent home should be able to observe firsthand a model of a two-parent family in his or her church family.

Dealing With the Problems of the Elderly

We must prepare people, at least when they are middle-aged, if not earlier, for the reality that there are unique problems they will face when they are older. What will they do when they are too old to work? What will they do if they are laid off and no one will hire them because of their age? What problems will they face being on a fixed income, and how can they prepare to overcome such problems? Do they have enough health insurance at an age when they can still purchase it? How can they be a blessing as a grandparent, rather than a hindrance to their children? What should be their attitude toward God and their family during illness?

We must prepare young adults for the possibility that they may have to take care of a poor, elderly parent. What resources are available to them, and how can they get outside help when their parents are sick? How can one organize sisters and brothers to help in taking care of elderly parents so one family member does not carry the whole burden or leave the rest to feel guilty later on because they did not help? Many adult sibling relationships have been severed because of the bitterness between them concerning the care of their parents.

WHO WILL DO THE TRAINING?

The members of the church should do the training, supplemented by volunteers and professionals from the community. This activity should be led by the pastor who cares for the flock.

God never intended the pastor to deal with every problem in the church. God, the Holy Spirit, has given gifts to each believer (Rom. 12:6; 1 Cor. 12:4–6), and the Bible makes it very clear that God's will is that the gifts be used for the common good of the members (1 Cor. 12:7). Gifts are not to be undiscovered or merely sitting on a pew.

The Bible teaches that Christians should love each other deeply and be hospitable (1 Peter 4:8–9). Each person should use his or her gifts to serve others, faithfully administering God's grace. More members of the church must be mobilized into this type of service.

The church must take action to help people avoid family problems. It is much easier to train people in preventing problems than it is to counsel them after a problem has taken root and has been watered by pride under the sunlight of ignorance, growing into a destructive monstrosity.

Over the past eighteen years, we have been developing such a ministry in our church and have helped many other churches to establish the same. However, we are still learning and have made some mistakes. Not all of our members participate or take advantage of what we offer, nor do they think they need the help. But most are involved, serving and being served. Here are some of the results of these efforts:

1. In the last eighteen years, we have had only one divorce among those who have been recipients of the family training ministry (church membership is over three thousand active members).
2. It is very evident to others that there are more good marriages in the church than before and that couples are deeply in love with each other.
3. Male church membership has been as high as 48 percent of our adult members. (This figure fluctuates, because the word has gone out to the single females that "they have men in that church.")
4. Many of our moderate- and low-income families are debt-free.
5. A number of young married adults who grew up in the church have families that are stronger than those of the past generation.
6. We have men who are competent in carrying out their roles as husbands and fathers.
7. Compared to other urban churches, we have fewer teenage pregnancies.

8. Part of our ongoing church growth is occurring because friends and relatives have seen the results of the family ministry in the lives of their loved ones.

The church can and must move out front, ahead of broken marriages and broken homes. The church has the Word of God, the Book of Life, and it has God-gifted members and God's power backing it up. What more do we need?

BOOKS FOR FURTHER KNOWLEDGE AND USE IN FAMILY MINISTRY

Abatso, George, and Yvonne Abatso. *How to Equip the African-American Family.* Chicago: Urban Ministries, 1991.

Jones, Reginald L. *Black Adult Development and Aging.* Berkeley: Cobb & Henry, 1989.

_____. *Black Adolescents.* Berkeley: Cobb & Henry, 1989.

June, Lee N. *The Black Family.* Grand Rapids: Zondervan, 1991.

Larson, Jim. *A Church Guide for Strengthening Families.* Minneapolis: Augsburg, 1986.

Money, Royce. *Building Stronger Families.* Wheaton: Victor, 1984.

_____. *Ministering to Families: A Positive Plan of Action.* Abilene: A.C.V. Press, 1987.

Sell, Charles M. *Family Ministry.* 2d ed.Grand Rapids: Zondervan, 1995.

Chapter 3

THE ROLE OF THE PASTOR IN FAMILY MINISTRY

THE PASTOR'S BURDEN AND VISION

> They said to me, "Those who survived the exile and are back in the
> province are in great trouble and disgrace. The wall of Jerusalem is
> broken down, and its gates have been burned with fire." When I
> heard these things, I sat down and wept. For some days I mourned
> and fasted and prayed before the God of heaven (Neh. 1:3–4).

The direction, quality, and effectiveness of the church's ministry to
families can be only as sound as the pastor's burden and vision for families. There is no doubt that there is a breakdown in the American family.
There can be no doubt that there is a family crisis in too many African-
American communities. I have spoken on the challenge that lies before
the church—not only in dealing with troubled married people and family crises, but also in taking the initiative through family ministry to prevent some of the problems and family breakdowns in the first place.

The pastor is key to the success of family ministry in the church,
which should also reach out to families in the community. Unless the
pastor has a burden for families that "are in great trouble and disgrace,"
there can be no family ministry that will help to change trends of the
downward spiral of African-American family life. After recognizing the

dilemma, conditions, and state of family life, the pastor, because of his faith in the power and love of God, can believe not only that the church of Jesus Christ can have a positive impact on family life but also that churches collectively throughout the United States can change the negative trend of the family. Each pastor must have a vision—driven by faith—of what family life can become in his church and community.

By nature of the pastor's position, he is already involved with families. He is the one the people come to with family needs, problems, troubles, and crises. He advises singles before he marries them, and he walks with them when their marriage is failing. What the pastor has to do is to mobilize the congregation, the church family, to get them involved in family ministry. The pastor himself will continue to be personally involved in family ministry through his pastoral counseling, preaching, and teaching on family issues. The principles of family life should be preached annually on a Sunday morning, in addition to guidelines on how to live a Spirit-filled life at home and how to love the people in one's own house.

I think it is very important that the pastor teach some classes on the family at least yearly in Sunday school, Bible class, or a church retreat. The Word of God is part of what gives the pastor his authority, and there should be no doubt in the church as to his concern and authority in the area of family ministry.

THE WORD OF GOD CAUSES CHRISTIANS TO GROW SPIRITUALLY

I believe that we are not coming anywhere close to the potential of the power of the Word of God in the life of the church. The Bible is more advanced than the practice and walk of the church. Many of the problems in the church would not exist if our people knew the Word of God. Very few deacons know their qualifications, duties, or roles as they relate to the pastor. Yet the Bible clearly spells these out. The shame is that these are leaders in the church. I am not trying to be critical, but I want to make a point that the church has to learn the Bible and live it out in the church, in the home, and in the world.

God's Word brings about change in people.

Preaching God's Word

If God's Word changes people, then it is crucial that we preach the Bible. I have heard preachers on too many occasions preach about the Bible instead of preaching the Bible. Expository preaching will keep us on target, for the message comes out of the Scripture. God has already given us the living Word, and it is inexhaustible. If we could preach in two lifetimes, we would never preach every theme, topic, thought, or idea of the Bible. Sometimes we get an inspirational thought, decide to preach from this thought, then turn to the Bible to see if we can find a verse to use. I have heard men preach from a verse that in context had nothing to do with the subject they preached. If it were not for their "great close," the sermon would have been a complete failure. Most closings elevate and lift the name of our Lord Jesus Christ.

Some men argue that expository preaching is boring. Some preachers make expository preaching boring because they are not preaching, they are giving a lecture. They have not distinguished between a "preaching stance" and a "teaching stance." I was visiting a church many years ago on my vacation. It was very hot, and the church did not have air conditioning. The pastor was preaching a doctrinal sermon. It had to be one of the most boring expository sermons I had ever heard. I think it is sacrilegious to fall asleep while worshiping God, but I found myself having to fight to stay awake. The content of the sermon was sound and excellent, but the illustrations were bland and the delivery was monotonous. I looked over at my wife and children to see if it was just me. My wife had a scowl on her face, laboring to concentrate. My three children were sound asleep, lying on each other like sacks of wheat. I was in torture trying to stay awake. A horrible thought came into my mind. Was I doing the same thing to my congregation? I prayed right then for myself and my congregation that I would never put them through such torture.

Expository preaching does not have to be boring. Such men as A. Lewis Patterson, E. V. Hill, E. K. Bailey, Jasper Williams, and Timothy Winters, just to name a few, are models of effective expository preaching. As a matter of fact, Jasper Williams of Atlanta, Georgia, recently told me that he switched to expository preaching a few years ago because it is more effective than his former method of preaching. E. K. Bailey of E. K. Bailey Ministries has a seminar promoting expository preaching. Lloyd C. Blue of Lloyd C. Blue Ministries travels full-time, teaching expository preaching in such a way that our culture is not lost.

What to Preach to Help Families Grow Spiritually

It is obvious that we are to preach the Bible, the full counsel of God. We must not be so concerned about families that we restrict ourselves and our congregation to a limited portion of God's Word. However, we must target some of our sermons for marriage, family, and the single life.

Salvation must be preached and made clear and plain. Many of our people attend church regularly and are not saved. Every member of the church is to be able to answer the question "What must I do to be saved?"

We must preach on what happens when God saves a person. Christians need to know that they still have a sinful human nature called the flesh, but they also have the nature of Christ, the "new man." Christ is in the believer, and the believer is in Christ. Believers' minds have been enlightened in order to understand the will of God for their lives by the indwelling Holy Spirit, who empowers believers to live the Christian life.

Christians need to know what to do when they sin. Married people need to repent, confess their sins to God, grant forgiveness to one another, and receive forgiveness from God and each other. They need to know that harboring bitterness and anger is destructive to the marriage and the family. And they need to know how to get rid of bitterness and anger, putting on compassion, kindness, humility, gentleness, and patience (Col. 3:12).

The following are a few suggested subjects and topics that should be preached:

- Salvation
- How to Live in the Spirit
- How to Grow in the Grace and Knowledge of Christ
- The Importance of the Bible
- God the Father, the Perfect Parent
- The Lordship of Christ in the Home
- The Work of God, the Holy Spirit
- Concern for the Lost
- The Sacrificial Love of a Husband for His Wife
- The Respect and Leadership Support of a Wife for Her Husband
- Christian Parenting
- The Christian Single Life
- God's Provisions for the Family
- The Holiness and Permanency of Marriage
- The Church's Teaching and Stance on Divorce
- God's Support of the Single Parent
- Lovers in the Bible
- Single Believers in the Bible
- Family Conflict Resolution

- Debt-Free Living
- Family Communication
- Expressing Love in a Family
- The Biblical Role of a Wife
- The Biblical Role of a Husband
- How to Keep Christ in the Family
- The Problems of Submission and Leadership
- The Ungodliness of Living Together Unmarried
- Winning Your Unsaved Mate to Christ
- Family Love and Loyalty
- Binding Our Extended Families
- The Destructiveness of Jealousy in a Marriage and Family
- Self-Image in Christ

Without salvation, families cannot experience what God intended when He created us. Without people clearly understanding God's Word, the Bible, they cannot come to Christ or live the Christian life, the results being the continual breakdown of the family.

We must have family revivals followed by training classes. We must have preaching week in and week out that exalts the Bible as God's Word, revealing God's will for the individual and family. It should be evident that our church members have been with Christ.

PREPARING SINGLES FOR MARRIAGE

Pastors and churches would go a long way in helping to reverse the divorce trend if it were mandatory that couples get premarital counseling or marriage training. The different facets of marriage, parenting, and family can be very complex. I would be a rich man if I had a dollar for every middle-aged person, elderly person, or divorcee who, after attending one of our seminars or marriage classes, has said, "I wish I had known this a long time ago. My marriage would have been different." Premarital counseling is a must. Traditionally, pastors have not done premarital counseling at all, or at most, couples have had two or three sessions of marital orientation. If we are going to establish solid Christian homes, more than this is needed. We need to do premarital training.

THE PASTOR'S FAMILY AS A MODEL

Whether pastors and their families like it or not, their families are in a fishbowl. People in the congregation are watching the pastor's family as the model Christian family of the church. The irony of looking at our families as a model is that we too are human beings—sinners saved by grace (assuming our children, who have a God-given free will, have accepted Christ as their Lord and Savior) and are sheep of the Lord's—like the rest of the congregation. Most of us were no better prepared or trained to be married than anyone else in the congregation. Clergy and their families are not devoid of sinful natures, which enable us also to be candidates to grow in the grace and knowledge of our Lord and Savior, Jesus Christ (2 Peter 3:18).

In light of our being perceived as a model family and taking into consideration our limitations and weaknesses, which are like those of any other Christian family, pastors must make their families a ministry priority. A more positive reason for making family a priority in ministry is that pastoring can be emotionally, psychologically, and spiritually draining, so the pastor must find his family life fulfilling, warm, and loving—for his own well-being. The reason I am describing the pastor's responsibilities as spouse and parent as a ministry priority is that we pastors have a tendency to expect our homes to be a haven of release from the pressures, disappointments, battles, and hard work of the ministry. The problem is that too often we haven't focused on building a family refuge of love and caring.

The Problems of Living in a Fishbowl

Some years ago, through our national ministry, Christian Research & Development (CRD), we surveyed some pastors and their wives and discovered that some of these marriages were experiencing the following problems:

1. Pastors said they were discouraged because their wives had little or no interest in their ministry.
2. Pastors were frustrated because their wives seemed not to understand the importance of their ministry.
3. The lack of some of the wives' participation in church activities was an embarrassment.
4. The pastors enjoyed being in the presence of women workers of the church more than with their wives because of the women's interest and support of the pastor's vision.
5. Some pastors experienced jealousy from their wives because of how the pastor related to other women in the church. It could simply be

due to the comparison of the pastor's pleasant attitude at church with women (and men) and his tired, exhausted, unsmiling face at home.

6. Some husbands, returning home exhausted from the problems of the ministry, desired peace, warmth, and love from their wives and instead received more problems relating to family life.

7. Some pastors reported that their wives had become withdrawn and unhappy.

8. Some pastors reported continual fights with their wives, and this embarrassed them because their neighbors knew.

9. Other pastors reported that although there was no fighting with their spouses, there was quiet tension in their relationship.

10. Some pastors had a sense of defeat and helplessness in their relationship with their wives.

11. Some pastors, because of the state of their marriage and family life, admitted feeling discouraged and depressed over their relationship with their wives.

In our effort to help pastors and their families, we have shared with them what we discovered from surveying the feelings and needs of some pastors' wives:

1. The pastor's wife is the only woman in the church who shares her husband with the entire congregation. His children are the only children in the church who share their father with the entire church.

2. The pastor's wife has the same need for a husband as any other wife in the congregation. Too often, because of the direct impact of the church on the home, the clergy marriage is merely functional rather than a developing, maturing relationship built on oneness.

3. The pastor is appropriately helping other women in the church with their problems but does not have the time, patience, or energy to help his wife and children with their problems, causing the wife to feel insecure.

4. Some pastors' wives never know when to expect their husbands home, though their husbands promise to be home at a certain time.

5. Meals lovingly prepared by wives for their husbands are not eaten at dinnertime with the rest of the family.

6. Some pastors are so caught up with their work that they do not inform their wives in advance when they have to travel out of town because of the ministry.

7. Some wives complain that people assumed she had firsthand knowledge of the pastor's vision, dreams, and plans for the church, when she knew less about them than some of the average members of the church, with whom the pastor shared more.
8. Some of the pastors are ignorant and insensitive to the slights and harassment their wives receive at the hands of women in the church who admire the pastor.
9. Some wives feel they are taken for granted by their husbands and are always expected to sacrifice themselves as martyrs.

The Pastor Ministering to His Family

Over the years, we have been able to help change the experiences of some pastors and their families through our national seminars and CRD Institute in Philadelphia. First, we believe that the pastor's family is a biblical priority. One of the biblical qualifications of a pastor is that he must manage his own family well, and if he does not know how to do this well, "how can he take care of God's church?" (1 Tim. 3:4–5). Married pastors, like all Christian husbands, are instructed, "Husbands, love your wives, just as Christ loved the church and gave himself up for her" (Eph. 5:25). This means the pastor must have a vision, plans, and goals for his family as well as for his church. It takes time to minister to the church, and it takes time to care for or minister to his family. God expects both ministries to be going on at the same time. It doesn't sound too romantic to pastors' wives, but if the pastor looks at caring for his family as another ministerial responsibility, it will help keep him on target. On occasion, I have reminded my children to share their needs with me, because I don't want to minister to everyone else and neglect them. To be accessible to my family, I have told my staff that whenever my family members call on the phone or need to see me, they are to have immediate admittance. We pastors are interrupted by others. I believe our children and wives have earned the right to interrupt us too. In spite of this policy, my family takes advantage of this only when it is a very important issue.

Scheduling Time for Wife and Children

Church ministry can be very demanding on a pastor's time, especially if a pastor is employed full time in a secular job. If, in addition, the pastor is going to college or seminary, family life can suffer severely. It is easy to allow ministry alone to crowd spouse and children out of the pastor's time frame. In order to control this, family should be officially placed into the pastor's schedule, the way we schedule a preaching engagement. I remember when I first started scheduling my family time—to be sure I did not neglect them. Other pastors and Christian leaders would ask me why I could not accept their invitation to preach or conduct a family seminar on a certain date or time. I would reply, "It is time I scheduled to be with my family." They would give me lectures on "seeking the kingdom of God first." So then, rather than going through a debate on the interpretation of Matthew 6:33, I started telling them, "I have a prior engagement." They assumed someone else asked me to preach or teach before they requested my services.

Scheduling a fixed amount of time on your calendar as a pastor guarantees making ministering to your family equally as important as ministering to the church. Here is what I have suggested to pastors in my classes and to those who attend our seminars:

1. No fewer than four hours weekly of dedicated time to talk with your wife.

2. At least one night a week for "family night," with the television turned off.

3. All family birthdays and your wedding anniversary must be written in your schedule and celebrated in some way.

4. As frequently as possible and with as much advance information as possible, list the times for activities at your child's school—activities in which parents are expected to participate, such as when your child's team will be playing and the date of your daughter's piano recital.

5. Schedule summer vacation with family away from home, even if it is only to drive a few miles from town and stay at a motor inn with a swimming pool.

6. Plan at least two weekends a year—six months apart—when you and your wife spend time together, taking inventory of your marriage and enjoying each other. Your weekend can be from Thursday to Saturday night, enabling you to serve your church on Sunday, if you prefer. Two questions that are to be laid on the table are "How can I improve as a husband and father?" and "How can I improve as a wife and mother?"

7. Do something together with your wife at least once a month (go out for dinner, entertainment, jogging, exercising, etc.).

8. Schedule time to talk with your children.

9. Take time to pray for and with your wife and children.

10. Schedule time for yourself—Jesus did (Mark 1:35–39).

Since it gives credibility to you as a pastor in leading other families, it is well worth it for you to allot time to build your own Christian home as you have been called to do, with God's help.

Chairman of the Communications and Problem Departments

Just as the church looks to the pastor as the great problem-solver, so does the pastor's wife—and rightfully so. The pastor has been called by God to help people with their problems. Certainly, he should be committed to helping his wife and children with their problems.

1. Stay in touch with home. Not only must the pastor ask his wife if she or their children have any current problems, but he must be approachable. His wife must have the freedom to bring family problems to him without feeling guilty that she is placing more burden on him on top of the problems of the church. I believe that if God called us to be husbands and pastors, He is saying to us, "My grace is sufficient for you, for my power is made perfect in weakness" (2 Cor. 12:9). When we stay on top of our family problems and keep them current, there are seasons when there are no problems, only sweet family fellowship.
2. The pastor should share his vision, dreams, and plans for the church with his wife. His wife should be his ministry prayer partner, so they will rejoice together because of God's faithfulness to the pastor, His servant.
3. The pastor should aid his wife in what her role and ministry will be in the church and protect her from the prefabricated molds that church leaders and the congregation would force her into. She should serve in the church according to her spiritual and natural gifts and what she believes is God's will for her life.

Chairman of the Love Department

According to Ephesians 5:25, the married pastor, like other husbands, is to be a sacrificial lover to his wife, following in the footsteps of our Lord Jesus Christ in His love for His bride, the church. The pastor should be an example to other men in the church in how to love a wife as Christ loves the church.

1. The pastor is to commit to being his wife's sacrificial lover. There should be no question that she is fully as important in his life as his ministry. He is not married to the church, but to his wife. He may

or may not be with a particular church for the rest of his life, but his wife will be with him until death separates them.

2. The pastor should honor his wife. He is to treat her like a queen. There should be no question in anyone's mind that he is deeply in love with his wife and that she is a special woman in his life.

3. Pray with your wife and pray for her. In praying with her, you are two lovers engaging the master lover, Jesus Christ, in a triad of holy communion. In praying for your wife, you are not taking her for granted but humbly depending on God to help you be a successful husband.

Being a Good Father

Again, God expects the pastor to understand that his children are no less a priority than the church. The pastor's children have an opportunity to grow up in a home under the authority and loving care of a man of God. Here are some rules to follow:

1. Imitate our heavenly Father in the way He loves His children. In spite of the fact that your children are the pastor's children, try to provide them with as normal a family life as possible. Challenge those in the congregation who would expect more from them than they would of another child the same age to help you love and encourage your children.

2. Not only should we live righteous lives before our families, but when we are wrong or have sinned, we must admit it and repent, as an example of what a Christian does when he has failed. We must not live in a way that our children or wife think we are hypocrites. When we stand in the pulpit on Sunday mornings as their pastor, they know better than anyone else that we are not perfect, but they are secure in knowing we are trying to practice what we preach.

3. Be a good provider. This involves meeting not only material needs, but also spiritual and emotional needs. Disciple your family spiritually and walk with them through their emotional challenges, from the dying of a pet to their first breakup in teenage courtship.

THE PASTOR NEEDS A PASTOR

Although we may be pastors, we are still spiritual sheep to God. We have to be fed and cared for like the rest of the congregation. Every pastor should have at least one pastoral couple that he and his wife can share with and from whom they receive care. The pastor needs another pastor who loves him and accepts him, someone he can go to when his troubles become overwhelming. I remember one time years ago that my wife and I got down on our knees and asked God to bring such friends into our lives. God not only raised up two couples for us then, but over the years God has brought others into our lives who have been special blessings to us in a time of need.

WHAT THE CONGREGATION CAN DO TO HELP THE PASTOR'S FAMILY BE A SUCCESS

Not only does the pastor have responsibilities to the congregation as shepherd, but the congregation also has responsibilities to the pastor and his family. Most churches do not know what these obligations are because they have not been taught. The only person to teach them this is the pastor, but most pastors feel awkward and embarrassed to instruct their congregations in the matter. For some reason, too many pastors think the church leaders, in particular, ought to know these things, when they don't. The pastor must open the Bible and train his church in their duties to him. The congregation must support and minister to the pastor's family.

Church leaders must
- Be the pastor's armor bearers in the ongoing war against sin, darkness, and the Devil
- Stand shoulder to shoulder with the pastor as co-laborers, carrying out the pastor's God-given vision for the church

Church members must
- Hold their pastor up in prayer before God
- Show appreciation to the pastor's family for the sacrifices they make in sharing the man of God with them
- Be supportive and protective of the pastor's children, not emotionally abusing them with a judgmental spirit
- Give the pastor and his wife words and notes of encouragement
- Protect the pastor's reputation by rebuking gossips and liars
- Be faithful in their giving and serving the Lord
- Submit to God by living godly lives
- Honor the pastor's day off and vacations to help him avoid burnout

Don't call his wife to share problems during these times. Allow the pastor and his wife and children to have some peaceful time together.

- Recognize that the pastor has been called, ordained, and given authority by God

  "No one takes this honor upon himself; he must be called by God, just as Aaron was" (Heb. 5:4).

  "Before I formed you in the womb I knew you, before you were born I set you apart; I appointed you as a prophet to the nations" (Jer. 1:5).

  "I became a servant of this gospel by the gift of God's grace given me through the working of his power" (Eph. 3:7).

  "Tell Archippus: 'See to it that you complete the work you have received in the Lord'" (Col. 4:17).

- Help the pastor to be able to do his work joyfully, not with grief

  "Obey your leaders and submit to their authority. They keep watch over you as men who must give an account. Obey them so that their work will be a joy, not a burden, for that would be of no advantage to you" (Heb. 13:17).

- Try to understand the difficulties of the pastor's position and responsibility

  In surveying some pastors, we found the following facts: They work on call seven days a week. Their average work week is 53.7 hours, the same as some of the chief executives of the top five hundred U.S. corporations. They visit hospitals and homes two to sixteen hours a week. They spend six to twenty hours a week doing pastoral counseling. Twenty-one hours a week or more are spent traveling from place to place; this is one reason that the IRS allows for car allowances, the same as salesmen. Pastors spend seven to fifteen hours preparing sermons, conducting funerals and weddings, teaching Bible classes, and being called on in emergencies.

The women of the church must

- Rally around the pastor's wife as sisters, blessing her as much as they can

Financial Support of the Pastor

As in any other family, the pastor should receive an income that will provide resources for the family. If we expect the church to be the primary institution that will help save our families, surely the leader of the church, the pastor, should reap the fruit of his labors. Too many of our pastors are working two full-time jobs—at the church and at a secular occupation. They work at church because of their calling and at the secular job because the church does not pay enough to live on. A church cannot expect its pastor to give leadership in saving their families and at the same time suffer fatigue and burnout as he and his family try to survive. A pastor should be a well-paid professional. Why is he considered a professional? Although the pastor is not to do all the work in the church, he is responsible for managing the church and for every ministry, organization, and activity in the church.

The pastor is an administrator, manager, counselor, teacher, preacher, and employer (in a large church). He must have a vision and, with the other leaders, work out the plans to bring the vision into reality. He gives leadership in setting church goals and priorities. He is involved in budget planning and is responsible for ensuring that financial records are accurate. He is responsible for training leaders and the congregation to do the work of the ministry. He is concerned with having adequate building space and facilities. One of the most draining of these is a new church building program. The pastor is concerned about Christian education, evangelism, discipleship, youth work, and the elderly, in addition to the sick and shut-ins. He must coordinate all church ministries, organizations, and auxiliaries so they are unified and have biblical objectives. He is responsible for regulating the music and worship services. He must prayerfully choose guest speakers who will contribute to the spiritual growth of the church. I believe all of the above and more warrants giving the pastor full-time pay.

The Bible Teaches That the Congregation Must Financially Support the Man of God

Instead, I give to the Levites as their inheritance the tithes that the Israelites present as an offering to the LORD. That is why I said concerning them: "They will have no inheritance among the Israelites." You and your households may eat the rest of it anywhere, for it is your wages for your work at the Tent of Meeting (Num. 18:24, 31).

When Jesus sent the twelve disciples out to minister, they were not to take provisions because the people they ministered to were to provide for them. "For," Jesus said, "the worker is worth his keep" (Matt. 10:9–10). The church must support the pastor with the right attitude. Paul would not allow the Corinthian church to support him because they did not have a spiritual love attitude concerning his support. But he makes it clear that it was their responsibility to support him (1 Cor. 9:3–23). On the other hand, the church at Philippi loved Paul, their first pastor, so he gratefully received their support (Phil. 4:10–19).

If you are benefiting from the pastor's ministry, you should support him financially. "Anyone who receives instruction in the word must share all good things with his instructor" (Gal. 6:6).

God has promised to supply the needs of those who are willing to support pastors, evangelists, missionaries, and other full-time workers of God (Phil. 4:19). How much should the pastor receive? In the Old Testament, the Levites lived from the tithes of the people. Jesus and His disciples were supported by His followers (Luke 8:1–3). In 1 Timothy 5:17–18, we are told not to muzzle God's man, but if he does his work well, he is worthy of a double stipend. I believe this adds up to more than an adequate wage, and the church is to be very generous to the pastor.

The pastor's salary should be in the range of the pay scale of other professionals, managers, and administrators. The following are some considerations for the financial support of pastors:

1. Base salary
2. Housing allowance. According to the IRS, this portion of the pastor's compensation is not taxable.
3. Fringe benefits for pastor and family:

   - Social security allowance
   - Pension plan
   - Health insurance
   - Disability insurance
   - Life insurance
   - Paid vacation (at least four weeks)

4. Professional expenses. A pastor should be reimbursed for the following expenses because they are professional expenses incurred while performing his duties:

   - Car allowance
   - Books and magazines

- Continuing education
- Postage, stationery, cards
- Printing and church advertisements
- Conventions and seminars
- Office supplies
- Travel expenses (conventions, church assemblies, etc.)

What Church Leaders Should Do to Help Maintain the Pastor's Family

1. The elders, deacons, stewards, trustees, or whoever are the primary lay leaders of the church must hold the pastor accountable to insist that the pastor not neglect his family for church work.
2. Church leaders should see that the pastor has at least one day off per week.

   > (The majority of other workers in our country get two days off from work.) The leaders should insist that the congregation honor this day by not troubling the pastor or his family unless it is a matter of life or death.

3. Leaders must insist that the pastor take vacations without the fear that there will be a coup in his absence.
4. If the pastor has a full-time secular job and is pastoring the church, the leaders must work out a plan with the pastor to move him toward full-time ministry. This means for the smaller church that evangelism and church growth are essential.
5. The pastor should have adequate help. Lay leaders must stand shoulder to shoulder with the pastor and share ministry responsibilities.

   > As Jethro told Moses, "What you are doing is not good. You and these people who come to you will only wear yourselves out. The work is too heavy for you; you cannot handle it alone" (Ex. 18:17–18; cf. vv. 13–24). As it was true with Moses, it is true today with every pastor with a God-given vision to carry out the Great Commission—one man cannot accomplish this alone. We will never be able to reclaim our families by burning out the pastor and neglecting his family.

Every pastor needs a secretary—part-time or full-time, depending on the size of the church. In the earlier years, I had a part-time secretary for seven years. Today, as we have over three thousand members, I have two secretaries and three administrators—in all, a full-time and part-time staff totaling thirty people. Our church would never have grown from six people to over three thousand active members if my leaders had not supported our vision with their commitment and had seen to it that I continue to have adequate help.

You start with people who love God and volunteer to help the pastor. As responsibility grows, these people should be paid as staff.

BOOKS FOR FURTHER KNOWLEDGE AND USE IN FAMILY MINISTRY

Langberg, Diane. *Counsel for Pastors' Wives*. Grand Rapids: Zondervan, 1988.

London, B. H., Jr., and Neal B. Wiseman. *Pastors at Risk*. Wheaton: Victor, 1993.

Mickey, Paul A., and Ginny W. Ashmore. *Clergy Families*. Grand Rapids: Zondervan, 1991.

Senter, Ruth. *The Guilt-Free Book for Pastors' Wives*. Wheaton: Victor, 1990.

Wise, Shirley D. *Sick and Tired of Being a Minister's Wife*. Columbus: Wise Works, 1991.

Chapter 4

HOW TO DEVELOP FAMILY MINISTRY IN THE CHURCH

GETTING STARTED

Like Nehemiah, the pastor should not only have a burden but must also know the present conditions of the church's families and those in the community by studying the current state of affairs. He can get this information by consulting the public library, local agencies that specialize in family concerns, the federal Government Printing Office, and the Census Bureau and by surveying the families in his church and community.

Although he will mobilize the church eventually, he needs to engage church leaders in the study of family issues and conditions. He can do this simply by presenting a workshop to church leaders of what he has discovered through his study. The pastor and the church leaders should evaluate what is currently being done in their church family ministry and then determine if more should be done. They should do all this with prayers.

FAMILY LIFE MINISTRY TEAM

If the pastor and church leaders decide that more should be done in their church's family ministry, they should inform the church congregation and establish a family life ministry team. The family life ministry team should consist of individuals selected by the pastor to identify, develop, and

51

execute family ministry based on a needs assessment of the congregation and the community. The individuals who make up the family life ministry team are individuals who are supportive of the pastor's vision for family ministry. This group will give leadership, training, and counseling in areas relating to family development. The pastor can determine the size of the ministry team and the extent of family ministry. For example, in a smaller church, the pastor alone conducts family ministry, or the family life ministry team consists of only the pastor and one assistant.

However, from our experience we generally recommend that the team consist of a minimum of four people and a maximum of eight. The entire church will be mobilized into family ministry (for instance, one group working in family evangelism and another specializing in biblical counseling), but the family life ministry team runs the family ministry. The team should represent different segments of the congregation. For example: leaders, men, women, married people, single individuals, single parents, blended families, widows, and if possible, teenagers. The pastor is the family ministry director, but he can delegate the operation of the ministry to an assistant or associate minister, a lay leader, or a staff person, or he may appoint a family life ministry team leader.

Qualifications of a Family Life Ministry

A team member, in general, is a person who

1. Is committed to the pastor's vision
2. Demonstrates a Spirit-filled Christian walk
3. Has a burden for the family and loves people
4. Is teachable and is able to be a disciplined student
5. Is willing to serve with enthusiasm
6. Is willing to use his or her spiritual gifts
7. Is available to make an investment of time to be trained to minister in the church's family ministry
8. Is cooperative and a team player
9. If married, models what he or she is trying to help other families to become
10. Possesses administrative ability, people management skills, and the emotional makeup to counsel people biblically

After the team members have been chosen, the pastor should present to them his state-of-the-family workshop and then present it to the church leaders.

PLANNING CHURCH FAMILY MINISTRY
Needs Assessment

In his book *A Church Guide for Strengthening Families*, Jim Larson gives suggestions for the family ministries task force (Family Life Ministry Team) meetings in assessing family needs and establishing a ministry.[1] He recommends the following meeting themes:

Session 1: The Importance of Families
(Why families are important. How families today are changing.)

Session 2: Family Wellness
(Qualities of a healthy marriage and family.)

Session 3: Consulting with Families
(Teams working together to develop a family survey. A list of questions for families in church and a list for families in the community. Questions should be concise and need only brief responses for tabulation purposes. [Royce Money, in his book *Ministering to Families: A Positive Plan of Action*, has great examples of such a survey.][2])

Session 4: The Needs of Families
(Tabulate the survey results, make a list of the most urgent family needs in the congregation, and determine the areas of greatest interest for ministry.)

Session 5: Planning for Ministry
(Planning is based on the list of needs which was developed at the previous session. Determine which needs are most urgent, which can wait until next year, which can be postponed for future consideration.)

Mission and Goals of the Family Ministry

The pastor and family life ministry team should now be able to come up with a mission statement and goals for the church's family ministry. Each church's family needs, priorities, and goals are different. Here is an example of what the mission and goals might look like.

Family Ministry Mission Statement

To assist families in living according to biblical principles that will bring glory to God and prepare single people to establish such families.

Goals of the Family Ministry

1. To evangelize and win families to our Lord Jesus Christ.
2. To educate Christians about biblical family principles.
3. To train Christians in how to live these principles in a practical way.
4. To aid families in problem-solving when needed.
5. To help improve the quality of life for poor and dysfunctional families.
6. To train Christian singles in courtship skills and the mate-selection process from a biblical perspective.

Program

In order to accomplish the goals of the family ministry, our next objective is to evaluate existing programs and establish new programs or ministries. The following is a sample of programming.

Training Program

Training of family life ministry team members:

1. Family Evangelism
2. Biblical Counseling: Issues in Family Development
3. Singles' Preparation for Marriage
4. Basic Marriage Training
5. Parenting
6. Family Financial Planning
7. Single Parents' Issues

Training of single people (including single parents):

1. Courtship
2. Mate-Selection Process
3. Marriage Preparation

4. Premarital Training (plus counseling)
5. Career and Vocational Development

Training of married people:

1. Basic Marriage Training
2. Family Evangelism
3. Parenting
4. Problem Solving and Conflict Resolution
5. Family Unity and Loyalty
6. Family Togetherness
7. Family Finances

Training of single parents:

1. Legal Issues
2. Single-Parenting Issues
3. Scheduling and Responsibilities
4. Emotional Issues
5. Courtship and the Involvement of Your Children

Marriage enrichment program:

1. Retreats
2. Seminars
3. Conferences
4. Couples' Growth Groups

Ministries:

1. Singles' Ministry
2. Single-Parent Ministry
3. Counseling Ministry
4. Family Evangelism

CURRICULUM DEVELOPMENT

Curriculum is determined by your church's needs assessment, goals, and objectives. No two churches would use the same curriculum. However, I have tried to assist you by listing books for further knowledge and use in family ministry at the end of each chapter and by listing additional resources at the end of this book. Also, Christian Research & Development and Resources for Better Families can be helpful because both organizations specialize in ministering to African-American families.

BIBLICAL COUNSELING MINISTRY

A counseling ministry supports pastoral care of the local assembly and serves as an outreach to non-Christians and the unchurched community. It operates under the authority and supervision of the pastor. God has given the church the gift to counsel (Rom. 12:7–8) and has given it the ministry of reconciliation (Matt. 18:15–17; Gal. 6:1–2).

Biblical counseling is not psychiatry, psychology, or psychotherapy, although a knowledge of human behavior is a component of its discipline. Biblical counseling is using the Bible to help people solve their problems or cope with them. It is allowing the holy Scriptures to change individuals and families when they submit to God's Word in the power of the Holy Spirit. Application of spiritual truth to one's life is foundational to church family ministry.

In the age of a growing number of dysfunctional families manufactured by the world's godless philosophies (sin and carnality), biblical counseling weeds through the confusion, getting to the root of the matter. This counseling deals with the soul and the spirit. In contrast, other forms of counseling deal only with the mind and the emotions. Biblical counseling is concerned with the mind, emotions, body, and spirit. I do not dismiss the psychiatrist, the psychologist, or the psychotherapist. There is a need and place for these counselors, but they are incomplete in dealing with problems of the souls of human beings. There is a need sometimes for cooperation between biblical counselors and secular counselors in order to help a client or family.

Biblical counseling has the ability to identify the problems from a biblical perspective and then apply scriptural solutions to the problems. The following are some of the areas of biblical counseling:

- Marriage and Family
- Addictions: Drug, Alcohol and Chemical Abuse, Sexual
- Depression
- Worry
- Occupational Concerns
- Premarital Guidance
- Blended Families
- The Elderly
- Youth Specialty
- Severe Bereavement
- Miscarriage and Stillborn Births

Suggested major categories of family ministry that should be represented by an individual or individuals on the family life ministry team are as follows:

1. *Spiritual Accountability*: The individual responsible for this should be the pastor, a deacon, or a pastoral designee. This individual would have the authority to call individuals into submission to the Word of God.

2. *Family Counseling*: This person would primarily be responsible for counseling individuals in areas related to family development, e.g., marriage, communication, parenting, etc.

    Background: This person should have completed, or be willing to complete, training in biblical counseling.

3. *Family Financial Development*: This individual would concentrate on developing programs and working with families in the areas of budgeting, money management, understanding of self as a resource, and occupational enrichment (career preparation and advancement).

    Background: The individual must have background, either professional training or self-taught, in this area.

4. *Family Training*: The one responsible for this area would be the specialist on issues related to marriage and parenting. This individual would conduct the training sessions on marriage and parenting as well as develop and supervise programs which would support the needs of the congregation in these areas.

    Background: The person responsible for this must exhibit a strong commitment to the biblical principles of marriage and parenting. A biblical counseling background is strongly recommended.

5. *Singles' Preparation for Marriage*: The one in charge of this area must be a specialist on issues related to preparing singles for marriage. He or she would develop programs and conduct workshops that would encourage singles to trust God for a mate as well as focus on topics related to the selection process, such as building godly friendships, courtship, marriage expectations, etc.

    Background: This person must have exhibited a commitment to the biblical principles for a godly single life. A biblical counseling background is recommended.

6. *Single Parent*: This person would be responsible for developing programs and conducting training on issues related to the single parent family. The goal of the program, training, and support groups is to encourage single parents to establish and maintain a family based on God's principles.

   Background: This individual must have exhibited a commitment to the biblical principles related to family life. The individual may be married or single. A biblical counseling background is strongly recommended.

7. *Senior Citizens*: In this area the team member would be responsible for developing programs and conducting workshops relating to issues that affect the senior citizen. The goal is to encourage senior citizens to continue to actively participate in the life cycle of the family, church, and community.

   Background: This person must be knowledgeable of the issues of senior citizens. Experience in working with senior citizens is recommended.

CONTRIBUTING MINISTRIES IN THE CHURCH

As part of the church family, all members of ministries, auxiliaries, and clubs must support the family ministry effort and not be in competition with it. The following are suggestions on how some other ministries in the church can contribute to the family ministry.

Christian education and the Sunday school can be responsible for teaching families biblical principles on family and marriage. Christian education can have a tutorial and literacy program to aid families in reading and being successful as students in school. This ministry could be given partial responsibility for development of the family ministry training curriculum.

Children and youth ministries can reach those inside and outside of the church with the claims of Christ. They can specialize in helping build healthy self-images in Christ. Programs can be devised for drug, crime, and violence prevention. Youths would be guided in a pure and chaste sexual lifestyle to prevent unwed teenage pregnancies and the spread of sexually transmitted diseases. Teens should be trained in the impact of education on family life as a motivator for school success. These ministries must play a vital role in keeping our children alive by providing peer activities to keep the children off drugs, out of jail, from having children, and from dropping out of school.

The evangelism ministry team must train families in how to win other family members to Christ. The discipleship ministry must disciple individual Christians, enabling them to be strong in the faith, and married couples should be taught to disciple each other in marriage and family concerns. Disciplers become surrogate parents to adults who did not experience nurturing and support when they were growing up.

MOBILIZING THE CHURCH

It is obvious that the pastor and the family life ministry team cannot evangelize all of the unsaved or unchurched relatives of the congregation, nor could they counsel and train all of the families in the church, regardless of the size of the church. The congregation must be enlisted to pray and get involved. There must be a steady flow of evangelism workers, disciplers, counselors, and trainers.

Resource People and Organizations

In the church or outside of it, there are professional people who can contribute to family ministry with vital information, experience, service, or leadership. The following are some of the professional persons who may assist the church:

- Doctors
- Nurses
- Mental health professionals
- Lawyers
- Law-enforcement officers
- Social workers
- Child guidance counselors
- Teachers from public schools, Christian schools, colleges, universities, and seminaries
- School guidance counselors
- Financial experts
- Business owners
- Insurance agents
- Personnel of preschool institutions and day care centers
- Professionals who specialize in the care of the elderly
- Probation officers

Other institutions and organizations that can be of service:

- Other churches
- Parachurch ministries
- Family service agencies
- Public welfare departments
- YMCA and YWCA
- Mental health hospitals and centers
- Senior citizens' care givers

FAMILY MINISTRY EVALUATION

Evaluation is essential to keeping a ministry vital, relevant, and effective. This eliminates outdated methods and less than enthusiastic, competent workers. This can be done by setting standards of performance for workers and programs. Periodically measure results as programs are in progress. Make corrections and changes in ministry plans when necessary.

Questions should be raised at least annually. Are we on target? What has been accomplished? What has not been accomplished? What is working well and what is not? What are the strengths of our family ministry? What are our weaknesses? Are we trying to accomplish too much, considering our personnel and resources? Should we be collaborating with another church or organization? Should we bring in outside trainers, speakers, seminars, etc.?

Use of original needs assessment and goals is indispensable in gauging achievement. Debriefing workers after an event is helpful for not repeating the same mistakes next time. Evaluation questionnaires distributed among those being ministered to is helpful. Case studies of individual families, using the families' needs assessment, tracks the family ministry's impact for favorable results—for example, tracking a poor family's ability to increase earning power over a period of three to five years.

GIVE GOD THE GLORY

Undertaking the challenge to establish or improve ministry to families in a negative environment is a formidable task. Continuing to diagnose the problems without doing anything about them will only hasten the demise of the family. Using our God-given gifts and abilities with the resources He supplies, we can face the challenge. God is willing to change the situation. God is not the problem. The Lord invites us to join the fray.

Some of us, as pastors and Christians, encounter seemingly impossible odds, but Jeremiah reminds us of the source of our strength: "Ah, Sovereign LORD, you have made the heavens and the earth by your great power and outstretched arm. Nothing is too hard for you" (Jer. 32:17).

As God gives us victory in ministering to families, we will give Him all of the praise and glory.

BOOKS FOR FURTHER KNOWLEDGE AND USE IN FAMILY MINISTRY

Adams, Jay E. *The Christian Counselor's Manual.* Grand Rapids: Baker, 1973.

_____. *Ready to Restore.* Phillipsburg: Presbyterian and Reformed, 1981.

_____. *Solving Marriage Problems.* Grand Rapids: Zondervan, 1983.

Birchett, Colleen. *How to Help Hurting People.* Chicago: Urban Ministries, 1990.

Broger, John C. *Self-Confrontation: A Manual for In-Depth Discipleship.* Nashville: Thomas Nelson, 1994. (An Instructor's Guide is also available.)

Crabb, Larry. *Effective Biblical Counseling.* Grand Rapids: Zondervan, 1977.

Ellison, Craig W., and Edward S. Maynard. *Healing for the City: Counseling in the Urban Setting.* Grand Rapids: Zondervan, 1992.

Fish, Melinda. *When Addiction Comes to the Church.* Old Tappan: Chosen, 1990.

Heitritter, Lynn, and Jeanette Vought. *Helping Victims of Sexual Abuse.* Minneapolis: Bethany, 1989.

May, Gerald G. *Addiction and Grace.* San Francisco: Harper & Row, 1988.

Moorehead, Bob. *Counsel Yourself and Others From the Bible.* Portland: Multnomah, 1994.

Rushford, Patricia H. *Caring for Your Elderly Parents.* Grand Rapids: Revell, 1993.

Strom, Kay M. *Helping Women in Crisis.* Grand Rapids: Zondervan, 1986.

Walker, Clarence. *Biblical Counseling With African-Americans.* Grand Rapids: Zondervan, 1992.

Chapter 5

HOW TO EVANGELIZE FAMILIES

REACHING FAMILY MEMBERS
Reaching Family Members in the Church

The greatest thing we can do for any family member is to lead him or her to a saving knowledge of Jesus Christ. I believe we have hope from the Bible that we can win entire families to Christ. This can happen all at once, or each family member can come to Christ over a period of time (Acts 10:19–27, 34–48; 16:14–15, 25–34).

The goal for the church is to try to see that every member of a family comes to know Jesus Christ as Lord and Savior. If we win one family member to Christ and bring him or her to our church for the purpose of joining, and develop him or her as a Christian, we should look at this as an opening for reaching the rest of that household.

We must not assume that every member of our church is saved. According to some of the passages in the New Testament, this is not likely. Evangelistic messages must be preached at least once a year on a Sunday morning, making the plan of salvation clear and plain. In these messages, the level of commitment that should follow a profession of faith in Jesus Christ should also be understandable. At the conclusion of each of these messages, an invitation should be given to receive Jesus

Christ. However, some church members who come forward to indicate that they are receiving Christ may be embarrassed to reveal publicly that they were not truly Christians. So, it is probably best to allow church members to pray silently to receive Christ.

We must especially follow up from time to time on children who grow up in the church and profess Christ at an early age. Most of the time, these children are genuinely saved, but they should not be left to grow on their own. The church must have a well-trained Sunday school staff to be sure these children are growing in Christ. There should be those in the church who specialize in children's work and youth ministry. Recently, I was conducting a Men's Retreat and asked all of the men to introduce themselves and state how long they had been a Christian and a member of our church. A young man who grew up in our church gave the information requested, revealing that he had been a member of our church longer than he had been a Christian. Parents should review a child's profession of faith at every birthday until that child is an older teenager.

Reaching Family Members Not in the Church

All church members should be trained to share their faith. All new members should be taught, among other things, in a new members' class how to witness for Christ. They should learn a very simple salvation outline such as the one listed below:

1. God Loves You—John 3:16
2. Your Need of God—Isaiah 53:6
3. What Christ Has Done for You—John 3:16
4. What You Must Do—John 1:12

There are many very simple outlines of the salvation message that can be used, but the reason the plan must be simple is that you don't want to overwhelm new Christians with learning a lot of Scriptures before they are allowed to witness. They should be expected to share their faith right away. This is natural for many new converts because of their new-found peace and joy in Christ. Some will tell people about Christ without any instructions. New converts must be advised that they will not be able to answer every question or challenge given them by non-believers, but they can get help from a more experienced soul winner at the church.

Ongoing Evangelism Training

There also should be a more thorough training in evangelism than that just described. The training should include

1. An understanding of what the Great Commission means
2. The importance of prayer with evangelism
3. Dependence on the power of God, the Holy Spirit
4. Salvation plan Scriptures
5. How to deal with objections
6. Strategy for getting new converts into the church
7. A follow-up plan
8. The recruiting of new church members to serve in the evangelism ministry
9. How to use gospel tracts
10. How to use evangelism tools such as *You Have Been Crowned With Glory and Honor*[1]

When I speak of ongoing evangelism training, I mean there should be continual training of every new member and training of older, experienced members in new methods and techniques of evangelism.

There Can Be Difficulties In Sharing Christ With Family Members

Teach new members what to expect from their unsaved family members. Family members can be some of the most difficult people to share your faith with, or they can be some of the easiest. Unsaved parents can take the position that you are their child and you can't tell them anything about religion, though you may be forty years old. Husbands can be full of pride and think that listening to their wives is not macho. A sister or brother may know you well enough to bring up your past sins. All of these things can be distracting, but the Christian must remember to make salvation in Christ the issue.

Pray for Unsaved Family Members

Church members should be taught to pray for their unsaved family members. Prayer is a powerful force. Sometimes prayer alone, without our involvement, can bring our unsaved family members to Christ. For example, I received a lot of resistance from an unsaved member of my family whenever I shared Christ with him one-on-one. I decided that instead of trying to tell him about Christ again, I would pray for his salvation. At my ordination examination, my family and church members were allowed to be present. Out of curiosity, my unsaved family member came. By the end of the examination, he had made a commitment to Christ. I had also prayed for thirteen years before my mother came to Christ. Prayer and evangelism go together.

Express Love to Family Members

Church members should be taught to express love to unsaved family members. It is not easy to express love to family members who are persecuting us because of our faith in Jesus Christ, but we must. Jesus is our example. From the cross He said, "Father, forgive them, for they do not know what they are doing." According to 1 Peter 3:1–7, husbands and wives can win their unsaved mates to Christ by their behavior. Certainly, other family members can do the same.

Invite Unsaved Family Members to Church

Church members should invite unsaved family members to church. This might be hard to believe, but some believers have never asked unsaved family members to come to church because they don't think they would be interested. Easter, Thanksgiving, and Christmas worship services are great for inviting unsaved members to church. Pastors should plan for this by giving the plan of salvation at some point in their sermon.

Family Day

Plan a Family Day worship service. This worship service is a Sunday morning evangelistic service geared to reaching family members. Visitors cards should be given out and collected for a home visit by the pastor or an evangelism worker.

Gospel Music Concert

Some unbelievers will attend a gospel music concert or something similar more readily than a Sunday morning worship service. During the concert, the plan of salvation and an opportunity to receive Christ should be presented. Weddings and funerals are other occasions to reach unsaved family members.

Children's Programs

Children's Sunday school, Easter, and Christmas programs are other opportunities to reach unsaved family members. Relatives will attend such programs to support a child relative the way they would for school programs.

Parents Should Lead Their Children to Christ

Parents should be trained in how to lead their children to Christ at home and not to depend on the church for their children's salvation.

Church Outings

Church picnics, a couples' Valentine's Day dinner, and other such events afford additional opportunities to reach family members.

REACHING BACKSLIDERS

Some family members have become backsliders and have dropped out of church. Don't forget about them. Make a list of them and start a prayer and visitation program to bring them back to God. Some of them are ready to return to Christ with some help.

REACHING NEW FAMILIES FOR CHRIST
Through Door-to-Door Evangelism

One of the most effective ways of staying in touch with new families in the community is door-to-door evangelism. Our society is mobile; people are moving in and out all the time. Even if you talk to some at their homes and they do not receive Christ, you have planted a seed that may bloom later. We visited a home at least four times over a period of eight years. During the ninth year, through our telephone evangelism, a sixty-five-year-old man came to Christ. Why should we leave such an opportunity for outreach to the Jehovah's Witnesses and the Mormons?

Through Youth Ministry

We can reach new families through children and youth ministries. I spoke at a church in Ohio some years ago and was impressed with the fact that the church was racially integrated and had been for twenty years. The church had a very good youth ministry and when black families began moving into the neighborhood, the youth director reached out to the black teenagers. Many teenagers from these unchurched families accepted Christ and joined the church. The teenagers' growth in Christ was noticed by their parents because of the obedience, honor, and respect that these young people gave them. The parents knew that the change in their children came about because of the youth ministry, which had some type of activity every week to keep the youth out of trouble. The parents felt guilty, so they started attending the church. They received Christ as their personal Savior and joined the church. The church did not plan to integrate. They only had committed themselves to obeying Christ and carrying out the Great Commission.

Through Community Outreach

We can reach new families through community programs such as daycare centers, tutorial services, summer camps for children, etc.

Through Bible Study Groups

Neighborhood and church Bible studies are other means to reach the unsaved. Unbelievers will attend a Bible study at church or in a Christian home if you have subjects such as

- Better communication in marriage
- Understanding and raising teenagers
- How to get more out of your money

Through Telephone Evangelism

Telephone evangelism is another way of reaching families in your community. You can use a Coles Directory to obtain names and phone numbers in order to share Christ over the phone or invite families to a church event.

REACHING MEN FOR CHRIST

Why should we single out men in evangelism? Women outnumber men in most churches. In some churches, male membership can be less than 10 percent. In my experience, it is a lot more difficult to get men to come to church or be committed and faithful than it is to get women. Much of the time when we lose a faithful single woman from the church, it is because she has backslidden because of her involvement with an unsaved man.

In this chapter, we are discussing how to evangelize families. The objective of this book is to establish and maintain Christian families. According to 2 Corinthians 6:14–18, we are not to be yoked with unbelievers. We teach that believers should not marry unbelievers, yet our churches are filled with single Christian women with only a few single Christian men or none at all.

We have wives in our churches who have unsaved husbands and sons at home. We must face Satan head-on and challenge him for millions of unsaved men. The church cannot build Christian families if we are not reaching our unsaved fathers and sons.

Training Men to Reach Men

The church must develop evangelism teams made up of men already in the church who will specialize in witnessing to men.

Training Wives to Reach Husbands

As I mentioned before, 1 Peter 3:1–7 instructs wives married to unsaved husbands that it is possible for them to win their spouses by their behavior. These women must be trained in the way to do this. A support group made up of these women plus women whose husbands have come to Christ must be organized for prayer, encouragement, and support.

A list should be made of these unsaved husbands, and the list distributed for prayer. The husbands' faults and sins should not be discussed in prayer groups. This is gossip and can cause a husband, when he does come to Christ, to join another church when he finds out that people have been talking negatively about him. If the wife has to talk to someone about her marital problems, it should be the pastor or someone else trained to handle such things.

A wife should ask other Christian men in her and her husband's family to share Christ with her husband as God leads them.

ADDITIONAL MEANS FOR REACHING FAMILIES
Family Revivals

We have had both church revivals and citywide revivals, and recently some other churches and cities have begun to hold family revivals. The first one I ever heard of and participated in was in Berkeley, California, under the leadership of Pastor Earl Stuckey. Not only did family members recommit themselves to Christ and each other, but there was an increase of men coming to Christ, and many who were inactive members returned to church. Pastor Stuckey followed up the family revival by visiting every unsaved husband of female church members. The goals of the family revival should be

1. To have all family members in attendance
2. To reach unsaved family members
3. To teach biblical principles concerning family life
4. To present biblical preaching that brings people to repentance so as to live a godly family life

Family Reunions

Family reunions are great occasions for leading family members to Christ. Workshops could be given to encourage Christians to participate in or organize a family reunion.

Family Gatherings

Family gatherings offer another opportunity to model and share the Christian life. Some Christians make the mistake of isolating themselves from their unsaved family members because they are offended by their lifestyle, yet, at the same time, they are praying for their salvation. I believe that we Christians ought to have moral standards for our homes. I think it is hypocritical to hang a plaque on the wall stating "God Bless This House" while we allow drinking, illegal drug use, and unmarried people sleeping together in our beds. As a matter of fact, I believe it is a stumbling block to a good Christian witness. However, we must express love to our unsaved family members. We should invite them to our homes for dinner, to birthday parties, or just for coffee and dessert.

Discipling Families

Evangelism isn't evangelism if we get only professions of faith and people do not join the church. Evangelism isn't evangelism if people join the church and receive no personal help in applying the Scriptures in their lives. To complete the Great Commission, we must "make disciples ... teaching them to obey everything ..." (Matt. 28:19–20).

There is a difference between the lifestyle of a Christian single and that of a non-Christian single. The lifestyle of married Christians differs from that of unsaved married Christians. However, there are single Christians who have not changed their ungodly dating habits. The church must make disciples for our Lord Jesus Christ. We must teach them biblical standards for every area of their lives.

Spiritual Sisters and Brothers

We are in the family of God. We are sisters and brothers in Christ. We should assign older, mature Christian men to guide new Christian men. We should do the same for the women. Mature married people can be a model for inexperienced husbands and wives. There used to be a time when a daughter would talk to her mother about marital adjustments. Her mother would give good advice with a commitment to contribute to the success of the marriage. Fathers used to hold their sons and sons-in-law accountable to carry out their responsibilities as husbands. There has been a breakdown in the extended family among us, and parental involvement toward the success of the marriage of their children is becoming far too rare. The church must get more involved by providing surrogate parents for those who need them, through a Spiritual Sister and Brother Ministry.

Couples Discipling Other Couples

There is a couple in my church who seem to be gifted in discipling other couples. They were able to make progress with a particular couple when our counseling ministry had gone as far as it could. Some people come from dysfunctional families in which as children they were not taught things such as personal care, being a homemaker, domestic financial management, child care, how to make simple repairs and maintenance, etc.

Small Groups

Small groups are very effective in discipling. These groups can be made up of married people of the same sex or mixed—with the purpose of developing better marriages.

BOOKS FOR FURTHER KNOWLEDGE AND USE IN FAMILY MINISTRY
Aldrich, Joe. *Lifestyle Evangelism.* Portland: Multnomah Press, 1993.
Berry, Jo. *Beloved Unbeliever.* Grand Rapids: Zondervan, 1981.
Bustanoby, André. *When Your Mate Is Not a Christian.* Grand Rapids: Zondervan, 1989.
Hyles, Jack. *Let's Go Soul Winning.* Murfreesboro: Sword of the Lord, 1962.
Lovett, S. C. *Unequally Yoked Wives.* Baldwin Park: Personal Christianity, 1968.
Richardson, Willie. *A Plan for Getting More Men Into the Church and Keeping Most of Them.* Philadelphia: Christian Research & Development, 1994.

Part 2

THE TRAINING OF SINGLE CHRISTIANS

Chapter 6

TRAINING SINGLE CHRISTIANS FOR MARRIAGE

More than eighteen years ago I met a young woman at whose marriage I had officiated nine months earlier. She had come to me to be married, recommended by her cousin who was a member of our church. I had met with this couple two times to tell them what would be expected of them as a married couple; then I married them. I asked her how she and her husband were doing. The question wiped the smile off her face. She said they were no longer together and had no hope that they could be reconciled. I was amazed that a marriage could fall apart so fast.

I conducted a survey of all the couples I had married up to that point. I had married people under an assortment of circumstances. Some were members of my church. More than half were not members of my church. Requests came from friends, neighbors, relatives, co-workers (I was a full-time mechanical-design engineer at the time and also pastored the church). Even my barber asked me to marry his niece. The results of the survey were as follows:

- 75 percent of the couples I had married had separated or divorced.
- Of the 25 percent who were still together, only 10 percent of the couples were happily married.

- Of the 10 percent who were happily married, only half of these couples knew why they were happy.

As a pastor, I was convicted and burdened by these facts. I was strongly convinced that married life should be better. I committed myself to not simply marrying people but trying to establish Christian homes. During the last eighteen years, we have had only one divorce among the singles who submitted themselves to our marriage training and preparation. We will not marry anyone without a commitment to complete our marriage training program. Not all of our single adults submit to this— 90 percent do.

The Christian life is radically different from a life without Christ as Lord and Savior. We know that when people are truly converted, a radical change takes place in their lives. The way they think changes. Their morality and values change. Their love of God, people, and self changes. Shouldn't Christian conduct in courtship also change?

I have spent a great deal of time in winning African-American males to Christ and discipling them. In their development, I have seen single men withdraw from dating to draw closer to Christ. Some have actually said, "I don't know how to relate to a woman as a Christian single man. I know how I used to relate to them as an ungodly person, but how do I relate now after receiving Christ?" The church and pastors need to answer this question not only for Christian single men, but also for Christian single women. All of them, men and women, need Christian guidance.

I believe that some of the conduct of some of our Christian singles is worse than when they were "in the world." Because of the shortage of single Christian men in the church, some women seem to be desperate when a single man joins the church. On the other hand, some Christian single men seem to be on a carnal ego trip because of their popularity with women in the church—a popularity they did not experience "in the world."

I believe that the success of a marriage is determined a great deal by what happens in a person's life before the marriage. I call this period before marriage the mate-selection process. This process includes the single's faith and trust in the Lord for a mate, friendships, courtships, marriage expectations, motives for wanting to be married, and clear thinking, rather than a feeling-oriented dating pattern. Singles need to be trained in how to determine when a relationship is not right for marriage. They need to know how to prepare themselves for marriage.

INDIVIDUAL PREPARATION FOR MARRIAGE

What is a single Christian to do until "Miss Right" or "Mr. Right" comes along? Enjoy the Christian single life. Too many single Christian people are unhappily waiting to get married. What causes them to be unhappy? There are two major causes. First, they don't have the opportunity to go on as many dates as they did before they received Christ and committed themselves to the Christian life. Most of the dating they did "in the world" wasn't very fulfilling or wholesome, of course, but the Devil has a way of helping them to forget past reality and glorify the past life of sin.

Second, some women don't have much hope because of the shortage of Christian men in the church. They constantly do addition and subtraction. They add up all the single Christian women, subtract the available single Christian men, and the remainder equals no chance for them to have a mate.

We are told in Philippians 4:4, "Rejoice in the Lord always. I will say it again: Rejoice!" This is God's will for all Christians, including single Christians. We need to help Christian singles to understand the radically different Christian single life.

CONFIRM THE SALVATION OF THE SINGLE PERSON

As I stated earlier, salvation in Christ is of the utmost importance. Before the single Christians came to Christ, they were dead in their transgressions and sins in which they used to live, following the ways of this world and the Devil, gratifying the desires of a sinful nature (Eph. 2:1–3). In their past life, some single men viewed women only for their own sexual pleasure. In their past life, some women viewed men only as a source for what they wanted to get out of life. In any case, God was not central to their lives—self was. Too often these godless attitudes continue in the church among some single people.

It must be confirmed that the single person has truly received Jesus as Lord of his or her life. If so, the individual is alive in Christ and has been created to live a godly single life (Eph. 2:5, 10). In the church we should not be working with spiritually dead people who are separated from Christ, without hope and without God (Eph. 2:12). Single people must be given a clear presentation of what it is to have salvation and be expected to grow in the grace and knowledge of Jesus Christ (2 Peter 3:18).

BECOMING A VIRGIN AGAIN

"Food for the stomach and the stomach for food"—but God will
destroy them both. The body is not meant for sexual immorality, but
for the Lord, and the Lord for the body. By his power God raised the
Lord from the dead, and he will raise us also. Do you not know that
your bodies are members of Christ himself? Shall I then take the members of Christ and unite them with a prostitute? Never! Do you not
know that he who unites himself with a prostitute is one with her in
body? For it is said, "The two will become one flesh." But he who unites
himself with the Lord is one with him in spirit. Flee from sexual
immorality. All other sins a man commits are outside his body, but he
who sins sexually sins against his own body. Do you not know that your
body is a temple of the Holy Spirit, who is in you, whom you have
received from God? You are not your own; you were bought at a price.
Therefore honor God with your body (1 Cor. 6:13–20).

Many marriages have broken up because of adultery. Sometimes
this is a carryover from a carnal single life of sexually permissive behavior, even among professing Christians. Even if the single persons have
lost their virginity, they should be instructed not to continue in sin.
Some years ago, we were having a special service in honor of women. All
the speakers were women who spoke for about fifteen minutes on a subject of interest to other Christian women. In one of the presentations, one
of the single women spoke of the joy she was having in her relationship
with Christ. She surprisingly spoke of her deliverance from an active sex
life and stated that she had "become a virgin again." She explained that
since she was assured by Scripture that God had forgiven her and does
not remember her sins any longer, God only saw what she had become—
celibate. Because of her celibacy, she was now a spiritual virgin, hence
she was a virgin again.

It is very difficult for some single people who have enjoyed sex in a
sinful context not to indulge in illicit sex again, for memories create
temptation. God is willing to help during times of temptation, and this
should not be forgotten (1 Cor. 10:13). Even if individuals weaken and
fail, they should not give up on living a righteous life and depending on
the Holy Spirit. "So I say, live by the Spirit, and you will not gratify the
desires of the sinful nature" (Gal. 5:16).

The church must speak out loudly against sexual immorality, not
only because it is God's will to do so, but also because immorality is
destructive to family life and is increasingly becoming a matter of life and

death because of the continual advancement of AIDS. Adultery has broken marriages. Living together without being married has fostered a new generation of adults uncommitted to the sanctity of marriage and to one another. When children are born into these illicit live-in relationships, their parents' lack of commitment can hamper them throughout their lives. Because of sexual immorality, the church faces a new problem today. Young Christian adults who grow up in solid Christian homes and know nothing of a wild, worldly, ungodly lifestyle are innocently marrying relatively new Christians who had contracted HIV years earlier. Should we require an AIDS test before we marry people?

A Christian mother of three who had been separated from her husband decided she wanted them to be reconciled. The husband had rejected Christ and continued his life of partying and womanizing after marriage. She reasoned, however, that her children should have both a mother and a father. The husband readily agreed to return home. But during their years of separation he had contracted AIDS and never told his wife. Within two years she died; in another year, he too died from the disease. Now the children have neither their father nor their mother.

EDUCATIONAL READINESS

Education is still the name of the game in America. Education does have an impact on the family, as I will explain in more detail in chapter 9, "Training Families in How to Use Their Resources." The best time to obtain as much education as possible is when we are single adults. It is more difficult when you are married because of family responsibilities. It is better to curtail dating activity as a single in order to pursue education than to lose a spouse because of neglect and financial pressures as a married person.

Single adults who are high school dropouts or still have not decided what they want to be when they grow up, are not yet ready to get married. These issues must be resolved first. Some of our poorest people don't stand a chance in the job market because of deficient education as a child or a learning disability that was never diagnosed. Sometimes adults, even those still in their thirties, say they are too old to return to school. We give them hope and encouragment to discover and develop through education and training what God has placed in them.

OCCUPATIONAL READINESS

You can't live on love. You have to have money, in spite of popular songs. Because of the cost of living today, some jobs, even if you have two of them, do not pay enough to support a family. We must help single people to acquire good occupations so they can earn wages that will not make them part of the "working poor." Even before they leave high school, there should be a strategy planned as to how they will move ahead in an occupation or career.

When one is a single it is the time to take risk with jobs, especially if the single person is still living with parents. This is the ideal time to change occupations because of dissatisfaction with a job or boss. This is also the time to leave even a good job for a better opportunity.

How can singles know if they are earning enough money to get married? Would a man's salary support a wife and one child? The man should make a budget based on the lifestyle of a family he knows and on the level of income he would like to receive. He may have to interview more than one family to get an idea of what it costs to support a family. We give this assignment regularly in our premarital counseling; we find that friends are honored to help.

It may be that a man does not earn enough money to support a family at this time. A couple can still get married with the understanding that for an agreed-upon period of time the wife will work to help support the family.

I believe that in the early years of childhood, from infancy to age six, children should have their mother at home nurturing, teaching, and developing them. I realize that some couples cannot afford to do this, but perhaps their lifestyles have to change. When we had less, as a people, we raised families this way. The value we place on our children and our commitment to family life must be such that we are willing to forgo some material conveniences or luxuries.

Long before singles find a person to marry, they should have wisely made up an estimated family budget and used it as a scale to measure financial progress as a wage earner.

RELATIONAL SKILLS READINESS

The Bible is the book on relationships—relationships with God, with other people, and with ourselves.

> Each of you should look not only to your own interests, but also to the interests of others (Phil. 2:4).

> He answered: "'Love the Lord your God with all your heart and with all your soul and with all your strength and with all your mind'; and, 'Love your neighbor as yourself'" (Luke 10:27).

If it is possible, as far as it depends on you, live at peace with every-one (Rom. 12:18).

Bear with each other and forgive whatever grievances you may have against one another. Forgive as the Lord forgave you (Col. 3:13).

In your anger do not sin; when you are on your beds, search your hearts and be silent (Ps. 4:4).

"Do not judge, or you too will be judged" (Matt. 7:1).

Therefore, encourage one another and build each other up, just as in fact you are doing (1 Thess. 5:11).

Interpersonal relational skills should be well developed before we are married. These skills should be developing in us as we grow up in our families. This is why it is good to have sisters and brothers. These skills should also be developed in kindergarten through high school and col-lege, if you are blessed to attend college. God further develops these skills in our church families. These skills pay off in dividends as we get along with people on the job.

By the time we marry, the maturity of our interpersonal relational skills should have been cultivated by love to evolve into marital bliss. But, of course, very few people experience this because, in general, we who are parents have not been trained. We do not deliberately train our children how to love, respect, and support others; however, single adults need to consciously try to develop these skills, such as

- Loving others
- Receiving love from others
- Being unselfish
- Handling anger
- Forgiving others
- Tolerating people whose personalities are irritating
- Sharing with and giving to others
- Submitting to others
- Being effective in personal communications
- Working through disagreements
- Appreciating how others differ from you
- Showing respect toward others

As you can see, our biological families and church families are the best places to develop these skills. Friendships with people of the same sex offer additional opportunities to produce these virtues.

SOME INDICATORS THAT A SINGLE PERSON IS MATURE ENOUGH TO GET MARRIED
The Willingness to Accept and Learn the Responsibilities of Marriage

Some men are willing to marry without the foggiest idea of what it means to be a husband from a biblical perspective. There are also some desperate women in the same boat. Women need to beware of a man who is not teachable. Many married men, regardless of whether they have children, will verbalize or think, "I don't want to be married any more," when they find out that marriage is not a lark.

Faith and Trust in God for a Mate

Without faith in God to wait for His timing and to trust in His willingness to guide our lives, singles can marry a person who is not suited for them. "Trust in the LORD with all your heart and lean not on your own understanding; in all your ways acknowledge him, and he will make your paths straight. Do not be wise in your own eyes; fear the LORD and shun evil" (Prov. 3:5–7).

Good Managers of One's Money

Good money management includes
- Being able to hold a job
- Living by a budget
- Saving money for marriage
- Owning something (car, etc.)
- Having good credit

Ability to Take Care of Oneself

Some adults allow their parents to take care of them. Some of these people are looking to marry someone who will continue to do so or who will join their team of benefactors.

Emotional Stability

Some people never grow up. They display outbursts of uncontrollable emotions such as anger, crying, and pouting when they don't get their way, then resort to shameful sulking, and either refuse to talk or become argumentative. We are to be in control of our emotions, rather than let emotions control us.

Continual Spiritual Growth

We should manifest the spirit of Christ by the fruit of the Spirit (Gal. 5:22–23): love, joy, peace, patience, kindness, goodness, faithfulness, gentleness, and self-control. We are not looking for perfect people; rather we are looking for signs that there is a Christ-life. We are looking for people who will bring Christ into a marriage—not the Devil.

Trustworthiness and Reliability

Intimacy cannot be built without trust. It is difficult to trust an unreliable person.

A Willingness to Face, Deal With, and Work Through Problems

The Bible teaches that the weight is on the man to give leadership. He is the chairman of the trouble and problem departments.

Industriousness, Orderliness, and Cleanliness

There is no place for laziness in marriage. Too often, single people marry people they don't know; for example, a neat, clean, and orderly person marries a slob. Felix and Oscar are great entertainment in *The Odd Couple*, but in real life this makes for a miserable marriage.

A Willingness to Give up a Singles Mentality

The attitude of "my life," "my money," "my vacation," "my things" has to be given up when you marry. Some husbands think it unmanly for their wives to know where they are at all times. This is silly when we realize that the man is the "head" of the woman (1 Cor. 11:3). The Bible speaks of oneness in a marriage. The single must think "we," "us," "our."

SINGLE PEOPLE SHOULD KNOW WHAT THEY ARE LOOKING FOR

Sometimes young, proud single people can be unrealistic in looking for the right person to marry. A young man in my church complained to me that no woman in the church would go out with him. He concluded that they were stuck up and unspiritual. I asked him whom he had invited to go out with him. He gave me a list of women who in my estimate were "tens." The women were attractive, well-groomed, stylishly dressed, professional, and sophisticated. He, on the other hand, was average and unkempt. His clothes did not fit him, his stomach was hanging over his belt, and he needed a haircut. I instructed him in ways he might improve himself and told him he was looking in the wrong part of the garden (women in our church). He was in the "ten" section when he should have humbled himself and looked in the "five" section. After some improvements, God blessed him with an "eight."

God created us and knows what type of person is suited for us in marriage. The reason I say "the type of person" rather than "a person" suited for us is that I do not believe the Hollywood idea of a "one and only person." My godfather, who is 102 years old, outlived two wives. Both marriages were successful. The women were different, but they were the same type of woman. When we submit to and practice the love of God in marriage, it reaps lasting benefits.

The question for the single person is, "What type of person is suited for me?" (Gen. 2:20). Singles should seek the face of the Lord in seeking the answer to this question. Then they should jot down some thoughts from the following categories.

Physical Characteristics

Although I list this first, I believe we are immature if this is the most important thing we are looking for when seeking a marriage partner. On the other hand, I do not think what a person looks like should be totally ignored. To punish a person later after marriage for what they can't change is an ongoing mistake of some couples. I once had a counseling case where the wife was displeased with her husband. She would call him a "sawed-off runt" or "shorty." I asked her if she resented her husband's height. She said yes. I asked her, "Was your husband taller before you married him?" She said no, but she thought she could adjust to him.

I once counseled a husband who continued to make jokes concerning his fat wife. He thought he could humiliate pounds off her.

I suggest to single people to take a good look at their girlfriend's or boyfriend's parents and grandparents to get an indication of what the physical future holds for them. Loving people should go beyond the physical.

Education

How much education is the single person requiring in a mate? Sometimes, for various reasons, more educated people badger their mates after marriage to obtain a higher level of education. The less-educated spouse may be satisfied with his or her education and have no intention of obtaining more.

Occupation

Sometimes married people are ashamed of what their mates do for a living or think that what they do is un-Christian. These issues should be resolved before marriage. It is good that single people make it a habit of knowing what a person they are dating does for a living, but, beyond that, when the relationship is very serious and there is talk of marriage, they should also know the other person's annual income. (It is good to know what a person does to earn money: it may involve some illegal activity, such as the drug trade.)

Some African-American women will have to face up to the fact that because of the oppression and lack of opportunity some black men have been subjected to, women may have to work all of their lives after marriage. I do not mean to say that these women will wholly support the family, but their income will have to subsidize the family income. We have a large population of men who are ex-offenders, uneducated, and in an occupational trade. Unfortunately, their prison record, too, is often held against them. However, as I have stated elsewhere in this book, we cannot let seeming handicaps defeat us. We are Christians, and our God can do the impossible through us.

Intellect

You should have noticed by now that all of the items on this list will make couples more compatible if considered before marriage. Intellect, too, is important. Some married people treat their mates like the village idiot. They are smarter, wiser, and more intelligent, and they never let their mate forget it. One of the problems is that most courtships are not long enough to really get to know a person.

I have a friend who purposely chose a college graduate with a lower I.Q. than his for a very practical reason. He has a very high I.Q. and is in a profession that requires that he continually use his mind. He did not want to come home to another "egghead" who would stimulate his mind further but chose someone with whom he could relax. They have great evenings together.

Social Life

It is very important that husbands and wives have similar tastes in what they do socially and recreationally. They need to do a lot of things together. They need to be best friends.

Financial Achievement

This has to do with knowing how a person handles money. Some people are immature and spend every dollar they receive. They say, "Trust God for tomorrow; let's live for today!" This is foolishness, for God has called us to be stewards.

Homemaking Skills

This area should not be taken for granted. Some of the biggest fights in marriage can be over a woman who does not know how to cook and a man who can't fix anything.

Temperament and Personality

This is one of the most important considerations, if not the greatest. There are some temperaments and personalities that are not very compatible. Again, some courtships are not long enough to really get to know the person. Matching the wrong temperaments and personalities can end in divorce or a life of misery with no peace. For instance, there are people who love debating and others who hate arguments. There are people who thrive on conflict and others who love peace. One of the mistakes people make is to choose opposites of themselves. I understand that this happens because we choose to compensate for our weaknesses. You should have a lot in common with the person you choose to marry, and your temperaments and personalities should be compatible. Again, we are not looking for perfect people. Nice people should marry nice people. Argumentative people should marry argumentative people. Slobs should marry slobs.

Spiritual Maturity

It takes three people to make a marriage—the husband, the wife, and Christ. We bring Christ into a marriage through our heart (John 1:12) and through obedience to God and His Word. We cannot expect to build Christian families without both husband and wife committed to Christ. Even if both people are saved, they still can be unequally yoked, based on commitment and submission to God, the Holy Spirit. A devotional life of praying together and sharing the Scriptures should be a must in the courtship of Christian single people. Such issues as the following should be raised and dealt with:

- Salvation and salvation experience
- Church membership and church involvement

- Family religious background
- Level of Bible knowledge
- Commitment to Bible teachings
- Spiritual gifts and the willingness to discover and use them
- Discussion on the difficulties of living the Christian life
- The importance of sexual purity and chastity, even if there have been past failures
- Discussion on specific spiritual growth goals
- Observance of the character of friends (birds of a feather do flock together)
- Knowing God's will for one's life
- Knowing who would lead in spiritual things (the man should)

Cultural Background

One's cultural background can be a blessing or a curse. In a counseling case I had with a married couple, one of the problems was that the wife was ashamed of her husband's eating habits, so she refused to go out to eat with him. He would eat with his chin almost touching his plate, using one hand to scoop the food into his mouth, while the other hand held a knife continually circling his plate like a prisonyard search light. We discovered that the reason he ate this way was that he grew up in a poor, large family, and if you did not guard your meat, it would be snatched from your dinner plate and gobbled down instantly. This husband was willing to be retrained in proper eating etiquette.

MEETING EACH OTHER'S NEEDS
What Needs Must a Partner Meet in Your Life?

Too often we think that just because the person we marry loves us, God has given that person omniscience to know what our needs are without our communicating them. What is worse is that when married people are dissatisfied and complain that their needs are not being met, they may not know what these needs are themselves. The needs should be thought through, written down, and discussed.

What Needs Are You Willing to Meet in a Partner's Life?

Selfishness is one of the destroyers of marriage. We marry to be loved by someone without any serious considerations for what needs we will be called upon to meet in someone else's life. Such needs should be clearly understood before marriage.

Marriage Is Permanent, But a Detrimental Courtship Should Be Broken Off

On the day of their wedding, people sometimes have doubts as to whether or not they are doing the right thing. Sometimes, planning for a church wedding brings out the true character of a person; however, this is ignored by some engaged people. The following are some possible indicators that a relationship is wrong and should be broken off.

1. The strength of the love is based on sexual pleasure. There is no sexual restraint as a Christian. Sex is the dominating factor in the relationship.
2. One or both people in the relationship do not trust the sexual faithfulness of the other.
3. When a partner does not show consistent spirituality to convince the other, without a doubt, that Jesus Christ is his or her Lord and Savior.
4. One or both have intentions of changing partners, if the marriage doesn't work out.
5. One partner is constantly critical of the other and seems to be searching to find fault.
6. If one partner dominates the other's personality and interest is primarily in self, there is ignoring and a lack of acceptance of the other as a person.
7. There are constant misunderstandings and breakdowns in communication. Communication is key for a successful marriage.
8. There are constant arguments.
9. A partner is vindictive and holds grudges.
10. A partner is jealous and there is a lack of trust.
11. One of the partners is too afraid of the other to break off the relationship for fear of bodily injury.
12. There is a deep-seated feeling about the relationship that blocks peace of mind.
13. One of the partners is struggling with drug or alcohol addiction.
14. One partner has trouble getting along with most people.

SOME WRONG MOTIVES FOR GETTING MARRIED

1. Fear of growing too old to get married
2. Being tired of working hard and wanting someone to take care of you and perhaps your children
3. Thinking it would be an easier way to get sex without a hassle
4. To get a permanent housekeeper
5. To get away from the family
6. Being turned down by someone else and wanting to prove you are marriageable
7. Being tired of being alone
8. To satisfy friends and relatives who say you should be married
9. To rid yourself of feelings of inferiority
10. To belong to someone or have someone to call your own
11. To have help with your children
12. Being aware that your biological clock is running down

BOOKS FOR FURTHER KNOWLEDGE AND USE IN FAMILY MINISTRY

Bustanoby, Andy. *Can Men and Women Be Just Friends?* Grand Rapids: Zondervan, 1993.

Inrig, Gary. *Quality Friendships*. Chicago: Moody, 1981.

McRae, William J. *Preparing for Your Marriage.* Grand Rapids: Zondervan, 1980.

Chapter 7

TRAINING SINGLES IN THE MATE-SELECTION PROCESS

I believe that God takes most people through a process of relationships before they meet the person who is suitable for them to marry. Sometimes it may be a few courting relationships and other times there may be many relationships. I believe sometimes we are not mature enough to know who is best for us until we have had some bad experiences with people we think are good for us—then we can appreciate God's choice for us. As I have conducted our *Developing the Christian Single and Family Life* seminars, I have surveyed Christian married people who, when they first met did not like each other, but are now experiencing a good marriage. It can be quite amusing to hear what God did to help a person see their partner as God's choice. It is also amusing to hear the high standards people in their twenties have in looking for a mate—standards that seem to dissipate as these people are still unmarried after their thirty-fifth birthday. The most important thing to remember during the mate-selection process is to trust God and take your time. I will repeat this fact in this chapter from time to time because it is a tragic mistake to do otherwise.

I recommend one to three years in getting to know someone. Some single people resist this suggestion. They say, "That's a long time." Even some of my fellow pastors disagree with me and continue to marry people who do not know one another. However, I would like to remind everyone to read the divorce statistics and look around in our families and churches at the marriages that break up in six months to three years. It seems to me more beneficial to invest the time in advance to know the person better before we swear before God in making marriage vows, which half of the people who get married don't keep.

I know that when two adults love each other, there is sexual pressure to make love. However, I don't believe God would have a prohibition on sexual relations outside of marriage if it were not possible for us to obey Him. In defense of getting married because of sexual pressure, some have even quoted 1 Corinthians 7:9: "It is better to [get married] than to burn." I think the idea in that verse is more than simply getting married to make sex holy; it is still important whom you marry. I know of some single Christian people who were so sexually hot for one another that they had to get married without delay, but sex did not hold their marriage together. They are now divorced. Sex alone cannot hold a marriage together, but learning to love, accept, and be supportive of a spouse will bond and unite a couple under the lordship of Jesus Christ.

I believe God needs time to bring about the right circumstances to reveal the person we should marry. It is easy to pretend and act for a few weeks or months; some divorcées would like to nominate their ex-spouses for an Academy Award. Some people have things they want to hide before marriage; given time, God has a way of protecting His own from disaster by revealing what the other person is hiding.

SELECTION LIMITS AND PROBLEMS
Believers Should Marry Believers

This principle is not only taught in the New Testament (2 Cor. 6:14–16) but was also practiced by Israel in the Old Testament (Deut. 7:3–4). It is also very practical that a family worship the same God, in the same church. Faith and worship are powerful in a family. So often it is the father who is unsaved or is a Muslim. Some fathers drop their wives and children off at church. Every family needs a father and mother who are fully committed to Jesus Christ as Lord and Savior.

Available Singles in a Social Circle

Sometimes Christian singles are limited as to the number of available singles of the opposite sex in their social circle. The Christian single often works on a job with unbelievers, attends college with unbelievers, lives in a neighborhood of unbelievers, and attends a church that has few singles, if any. This can be very discouraging to Christian single women. However, I remind single women that they should not count the number of single men in their church or at a social gathering in comparison to single women, but trust God for a spouse. All they need is one man to marry. Jesus walked on water (Matt. 14:25) and turned water into wine (John 2:7–9), and God divided the Red Sea (Ex. 14:21). Since God has performed these great miracles, He certainly can raise up one measly man for a woman to marry.

Singles must broaden their social circle if a single person of the opposite sex is not available. Singles should not be embarrassed to let it be known among family, friends, and church members that they would like to be married. God encourages marriage. Singles should ask people who love and care for them to pray for them as they go through the mate-selection process. Some of these people will not only pray but will try to introduce them to singles of the opposite sex if they are humble enough to receive the help. The single person should also attend gatherings of other single Christians and get involved in Christian activities with other singles.

The church can help by organizing a singles' ministry that includes opportunities to meet other singles. The church in particular should seek the salvation of African-American males and disciple them into the singles ministry.

Wisdom for Single People Who Want to Get Married

Whom you marry may be the most important decision you will ever make, with the exception of deciding to receive Jesus Christ as your Lord and Savior. During my thirty years of ministering and pastoring, too many single adults seem to be void of wisdom. Throughout the book of Proverbs, God contrasted the fool with the wise person, and Jesus did so as well in some of His parables (Matt. 7:24–27; 25:1–13). We have but to look at the results over the last thirty years to see how many people have been foolish when it comes to family life choices.

God promised He will give us wisdom liberally if we ask (James 1:5). Every single Christian should take advantage of this benefit from God. Wisdom must be lived and practiced. There is protection in wisdom.

> For the LORD gives wisdom, and from his mouth come knowledge and understanding. He holds victory in store for the upright, he is a shield to those whose walk is blameless, for he guards the course

of the just and protects the way of his faithful ones. Then you will understand what is right and just and fair—every good path. For wisdom will enter your heart, and knowledge will be pleasant to your soul. Discretion will protect you, and understanding will guard you. Wisdom will save you from the ways of wicked men, from men whose words are perverse, who leave the straight paths to walk in dark ways, who delight in doing wrong and rejoice in the perverseness of evil, whose paths are crooked and who are devious in their ways (Prov. 2:6–15).

Get wisdom, get understanding; do not forget my words or swerve from them. Do not forsake wisdom, and she will protect you; love her, and she will watch over you. Wisdom is supreme; therefore get wisdom. Though it cost all you have, get understanding (Prov. 4:5–7).

Instruct a wise man and he will be wiser still; teach a righteous man and he will add to his learning (Prov. 9:9).

Godly Motive

The first consideration for the single Christian is to ask, "Is God leading me to be married or is this a desire of my own? If I have the desire to be married, do I have the right motive?" Your motive for marriage should match God's reasons for instituting marriage. Since God is the one who instituted marriage (Gen. 2:18, 22–24), we should submit to His authority when making decisions about it. God's purpose for marriage is for two people to intimately love each other and grow together in companionship (v. 18). God's goal in marriage is the unity of oneness (v. 24) and that this relationship should only be broken by death (Rom. 7:2). Therefore, the godly motive for wanting to marry is to find someone to whom you are willing to give yourself, to love by meeting his or her needs as a companion with lifelong commitment, oneness, and faithfulness. Notice, this is giving 100 percent with no strings attached. It is not fifty/fifty, but loving a person with the love of God (1 John 4:7, 12) until death separates you. The question is, are you ready right now to make that kind of commitment?

Be Educated About Marriage

What you know about marriage from a biblical viewpoint and your firsthand experience of what a Christian marriage and family looks like will give you hope and help you select the right person to marry. One of the reasons so many marriages break up is that the only examples of marriage we know is the family we grew up in, which can be a very dysfunctional family or a single-parent family. Even if we grew up in a good Christian home and our parents truly loved one another, it is still important to learn God's biblical teaching on marriage and family.

I have already stated how complicated marriage can be, so the wise single person will want to be informed and educated concerning the subject of marriage and family.

The single person should read books on the subject, participate in relevant classes at church, and attend seminars. Another blessing to a single person who wants to be knowledgeable is to develop friendships with successful married people. Not only will this benefit you as a single but after you are married, you can seek their counsel as you go through your periods of marital adjustment, which are inevitable in all marriages. Unfortunately, newly married people who are ignorant of what to expect during these periods often bail out and quit the marriage because of a lack of marital education and preparation.

God Is Your Lover

We are told, "Love the Lord your God with all your heart and with all your soul and with all your mind and with all your strength" (Mark 12:30). This is for our own good, whether we are single or married. Because we do not visibly see God, there is the tendency to put more importance on relationships we have with boyfriends, girlfriends, or spouses. Oh sure, when we get into trouble in these relationships, we turn back to God, but sometimes God doesn't seem to be able to relieve our pain, hurt, and depression fast enough. The problem is that our relationship with the Lord is not very strong.

A relationship with God needs our attention the same as any other relationship. We need to spend time with God. Talk with God. Listen to God. Walk with God. Get to know God. For singles to experience a joyful, meaningful life and not go through unnecessary disappointment, pain, rejection, hurt, and being misled, misused, and depressed, the Lord must become their lover.

God can meet love needs in our lives that no one else can meet. I believe that because God created us and He is omniscient, omnipresent, and immutable and loves us with a perfect love, our deepest love needs can be met only by Him.

I have witnessed single people not having time for God after they fall in love. Christians who were faithfully worshiping and serving God just drift away. They can't get to church and are too busy to serve. They don't remember to pray. Their Christian testimony is ruined with their lover. Fellowship with Jesus is broken because often there is sexual involvement. They don't have time for Christian fellowship. Sometimes, when it does not work out with the lover whom they substituted for God, they are too embarrassed to return to the church of which they are a member.

There is no relationship on earth worth breaking our relationship with our Lord and Savior, Jesus Christ. Even if mother, father, and lover forsake you, God will pick you up (Ps. 27:10). We do ourselves a favor if we love the Lord with all our heart, soul, mind, and strength.

If we are that close to God, we can trust Him for a mate. We will not have to be anxious about it, worry about it, or become desperate and marry someone outside of God's will for us. If you are convinced that the Lord is real and that He loves you, you can rest in His love. You can patiently wait for Him to bring his choice into your life; until then, enjoy the single life.

A Serious Decision

Again, I stress that the matter of choosing a person to marry is a very serious one for a Christian. You are entering with another person into an institution and union with God that is to bring Him praise and glory. Your decision will affect not only you, but also the person you marry, your children, your extended family, and your church. Normally, we do not think this way. I have heard single people tell their parents, "Who I marry is my business." This may be true, but your choice of the person you marry does affect the people I listed above, especially your parents and family.

The decision as to whom to marry is serious because according to God's will it is permanent "until death separates you." The world's attitude is if it doesn't work, I will get a divorce. If this person does not work out, I will get another. What is worse is that sometimes people simply walk away and disappear, never to return, abandoning their spouse.

When we make wedding vows, we are making a covenant with the person we marry and with God. You can't leave God out. He instituted marriage; man instituted divorce and living together without commitment. "'I hate divorce,' says the Lord" (Mal. 2:16). Marriage is permanent, until death.

When the time comes to make the decision of whom to marry, it should be made advisedly, reverently, prayerfully, and in the fear of God.

Friendship, Courtship, and Companionship

Single women have said to me, "Pastor, men are not committed to a serious relationship." I ask, "Why do you say that?" "After I've been going out with them for three months and want to know where the relationship is going, they tell me they just want to be friends, or they say I'm a good sister in the Lord," the single woman replies. I have heard this over and over. One woman was so exasperated she said, "I'm tired of being a man's friend or his sister. I want to be somebody's wife." I told her to be patient and wait. She is now happily married to the man who said he just wanted to be friends.

Some years ago a single man came to me discouraged. "It's happened again," he said sadly. I asked him, "What are you talking about?" "Women," he shrugged. "I'm not ready to get married. For no reason at all they keep talking about marriage. I tell them from the start I want to be friends and that's all. I make it clear in the beginning that I am not ready to settle down. All I want is to go out with a sister and be friends," he explained. "Do you kiss these women?" I asked. "Yes," he answered with a puzzled expression. I knew that his entire family were outwardly affectionate people, so I asked, "Do you kiss them the same way you kiss your sister?" He immediately said, "No!" with some embarrassment. I said, "So you want to be friends with these sisters, but you kiss them like lovers." I smiled.

Develop Your Relationships Instead of Letting Them Happen

Relationships evolve in steps of which we are not always conscious. Between the time a couple meets and the day they marry, key intervals have taken place. From the time you meet a person until you agree to go out on a date is one step. From the time you go out until there is the first intimate kiss is another step. From the first intimate kiss until the first time you have a sexual relationship (unfortunately, this is modern, ungodly dating), is another step. From this point until you marry may be the final step. The problem is that some Christian singles follow the model of the world and do not include God, wisdom, and righteousness in their dating life. Rather than letting the steps happen, wise singles will be in control of their emotions, clearly understanding when the relationship is moving from one interval to the next. This is clear thinking, and decisions must be made at each stage for fewer misunderstandings and less disappointment, hurt, and pain.

There are many married people who have never been friends. They have children together, pay bills together, go to church together, but do not experience togetherness, because they are not friends. They have never felt totally accepted by their spouse. When they were single, the steps just happened; they moved through courtship to marriage and now long for companionship. They were never friends, so they can't become real companions. I don't mean to say that all who went from courtship to marriage are not friends or companions, for I know that this is not true. I believe that some of us married people are friends and companions with our spouse only by the grace of God, because for most of us, it was not planned—we were too much in love.

I want to suggest that single Christians should start with *friendship*, move to *courtship*, enter *marriage*, and grow into *companionship* as illustrated in Figure 1 below. Single Christians need to consciously develop these intervals or relational steps.

Friendship

Friendship is no light matter from the biblical point of view. God calls believers to a level of friendship that is rare in the world.

> A friend loves at all times, and a brother is born for adversity (Prov. 17:17).
>
> Wounds from a friend can be trusted, but an enemy multiplies kisses (Prov. 27:6).
>
> As iron sharpens iron, so one man sharpens another (Prov. 27:17).
>
> After David had finished talking with Saul, Jonathan became one in spirit with David, and he loved him as himself. And Jonathan made a covenant with David because he loved him as himself (1 Sam. 18:1, 3).

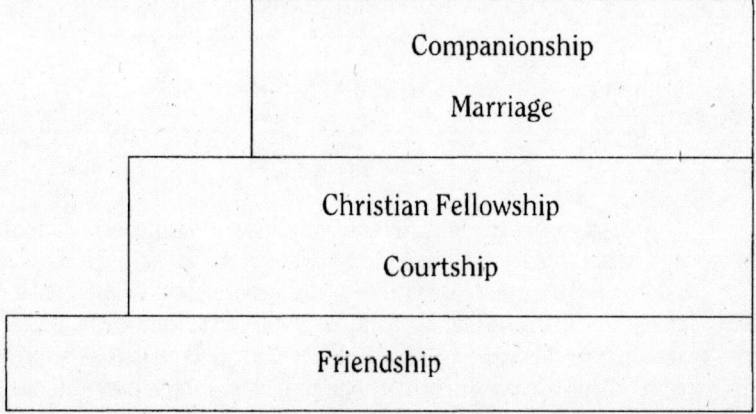

Figure 1

There are advantages for single people to start with friendship rather than courtship. Women who would like to be married will not be accused of wanting to go out with a man to trap him into marriage if she makes clear that her interest is friendship. Such a woman is trusting the Lord and His direction if the friendship should evolve into something more serious. Christian men who are not ready to be married will practice honest friendships that do not include intimate kissing, petting, and sexual intercourse.

I want to suggest that the following intervals or steps be developed in friendship rather than letting things just happen. These steps are illustrated below in Figure 2.

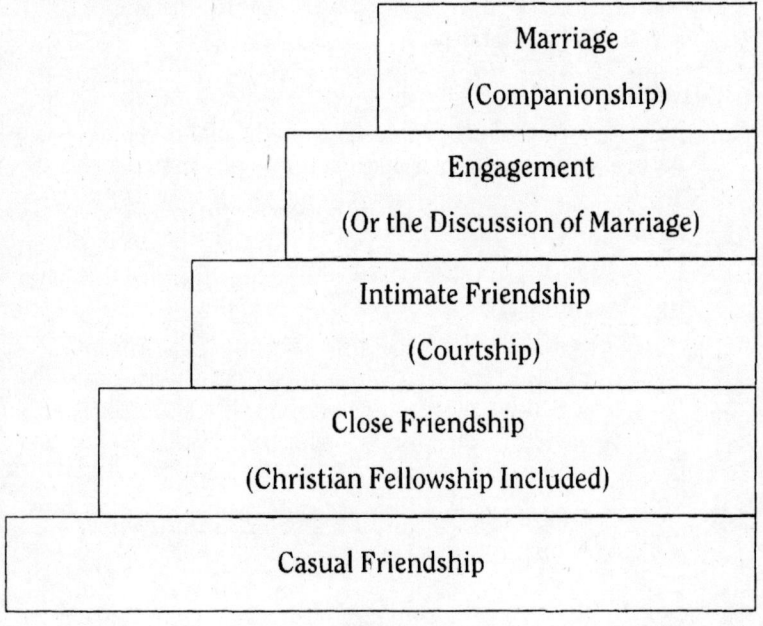

Marriage

(Companionship)

Engagement

(Or the Discussion of Marriage)

Intimate Friendship

(Courtship)

Close Friendship

(Christian Fellowship Included)

Casual Friendship

Figure 2

What makes this so different from the world's model of courtship is that Christ is not left out. Developing a wholesome friendship is the best way to start a relationship, for in this way two people begin to know each other before there is an expectation of intimacy without commitment. Each interval is discussed honestly, with a decision made by both parties before moving to the next step, rather than assuming these intervals by inner feelings that are not discussed. This helps to avoid misunderstandings, hurt, and pain. This system is no guarantee against relational pain that is experienced in the mate-selection process, but it does cut down on some of the unnecessary suffering and some foolish decisions that lead to bad marriages. Hundreds of former singles who are now married and members of my church as well as many others across the country who have attended our national seminars have practiced this and are now teaching it to their teenage children.

Gary Inrig, in his book *Quality Friendship*, lists five essential features of biblical friendship:

1. My friend is the one whose needs I can meet, not the one who meets my needs.
2. A friend encourages his friend in God.
3. A friend is someone with whom I share a deep common interest.
4. A friend is someone committed to help his friend realize God's purpose and potential for his life.
5. A true friendship involves declared loyalty and commitment.

Casual Friendship

At this interval, you do not know enough about a person to agree to a date. A casual friendship begins when one or both single people have an interest in or are attracted to one another. Believing in love at first sight is playing Russian roulette with your life. Don't be misled when someone who is interested in you tells you, "God laid you on my heart" or "God promised you to me." Just remember, God is intelligent enough to tell you Himself. During this casual friendship interval, too much is assumed about people whom singles know very little about.

The only commitment that should be made at this level is to find out more about the person in whom who have an interest. If neither is interested, then move on graciously.

To get to know someone, you have to ask pertinent personal questions. At the outset, you want to establish whether the person is married or single. Often single women get deeply involved with a man before they find out he is married. Is the person a committed Christian, a non-Christian, or just a religious professing Christian who is not submitting to the authority of God and His Word, the Bible? Some women want their husband to give spiritual leadership after they marry, but before marriage the man's spirituality is not an issue.

You want to know what a personyou're interested in does with his or her time. If employed, by whom? If not, why not? Has the person ever been in jail? For what? Is the person in school? Why? What does the person do for recreation?

Obtain this kind of information before you go out with someone. Such information can be obtained over the telephone. If possible, verify as much as you can before you go out with this person alone. It is good to know individuals who know the person you have an interest in or who has an interest in you. Although this is not always possible, several phone conversations over a period of time will suffice. Perhaps you could call the person on the job to verify employment or call his or her pastor to learn more.

We are taught in God's Word to use discretion in choosing friends (Prov. 22:24–27); if we do not, we could be adversely affected by the relationship.

It is also wise to invite someone you do not know to a group event such as a social gathering of other Christian singles, where adult games or icebreakers invite people to give information about themselves. For this purpose an official church singles' ministry is also a blessing. Nevertheless, a few single friends can take the initiative to help each other by having such gatherings among themselves.

Close Friendship

This is the interval in which you begin to date, but the emphasis is still on friendship, and you are not dating one person exclusively. This is especially good for those who do not want to get serious about anyone at this time but would like to go out with someone occasionally. It is made clear to the person you go out with that you are going out with other friends and are not serious about anyone at this time.

It is during this interval that many single people back away from a relationship, for different reasons. For Christians this stage is different from the worldly way of meeting people and going out with them exclusively. Some singles simply are insecure. They feel that if they don't rope and tie their catch down, someone else may beat them to it. My position is that the worldly way of courtship is not very effective in mate selection as proven by the high divorce rate. People who are not compatible often choose the wrong person to marry; then, after getting to really know each other after marriage, they find they don't like each other.

Also, at this interval two matters must be taken into consideration. First, there is the prohibition against dating non-Christians. As a Christian, you should not date non-Christians. You might be attracted to a nonbeliever, but the major person in your life is not accepted by the non-Christian. The major person in your life is Jesus Christ. The apostle Paul states this very clearly:

> Do not be yoked together with unbelievers. For what do righteousness and wickedness have in common? Or what fellowship can light have with darkness? What harmony is there between Christ and Belial? What does a believer have in common with an unbeliever? What agreement is there between the temple of God and idols? For we are the temple of the living God. As God has said: "I will live with them and walk among them, and I will be their God, and they will be my people.
>
> Therefore come out from them and be separate, says the Lord. Touch no unclean thing, and I will receive you (2 Cor. 6:14–17).

The second matter is that of Christian fellowship, which must be an emphasis in Christian dating. We can gain some insight from 1 John 1:5–7:

> This is the message we have heard from him and declare to you: God is light; in him there is no darkness at all. If we claim to have fellowship with him yet walk in the darkness, we lie and do not live by the truth. But if we walk in the light, as he is in the light, we have fellowship with one another, and the blood of Jesus, his Son, purifies us from all sin.

To actively have Christian fellowship as a goal in courtship means

1. Dating people who know Christ
2. Dating people who are in fellowship with Christ
3. Being friends as a willing acceptance until God leads the relationship into something more serious
4. Sharing the Word of God with each other in addition to praying together
5. Worshiping God together
6. Being godly and honest
7. Rejecting sexual intercourse as sin and "walking in darkness"
8. Acknowledging the lordship of Jesus Christ
9. Being committed to walk together in the Spirit and be filled with the Spirit
10. Mutually trusting God for a mate

To maintain the emphasis of friendship, there must not be any intimate kissing or petting. Such behavior changes the relationship emotionally without necessarily changing the will to a deep commitment. Intimate kissing changes the relationship from close friendship to intimate friendship without the proper commitment. You may verbally say you do not want to get serious, but intimate kissing communicates the opposite. It is also important to realize that any talk of marriage at this point is premature. Like kissing, talk of marriage too early in the relationship can be misleading and distract you from focusing on getting to know the person. Some men use the talk of marriage to manipulate women.

Do not accept expensive gifts because this also can communicate more of a commitment than you are willing to make or than the gift giver is making.

Remember, as you move through the intervals, you are allowing God to move and reveal information about the persons you date and about your reaction to them before there is a permanent marital relationship.

There should be a three- to six-month investment of time in this interval of close friendship.

Intimate Friendship

At this interval, you have made the emotional commitment to date one person exclusively. This commitment must not be assumed but clearly discussed and committed to by both parties. During intimate friendship there must be the self-discipline of not being led by your emotions alone or by sexual lust, but by clear thinking and wisdom, guided by God, the Holy Spirit.

There should be a commitment to invest at least twelve months at this level. Things have begun now to get serious. The two people must be very inquisitive; you cannot learn too much about each other. This is precisely the reason that some single people want a quick courtship; they are afraid something will be discovered that they want to hide. In getting to know the person better, explore the following:

1. Observe the character and behavior of best friends.
2. Is personal time spent with God in prayer and Bible meditation?
3. Find out attitudes on handling money, including spending and saving.
4. Get to know family members and learn family background.
5. Determine if the person is trustworthy concerning dating only you.

6. What are the strengths and weaknesses of the person you are dating? When you don't know of any weaknesses, it is a sign that you don't know the person very well or that the person is acting out a role and is not being honest. The Bible reveals that the most holy saints were not perfect. Everybody has a sin nature.

CHILDREN

The following questions concerning children should be discussed when the relationship starts getting serious, but before the commitment to marry.

1. Do you want children?
2. What are your family-planning views?
3. Does either of you have medical problems that would hinder you from having children?
4. How long after marriage would you like to have children?
5. Suppose God does not bless you with children?
6. How many children do you desire? Boys? Girls?
7. Suppose you are not able to have boys and/or girls?
8. What are your thoughts about adopting children?
9. Does either partner have children already through a previous relationship:

    a. What obligations are involved?
    b. What arrangements have been made for child visitation?
    c. Under what circumstances is there to be contact with the child's mother or father?
    d. What are the financial obligations and for how long?
    e. If the two of you decide to get married, is the one partner willing to legally adopt the other's children?
    f. If so, do you agree on child discipline?
    g. Will one partner be allowed to discipline the children of the other?

FAMILY BACKGROUND

All of us are products of the families we were born into. We have been greatly influenced by our home environment for better or worse. It is most important that we understand the home life of our partner, and our partner should be knowledgeable of our family background. These are some questions that should be asked:

1. Are your parents still married, were they divorced or were they never married?
2. What kind of relationship do you have with your parents?
3. Is there emotional stability in the family? Is there mental illness in the family?
4. What are the dominant family traits?
5. How well does your family communicate with each other?
6. How well does your family receive me?
7. Are you too close to either parent, being dominated as an adult?
8. Are there signs that you will have difficulty with your partner's family members if they become your in-laws?
9. How are differences and problems solved in your family?
10. What are the family members' beliefs in God?

Even if the answers to some of these questions are negative, it does not mean that you should not marry your partner, but understanding these family defects beforehand does help you make an honest decision about whether you love your partner enough to get married.

The investigation of family background will also reveal positive family history that sometimes family members don't know because they never asked. It could reveal a hardworking father who never finished high school because of oppression or a dysfunctional family but who vowed to himself that all his children would attend college and accomplish higher goals.

I believe that it is important to have an ongoing, active relationship with our extended family. The strength of the extended family is what has enabled us to survive from slavery to the great migration to the North, then to the West, and more recently back to the South. The extended family is also enabling many of our single-parent families to survive.

THE BIBLICAL MODEL OF MARRIAGE REVEALED IN COURTSHIP

During courtship single Christians must try to develop their relationship guided by biblical teaching. One of the key principles is distinguishing between human love, *phileo* love, or *agape* love. Human love is love based on what the person doing the loving expects to get out of the relationship. This is the reason that two people who marry because they love each other can, within a few weeks, months, or years of marriage, fall out of love. It is an emotional, selfish love that comes from the flesh. *Phileo* love is better, but it takes more than a brotherly or friendship love to suffice in a marriage based on God's standards. What is needed is *agape* love, unconditional love. What is needed is a selfless love, a persevering love found only in God himself and supernaturally given to believers through the Holy Spirit.

Short courtships do not give *agape* love an opportunity to develop or be manifested. Some of us who have lived long enough know that you do not know who really loves you or who is your friend until testing circumstances come along. Those Christian singles who trust God enough to take time to patiently develop a relationship during courtship allow God to bring about circumstances to test the reality of love and levels of commitment.

If a person is born again and willfully practices God's *agape* love, the love will display itself in a way similar to the way God reveals His love. Such love is driven by our love for God and our obedience to Him.

BE YOURSELF

One of the most devastating discoveries after marriage is that your spouse does not accept you or respect you as a person or is constantly trying to change your personality, the way you think, and the way you look. One of the reasons this happens is that too often during courtship one or both people are trying to impress the other. Certainly, this is human when you first meet someone. However, we have now moved to the intimate level of friendship. At some point during this interval, intimacy is to have matured at least to the best-friends stage, which includes acceptance. Best friends of the same sex do not waste time trying to prove anything to each other. As a matter of fact, such friends will see through any pretense and challenge you if you try.

If it is real love, why pretend? Be yourself. If you don't trust the person enough that you can be you, you are playing a dangerous game, believing your mate is going to accept a stranger after marriage. You can pretend to be someone else during courtship, but you can't keep it up for the rest of your life.

If it is real love, the commitment to the person loved ought to be similar to Ruth's love for her mother-in-law, Naomi:

Ruth replied, "Don't urge me to leave you or to turn back from you. Where you go I will go, and where you stay I will stay. Your people will be my people and your God my God. Where you die I will die, and there I will be buried. May the LORD deal with me, be it ever so severely, if anything but death separates you and me" (Ruth 1:16–17).

POTENTIAL AS A HUSBAND OR WIFE

Being married is a great responsibility. It is important that single people who have intentions of being married learn what the responsibilities are before they get married. It is even better if one knows the responsibilities before selecting a mate. The single person must know marriage responsibility from a biblical perspective. When selecting a mate, one must love the other person enough to know, accept, and be willing to carry out his or her responsibility in the marriage. There is nothing romantic about this. It is work. It takes more emotional and psychological energy than physical energy.

Although in a courtship a single person does not have the opportunity to live as a husband or wife, there should be some indication that each has the potential to be a good Christian spouse. I want to just talk about a few major responsibilities and how evidence of a person's commitment to the responsibilities reveals itself in courtship.

In 1 Corinthians 11:3, Paul says, "Now I want you to realize that the head of every man is Christ, and the head of the woman is man, and the head of Christ is God." It is basic that a man who expects to exercise headship in his home has the responsibility to submit to the headship of Christ. Christ has set the example of submission. In an intimate relationship, it should be abundantly clear to a woman that her partner is submitting to Christ, loving Christ, and submitting to His Word. A man who is not devoted to Christ can never be the kind of husband that God demands. Likewise, Ephesians 5:22 says, "Wives, submit to your husbands as to the Lord." A single man should see in his partner a single woman who takes seriously her responsibility in submitting to the Lord. In other words, it takes a husband, a wife, and Christ to have a good Christian marriage. If Christ does not have a dominant role in a single person's life, He will not have a dominant role after marriage. It is common for some women to compromise at this point for the sake of being married, only to be disappointed with the marriage later because the man is not spiritual. Many single men did not mind it too much when their girlfriend readily had sexual relations with them before marriage, only to discover after marriage that the woman only professed Christ and has made carnality a way of life.

A man is told to love his wife "just as Christ loved the church and gave himself up for her" (Eph. 5:25). A man must model Christ's commitment to the church by meeting his wife's needs, expressing love, and making sacrifices out of agape love. There should be signs during

104

courtship that the male shows enough love to find out what needs his partner has—needs that, if they marry, he is willing to meet. His expressions of love must go beyond giving a gift or taking her out every now and then. In a courtship that is given adequate time, there will be occasions where the male will have opportunities to sacrifice for the female if he really loves her. A woman should not try to manufacture such occasions but trust God to handle it, provided the relationship is not being rushed.

Another responsibility is stated in Ephesians 5:24: "Now as the church submits to Christ, so also wives should submit to their husbands in everything." No woman should marry a man whom she does not love or trust enough to lead in the home. During courtship she needs to examine his track record as to how successful he has been in making decisions concerning his own life. If he has responsibilities for the welfare of others, this too should be examined. Some women are disappointed after marriage because their husband will not lead, take the initiative, and deal with problems. Had they considered this before marriage, they would have discovered this is simply the way the man handles life.

Many men are shocked after marriage because the woman who was so sweet during their whirlwind courtship—Miss Kissy-Kissy, Miss Huggy-Huggy, Miss "You-Are-So-Wonderful"—turns out to be a dragon whenever she does not have her way or when he asks her to do anything she doesn't want to do. If he had taken his time to develop the relationship during the courtship, he would have discovered that her parents always had a problem with her rebellion. Her parents were relieved when she became an adult, moved out, and got her own apartment. This new husband realized too late that at the wedding ceremony his in-laws were crying, not because they were losing a daughter, but because he didn't know whom he was getting for a wife. If he would have taken his time in the relationship, he would have discovered that she has trouble with co-workers on her job, ignores her parents' advice, is mad at her pastor because he corrected her, and her best friend is a woman she dominates.

ENGAGEMENT PERIOD
Wedding-Day Deception

There are people who meet each other for the first time and are engaged to be married within one month. This can be deceptive because it is assumed that because a person has agreed to marry another, there is deep love and commitment. As I stated earlier, some people marry for wrong reasons. The minute there is talk concerning the possibility of two people marrying each other, it has a tremendous impact on the relationship.

The focus in the relationship turns from getting to know one another better to a wedding day. The emphasis becomes preparing for a wedding day rather than preparing for establishing a Christian home. I have known couples to spend hundreds of dollars on a wedding and then move in with relatives because they could not afford to live on their own. Living with relatives after marriage violates Genesis 2:24: "A man will leave his father and mother and be united to his wife." I know there are justifiable reasons for newly married people to live with relatives for a short period, but most of the time it comes about because either the bride is pregnant and they did the right thing by marrying after the mistake or there was no planning or preparation for setting up a Christian home that honors God.

Single Mentality

Once there is an agreement between two people that they are going to be married, they must move from a "single mentality" to a "marriage mentality." In other words, the single person must stop thinking "I, me, mine" and begin to think "we, us, and our." Single mentality in marriage is divisive and selfish. For example, a wife may ask her husband where he is going or where he has been. He may reply that he is a grown man, and he is over twenty-one years old. The issue is not his masculinity but whether he is carrying out his duties as head of the house. It seems reasonable to me to know at all times where your head is. We would look very silly walking around without a head. We would sound even sillier if we were asked the location of our head and we said we didn't know.

Some women are offended when they get home late and their husband is waiting up for them to inquire where they have been. The wife may reply, "You're not my father, giving me a curfew time to be home." Depending on the spiritual condition of the husband, a reply such as this would not only be an affront to his masculinity, but could be grounds to fight for a boxing championship, with the wife as the opponent. Engaged couples must practice thinking in twos, transitioning from singleness.

When thinking about existing friends, there has to be a transition to "our friends." After marriage some friendships with single people are no longer practical because interests of single people and married people are not the same. I am not saying that you can no longer be friends with singles, but the only friendships that work after marriage must include both husband and wife or have mutual approval. A wife could not have a girlfriend who does not like her husband. A husband could not have a close relationship with a male of whom his wife does not approve. There are exceptions, but very few that don't block the progress of the marital relationship.

It Is Better to Break An Engagement Than to Break Up a Marriage

Earlier, I spoke of reasons why a relationship should be broken off. Sometimes negative relationship symptoms do not surface until the engagement period. One of the reasons is that once a wedding date has been agreed upon, some people have a sense that they have won, they own their partner, so they relax and let their hair down. Another reason is that preparing for a church wedding can be very expensive and an intense experience. Not many people would admit it, but after the draining ordeal of a church wedding, the only thing that two exhausted people did was sleep on the first night of their honeymoon.

Some people have had serious doubts on their wedding day, but still went through with the wedding because they did not want to disappoint "the people." However, within a few months or years they were divorced. I can understand that there would be some embarrassment after invitations have been mailed, dresses have been made, tuxedos have been rented, and caterers have been contracted, but I think it is more important to obey and honor God. "I hate divorce," says God in Malachi 2:16.

A marriage should be postponed, if possible, to allow the couple to work through problems that cause doubts, or the engagement should be broken and the relationship ended. This is not an easy thing to do, and it takes some time to heal from the hurt of a broken relationship, but more damage is created when there is a divorce—for the couple, their children, the church, and God.

PREMARITAL COUNSELING

Premarital counseling is a must. The couple need to involve a neutral party to help them to assess whether they should get married and to help prepare them for marriage. Most of the time, this should be the pastor or someone he assigns. Couples need to be trained in married life before they are married.

BOOKS FOR FURTHER KNOWLEDGE AND USE IN FAMILY MINISTRY

Eble, Diane. *The Campus Life Guide to Dating*. Grand Rapids: Zondervan, 1990.

Cross, Haman, Jr. *A Manual for Christian Dating and Courtship*. Philadelphia: Christian Research & Development, 1986.

McAllister, Dawson. *How to Know If You're Really in Love*. Dallas: Word, 1994.

Stafford, Tim. *Love, Sex and the Whole Person*. Grand Rapids: Zondervan, 1991.

Talley, Jim, and Bobbie Reed. *Too Close, Too Soon*. Nashville: Thomas Nelson, 1982.

Warren, Clark Neil. *Finding the Love of Your Life*. Colorado Springs: Focus on the Family, 1992.

Chapter 8

PREMARITAL COUNSELING TRAINING

It would be very helpful if the couple that comes to the pastor for pre-marital counseling has practiced the things I have talked about concerning courtship and the mate-selection process. It is a lot easier counseling these people than those who have not. Let's take the position that we have not had the opportunity to prepare them for marriage, which will be the case of some who come to us regardless of our ministry to single people.

THE COUNSELOR'S OBJECTIVES

1. To train couples for marriage.
2. To teach God's purpose for marriage. We live in times when people want to get married for many different reasons. We would like to teach them God's purpose for marriage because God, not man, created marriage. God is the one who set up the institution of marriage and sanctified it.
3. To teach the biblical role of the husband and wife. For too long, the Bible has been neglected regarding God's teachings as to what the family is to be like. The foundational passage for this teaching is found in Ephesians 5:21–6:4.

4. To teach the responsibilities of being a husband and wife. Many people want to get married but do not realize that there are responsibilities involved in marriage. There are those who do not want any responsibilities, yet they want to get married. We must prepare them to understand their responsibilities in marriage.
5. To be sure couples are getting married for the right reasons. Of course, the most important reason would be that they genuinely love each other with mature, godly love, not infatuation. They must be in love not merely for a physical or sexual relationship but truly for the right reasons.
6. To teach them how to develop good communication with each other. Communication is extremely important in a marriage. Every marriage that breaks down does so first in communication. We want to help the couple develop good communication skills and train them in how to work through problems after marriage.
7. To teach family financial management. A recent statistic showed that 90 percent of all the people in America are having some type of financial problem. This is not because most people in America are poor, but it does mean that most of them are not disciplined when it comes to spending, planning, saving, and investing their money. At the very least, we want couples to get off to a good start in planning for their marriage and being prepared financially.
8. To teach the principles of child rearing. If we need training in how to be married, we certainly need training in how to raise children. We are having more and more problems with children and teenagers today because many mothers and fathers are not practicing biblical principles in bringing up their children.
9. To help couples establish their marriage on the foundation of a personal relationship with the Lord Jesus Christ (salvation and spiritual growth). I believe that marriage is a triangle and that it takes the husband, the wife, and the Lord Jesus Christ in order for us to experience the kind of marriage God wants us to have. I do not believe that anyone can experience joy, love, peace, and unity in a home without the Lord Jesus Christ. Therefore, it is very important that we, as counselors, be Christians ourselves. In other words, we must have a personal relationship with Jesus Christ as our Lord and Savior. We must also know how to lead someone else to Christ. We want to try to lead each person who comes to us for counseling to the Lord Jesus Christ if they are not already a Christian.

It is my belief that there is a tremendous ministry in premarital counseling, even in counseling those who are not Christians. When we discover that they have not received the Lord Jesus Christ, we ought to make every attempt to lead them to Christ. If you do not know how to do this, you will have to learn by either going to a Christian bookstore and purchasing a book on this subject or perhaps learning through a training program, if it is available. It is essential that we try to lead all people who come to us to the Lord Jesus Christ. If they reject Christ and do not want to become Christians, I still believe that we should go through all of the premarital counseling and try to train them in how to be married if they are willing to go through with it. As we attempt to train them biblically and give them God's directions, we must be aware that they will not be able to carry out these directions because they do not have the power of God in their lives. Perhaps at the conclusion of the premarital counseling, you might again try to lead them to our Lord and Savior Jesus Christ. Often they are ready to accept Christ at this point because they have been impressed with the Bible. They did not know that Bible knowledge can be relevant for life today.

10. To teach the biblical view on sex in marriage. We need to teach morality today because immorality is tearing down the marriage commitment. Adultery is destroying many homes. We want to teach people the biblical view of sex before they get married. On the other hand, we want to teach them also the pleasure and joy of sex in marriage. Married love is sanctified and holy. Some are misguided into believing that somehow sex is sinful, even in marriage.

11. To ascertain the couple's expectations of the marriage. We need to find out what each person expects to happen after the wedding vows. Many people have very unrealistic ideas of what marriage is all about and also what the expected role of their mate is. We must deal with these unrealistic ideas before the couple marries.

12. To ascertain the couple's knowledge and understanding of each other. One of the things that is so alarming today is that many couples are marrying after very short courtships. We can't very well do much about that before people come to us for premarital counseling, but one thing premarital counseling will do is help the couple obtain more knowledge about and understanding of each other.

13. To show the couple the strengths and weaknesses of their relationship, we should discuss the possibilities of future problems in the marriage

and how to resolve problems, if possible. Too often people who are in love cannot do this for themselves. It takes courage from the counselor to probe, reveal weaknesses and faults, and try to get the couple to face up to them.

14. To teach them how to further develop and express love to each other. Most people who get married at least start off liking each other, but after they are married, many become strangers living in the same house. One of the objectives of premarital counseling is teaching people how to continue to develop their love for one another, how to continually express love to one another, and how to develop continued friendship that will grow so deeply that it will become companionship.

15. To help them establish good worship and devotional practices as a family. Without the Lord Jesus Christ no home or family can have the joy, peace, and unity that God would like each family to have. Therefore, the worship of the family is extremely important under the leadership of the man, whom God has designated to be the priest in the home. We want also to encourage husband and wife to worship together, to have some kind of devotional practices in the home and not to depend totally on what the church gives to the family in the way of ministry.

16. To ascertain the marital readiness of the couple. Sometimes, without the counselor's saying so, it becomes clear to one or both people that they are not ready for marriage. However, sometimes the counselor must point this out and give concrete reasons. Sometimes it becomes clear that although they are two fine Christian people, they have severe personality conflicts and are better suited for another person with a different personality. A counselor must have the courage to speak the truth in love. If people are determined to marry no matter what, they will not appreciate hearing the truth and sometimes will become angry with the counselor. At this point, the counselor's job is done. The final decision to get married is left up to the couple.

The major qualification in the Bible is that we marry Christian to Christian (2 Cor. 6:14–18). A pastor can marry two unwise Christian people; but it should be against his conscience to marry people when he has no hope for their marriage. In such a case, the pastor must not violate his conscience.

Couples' Considerations During the Engagement Period

1. The engagement period is the last opportunity to get to know the person before marriage. It is the last chance to determine if this is the person you want to spend the rest of your life with. God hates divorce (Mal. 2:16). Choosing a marriage partner is a serious, permanent decision.

2. Couples should take advantage of the premarital counseling opportunity by fully cooperating, doing assignments, and being truthful in the sessions. The counselor will raise important issues you would never raise because you are in love.

3. Determine what each person wants out of a marriage and what each person is willing to contribute to the marriage.

4. It is an opportunity to practice sexual discipline, which builds trust and strengthens fidelity after marriage. It is not the time for sexual experimentation. It is difficult to exercise self-control when two people love each other. It is natural to want to make love to each other. However, many heartbroken married people have mistaken sexual pleasure for genuine love, to their detriment.

5. Discover likenesses and differences for potential compatibility after marriage. Immature people notice and love only the things they like about a person before marriage. The key thing to remember is everybody has a sinful nature in spite of salvation; therefore, everybody has weaknesses and faults, and these need to be recognized before marriage as much as possible. After the honeymoon period is over (three months to a year), weaknesses and faults are amplified a hundred times. The decision to marry is "for better or for worse." Do the parties love each other enough to commit to live with each other in spite of weaknesses, faults, and imperfections?

6. Begin to try to build a positive relationship with in-laws and extended family. Marriage affects not only the two people who marry each other, but also their parents, other family members, and friends. This is an area that, if neglected during courtship, can cause serious problems after marriage. The people who really need to be impressed during courtship are in-laws. What is missed too often is that most parents love their grown children and still care about their welfare, yet sometimes they know nothing about the person their son or daughter is going to marry. This is especially true if adult children do not live with their parents. Ideally, relationship building should be done face-to-face, but in the case of relatives who

do not live in the same city, the phone should be used to build a relationship with in-laws.

7. Study, understand, and discuss the roles and responsibilities of a husband, father, wife, and mother.

8. Discover emotional, spiritual, and psychological needs of the partner and honestly determine whether you believe you can meet these needs.

9. Establish and plan financial management for the new home and family that is being created.

10. Observe how your intended expresses love to you and if this is satisfactory to you. Openly discuss how your intended should express love to you and not expect this to miraculously happen automatically after marriage without your giving information.

11. Discover and discuss life and future family goals.

12. Plan for setting up housekeeping and the wedding. Most people put too much emphasis on the wedding day rather than setting up housekeeping. Some couples have big, expensive church weddings without being able to afford it. Planning for the wedding should start at least six months before the wedding day, especially if it is going to be a church wedding. Couples should not have a church wedding if they cannot afford it or if they put their parents in debt to pay for it. That can be the beginning of in-law problems.

13. Determine what church you will belong to if you do not belong to the same church. This should be thought through and agreed upon before marriage. God wants oneness in a marriage. Not being taught the same thing about God and the Christian life can be divisive in a family. Certainly, we should be able to pray for a Christian couple, "May the God who gives endurance and encouragement give you a spirit of unity among yourselves as you follow Christ Jesus, so that with one heart and mouth you may glorify the God and Father of our Lord Jesus Christ" (Rom. 15:5–6). If there is an impasse concerning which church to belong to, the woman should submit to the man as head of the family and join his church.

Not belonging to the same church can also hinder family unity when children are born. What church will they attend? Usually, it is the wife's church because the husband doesn't want to be the babysitter at his church or be stuck with the kids. Sometimes, when children become teenagers, they join a church that has a good youth ministry. What can happen is that the dad is in one church, the mom in another church, and the children in yet a third church. On the other hand, they may not be attending church at all because they don't like anybody's church. As you can see, this does not advance family unity.

14. The end of the premarital training is the last opportunity for you to decide whether you believe this relationship has the potential of becoming a good marriage.

   a. Don't rush yourself into coming to a final decision. Sometimes the counseling reveals new issues you must work through in your mind and heart.

   b. Don't worry about what people will think or say if you decide not to marry your intended. They are going to talk about you more if you marry the wrong person and get a divorce later.

   c. Break off the relationship if you have serious doubts about your intended. Don't deceive yourself into thinking the marriage will work when God is telling you differently.

ISSUES THAT NEED TO BE DISCUSSED DURING PREMARITAL COUNSELING

The following questions are some that we ask during premarital counseling to help couples become more knowledgeable of each other and uncover information that would have a disastrous effect on the marriage if not known before the marriage. Some married people feel they have been deceived when they find out some information about their spouse after marriage, such as their being married before in another state, their being the parent of children the other partner knows nothing about, their having a prison record, or being a former homosexual.

Marital Data

1. *What is your marital status?* Counselors need to know the present situation of the two people who are intending to marry each other. We need to know if they have ever been married or if they are separated from a present spouse, married, engaged, divorced, shacking up, living together, going steady, or widowed. There are people who come to premarital counseling who are tired of their present spouse or don't want to be married any longer and want the marriage to the new lover to be blessed by God and the church.

   Some people come to counseling unofficially engaged (most women don't think it is official until they receive a ring). They have not made the final decision to marry the person—they have some doubt. Wisely, they believe counseling will help them in making up their mind.

Some divorced people continue to marry and continue to divorce. Some of these people have problems within themselves that need to be resolved. Some of them have serious emotional problems with the opposite sex or other problems that need to be dealt with.

2. *Why are you getting married?* We want to know why people are getting married. For example, they might be getting married because there is a pregnancy. If there is, and that is the reason they are getting married, we want to really find out whether or not they truly love each other. Many people have gotten married because of a pregnancy, and it did not work because they didn't love each other. They were not committed to each other, and so one bad mistake was piled onto another. However, if the couple are mature enough, they can develop and grow in their love relationship. Certainly, we recommend that people do marry one another when there is a pregnancy involved and they are mature enough to want to build a relationship, though they might not feel very strongly in love with one another at the time.

3. *Do you understand that your choice of a spouse will determine the success of your marriage and that premarital counseling is only an aid, not a guarantee of success?* We want to make this clear to them. As I have said more than once already, we want couples to understand that the success of their marriage depends on the spouse they choose and not the counseling itself. Counseling will help them only if they have made a good choice in a marriage partner.

Dating Data

1. *When did you first meet each other? Where?* This will help you determine how long these people have known each other. So often today, people really don't know one another well enough to get married. Now, there have been times we have recommended that the couple postpone their wedding date until they have had enough time to get to know one another a whole lot better.

2. *Have you been engaged before?* We want to find out how many times, who broke any previous engagements, and the circumstances of the breakup(s). The answers to these questions may also indicate the stability and maturity of the parties who have come for counseling. A person may simply be marrying on the rebound or desperate to prove they are marriageable after being rejected by someone

else. Also, a past breakup may uncover some glaring negative trait, such as jealousy, that needs to be dealt with before one of the parties is eligible to get married.

3. *Have you and your fiancé(e) ever broken up?* We want to know whether this has been an up-and-down relationship. In some marriages, there are up-and-down situations where people separate, come back together and struggle to maintain the marriage, then finally divorce. The fact that they have broken up and gotten back together again might be an indication that they are not suited for each other. However, each case is different, and you will have to deal with the facts in each particular situation.

4. *Do your parents approve or disapprove of your marriage?* So often today the attitude of many couples is that they don't care what their parents think or what they say about whom they will marry. I am referring not only to people who are eighteen or nineteen years old, but also to those who are twenty or thirty years old and older. The idea of having the approval of one's mate by parents is very important for continued relationships with the rest of the extended family. Many children do not have a relationship with their grandparents because their grandparents do not like their father or mother. One of the weaknesses in the family today is that we have not honored our parents, nor have we considered our parents' opinions. On the other hand, sometimes parents can be wrong. What I recommend to couples is that if their parents do not approve of their relationship, they should spend more time with the parents, making every attempt to work at the relationship with the parents, enabling the parents to learn the positive traits of the mate. The marriage will affect both sides of the family, and if they can build a good relationship with the parents, they should try to do so. Sometimes it is simply because the parents don't know enough about the person. As the couple develop a relationship, they know each other, but the mother and father do not know the person their daughter or son wants to marry, and they are apprehensive about the newcomer. I recommend to couples that they spend time with the parents so they can get to know the fiancé(e) much better. However, sometimes parents can be totally unreasonable and want to be dominating in choosing a mate for their son or daughter. In such cases, the adult children will have to marry without the parents' approval. However, most of the time, the parents just don't know the fiancé(e), and the problem

can be resolved as they all spend more time together. Couples should not have an arrogant attitude when their parents do not approve of their fiancé(e). They need to be patient, postponing the wedding date and the engagement until they can win their parents over and get their approval. After parents get to know the fiancé(e), they will have a better idea whether or not this person might be good for their son or daughter because they know the weaknesses and strengths of their child.

5. *What do you expect to get out of this marriage?* Sometimes, people have unrealistic, selfish, and naive expectations that need to be corrected.

6. *What do you expect to give to the marriage?* Now, this particular question really catches people off guard sometimes. They have no problem answering the previous question, but most people have never even considered what they are going to give to a marriage relationship. Most of us are self-centered and selfish. We get married with the idea of having someone love us and keep us happy. As counselors we want to challenge the couple to think about what they intend to give to the marriage.

7. *What will be the advantages of your getting married rather than being single?* We want them to think through getting rid of the single life and moving from being single to being married. Some people want to be married while at the same time having the advantages and freedom of being single.

8. *What are some of the conflicts you have with your fiancé(e)?* If they say they have no conflicts or no problems, then you let them know they really don't know one another well enough or they are being naive. All couples have some weaknesses or problems in their relationship or they have some things that bother them. You want to pursue this issue.

9. *What has been the most serious problem in your relationship? If it has been resolved, how did you resolve it?* There might be a serious, ongoing problem or one that they push under the table for the sake of getting married. You want to hear about it even if they think it has been resolved. Many times it has only been glossed over or someone has given in, but there really has not been a resolution to the problem.

10. *What has been the worst disappointment you have experienced in the relationship so far?* When people are in love and really want to get married, especially introverted people, they will not even discuss such

things, but will keep them to themselves. I remember a couple who got married, and after they were married for about a year, they had a fight. The wife confessed to her husband that while they were going together, she never had an opportunity to choose where they should go on a date, and therefore, she was bitter about it. She also did not like the idea of living in his mother's house, which he thought would save them a great deal of money. She kept these things to herself until deep bitterness had built up within her after the marriage. We want to try to get people to talk about these things.

Health Data

1. *Rate your health (circle one): very good, good, average, or declining.* Many times, when people want to get married, they are not honest about their health situations. We want to get them to discuss this before marriage. Also, after they are married to someone, they find themselves not willing to be married for better or worse, in sickness and in health. We really need people to be honest. If they say they love each other, they should have no reason or problem honestly answering these types of questions.

2. *Are you using, or have you been using, drugs such as marijuana, cocaine, heroin, or others?* This might be a person who is currently using or who formerly used illegal drugs. In any case, the fiancé(e) needs to know about this. If the person is a drug user at this particular time, the fiancé(e) has a right to know that he or she is marrying a drug addict or an ex-drug addict who, at any point in time, might under certain pressures go back to being a drug addict. We need to get people to be frank and open about these matters. At our counseling center, we constantly receive calls from people who are married to drug addicts. They are living very horrible lives because, in some cases, they were dealing with drugs before they ever got married but never told their mate prior to marriage.

3. *Do you know if you cannot give birth to children?* Sometimes, women know in advance that they cannot give birth to children and decide not to tell to their fiancé. This can be a very tragic decision if the man really wants children and feels his wife deceived and tricked him. There must be honesty in these relationships. If the man wants her even though she cannot have children, he may love her enough that it does not make any difference. We have had many cases where it did not make any difference whatsoever. The couple had already

made up their minds that if they could not have children, they would adopt.

4. *If you are a man, do you know if you are sterile?* Of course, the same thing holds true as discussed in the previous question. If the man knows that he cannot father children or there might be a possibility that he cannot, he needs to be frank with his fiancée.

Personal Data

1. *Are you a parent of children from a previous relationship?* When we speak of children from a previous relationship, it could mean children born out of wedlock or children from a previous marriage. It could be from other types of situations, such as a one-night stand, a rape, or incest. We want to deal with this because it can really be a source of problems in a marriage.

2. *What is your legal situation with the children?* We want to know whether the previous child has been adopted and whether the parent has visitation rights. We need to help people check out the legal situation because this can be a source of problems later on in the marriage, especially if the former spouse is jealous or wants to get revenge and wants to create problems in the new marriage. There might be some things these people need to do legally in the new marriage for the new family. It might be wise for the new spouse coming into the relationship to adopt the children if they are young, so that the family members will all have the same last name. However, this might not be good for older children who have a relationship with their other parent.

3. *Are you financially supporting your children? How much do you pay each month?* This is very important in the financial building of the new home being set up. It should also be included in the budget the couple is working through.

4. *What are the arrangements for seeing the children?* We need to know the arrangements or if any arrangements have been made. Many times a spouse may become jealous because the mate goes to see his or her children while the ex-lover or the person with whom there was a former relationship is present. This can create problems in the new marriage.

5. *Will you trust your fiancé(e) to love and discipline your children?* This comes up as a problem because sometimes the person will say, "These are my children; they are not your children. You cannot dis-

cipline my children; you cannot spank my children." This can definitely be a cause of division and many pains for the family in the future if this is not discussed and dealt with prior to marriage.

6. *Do you have any type of venereal disease?* Of course, the couple need to be honest with each other about VD, especially herpes and AIDS. I have had at least two cases in which the men had herpes and it made no difference to the women. The women still wanted to marry them, regardless. A person can have contracted VD in the past, then received Jesus Christ and be living a good Christian life now, but still have the disease.

Educational and Occupational Data

1. *Discuss your education, last year completed, grade, degree and major, other training and year completed.* The reason we need this information is that sometimes one person is more educated than the other, which may be a conflict after marriage. One person begins feeling inferior to the other. You will need to see if there is a great difference and discuss it to see if it is a problem.

2. *Do you have any future educational plans?* If there are any future educational plans, they need to be discussed fully, especially how the education is going to be financed. Many couples have gotten married and one or both intend to finish their education after marriage. Since there were no prior plans made, one may become bitter because of home finances, having children, and not being able to afford further education. They begin to blame each other because they could have gone further in life if they had had more education. They believe it is the other person's fault and they should have never gotten married to them. You want to point out that if there are any future plans about education, there needs to be an understanding before they get married about how they will go about continuing their education.

3. *Are you employed?* We want to find out if the person is employed, especially the male, who, according to the Bible, is supposed to be able to support the wife and family after marriage. We need to deal with and go over this with couples.

4. *If you are unemployed, how long has it been? How much time have you been spending weekly in trying to obtain a job?* If it is the man, this may be an indication that he is not employable and needs to get training, or maybe he is lazy and really doesn't want to work.

5. *What are your occupations or trades?* This is especially directed to the man. Every man needs to have an occupation. It might be that he may not have a very good job at the time of the counseling. The man and the woman both may need to plan to go on for further training so they will not have future problems supporting their children.

6. *Have you ever been asked to leave a job? If so, for what reason?* This question should help you if there is a pattern of losing jobs and if the person has a bad attitude or an unsubmissive attitude on the job.

7. *How much are you paid?* This is a very important question because often people are so much in love that they never get this kind of information. One of the things that is so devastating is not having the proper income to support a family. Sometimes the reason may be that there has not been any real planning to find out how far a person may go in a present job, whether or not he needs to change jobs or perhaps even change careers.

8. *If you are a woman who works, do you intend to work after marriage?* Again, this can create a problem after marriage if a woman has made up her mind that as soon as she gets married she is not going to work anymore and they have never discussed it. The man may assume that she is still going to be working after the marriage.

9. *Do you foresee how your career could affect your marriage in a negative way?* In these modern times, there are careers in which either the man or the woman spends a large amount of time away from home. That, in itself, is not a reason for not getting married, but it is something they need to be aware of and discuss. I remember a particular case in which the man had just started his law practice as an attorney, and, of course, to build up that kind of business, he would have to put in a lot of extra time. The couple were committed to this. Sometimes people have jobs that will take them on out-of-town trips, and there must be understanding and commitment to that ahead of time so travel should not be a problem in the future.

Marital Roles Data

1. *Should the husband help domestically (washing dishes, cooking, etc.)?* You must certainly look at this because, so often in Black families, the husband and the wife both have to work. Many men think the wife should work, then go home and do all the cooking and cleaning. Men feel this is domestic work and it is the woman's place

to take care of this type of work. However, if the woman is going to work to help support the family, the man should help do the domestic work. You must make this very clear to the couple.

2. *Who has the greatest responsibility for caring for and raising the children?* As we read the Bible and other books on parenting, we understand that there is certainly a role for the father as well as the mother in raising the children. Both have equal responsibilities; however, when it comes to disciplining, the Bible seems to give the husband the greater responsibility in seeing that his children are trained in good behavior.

3. *Should the husband and wife combine checking and savings accounts in both names?* Again, this can be a bone of contention after marriage if the husband and wife do not trust each other with money, or trust each other enough to share and be candid about how much money they have. This definitely needs to be discussed before marriage.

4. *If the two of you cannot agree on a major decision, whose decision will be followed?* Again, this will stop many fights after marriage, if a couple can agree ahead of time. The couple should discuss all major decisions together, but when they cannot agree, according to the Scriptures (Ephesians 5 and other places in the Bible), the wife should submit to her husband.

5. *Should the husband give his wife a break from the children?* Again, we like to encourage the husband to be sensitive to his wife by helping with the children and giving her a break from the children. She may want to go out with some friends or relatives, especially if the children are two years or less apart. He needs to be sensitive to the very difficult job she has in being a mother and a housewife.

6. *Should the husband manage money and make financial decisions alone?* Of course, the answer to this is no. Couples should discuss finances together. In terms of who will actually keep the financial records, it could be either the man or the woman. Most of the time, women seem to be better record keepers than men. However, there are men who keep better records or who might be more disciplined than their wives in spending money. Couoples should discuss financial matters together and come to an agreement prior to marriage.

Financial Data

1. *After marriage, if the wife stops work because of pregnancy, will the husband's salary be adequate?* This question is very helpful in

getting the couple to plan for the future, in determining when they will start having children, and in not taking things for granted. I remember a time when, until this question was asked, one couple had never even thought about it, and at the same time planned to have children right away. The man realized that if his wife became pregnant, he could not support the family. In this particular case, it turned out to be very helpful to him to have discussed this question ahead of time. He went to work and talked with his boss and received not only a raise, but also a promotion.

 2. *What debts do you have?* We want to find out early where the couple stands financially so that if the wedding is months away, there is time to begin planning to get out of debt. It is actually best for the couple, if possible, not to start their marriage in debt. The only exception is a college or school loan or if one of them is purchasing a home. We want to try to help them, especially if they plan far enough in advance of the wedding, to be out of debt when they start their marriage. There are times, however, when it is utterly impossible for a couple who want to get married within a few weeks or months to get out of debt before marriage. The marriage should go on; however, the advantage would be that they know the kind of debt they are facing together. As counselors, it is our responsibility to help them with a budget so they will know how to include the debt in the budget and have as their goal to get out of debt.

 3. *What will be your insurance needs?* There are four basic insurance needs (and there might be others) that we feel married couples need to look into in order to avoid some of the problems married people face. The first one is life insurance. All families should have adequate life insurance. It should certainly cover burying someone and paying for a funeral, but there should also be enough insurance to liquidate any debt the couple may have. If the couple are in their twenties or thirties, life insurance is much easier to get than if they were in their forties or fifties. If you have an ongoing counseling ministry, you should have an insurance agent you can recommend to couples to guide them. Of course, you want an insurance person you can trust to be honest with couples and one who will not try to sell them things they cannot afford or really do not need at this particular time.

For those couples who own an automobile, it is very critical in some states that they have automobile insurance. Men especially sometimes have their financial priorities mixed up and feel they can drive a car without insurance. I like to remind people who like to drive without insurance that an accident is an accident and it is not something you plan. I have had several cases in which, because of not having auto insurance protection, men have had to pay out of their own pockets, and it has been financially disastrous for the family.

The third type of insurance is family health insurance, including a dental plan. The fourth is mortgage insurance in case of loss of income due to the death of a spouse. Sometimes, this means both the husband and wife should be insured because both are wage earners contributing to the family's welfare.

4. *Where will you live? Will you buy or rent a home?* Again, we are helping the couple to establish a home and helping them to plan in advance. Surprisingly, there are a number of people who make up their minds to get married and never even plan where they are going to live. Some of them live with friends or relatives, which is not the way to begin a marriage.

Data About Older Adults

1. *Do you own the house you live in? Whose name is it in?* This is very, very important because a lot of times, people don't take the time to legally change the name on a deed. The person may be a widower and the house is in his and his deceased partner's name. That has to be changed. The house may be in the names of the children because the parent who is now getting married decided to leave it to the children. The new spouse may not know anything about it and assume that the house is in the partner's name. When the partner dies, the survivor is under the impression he or she will automatically receive the house and have a place to live. I had a case in which a widow sold her house, shared the proceeds with her new husband, and moved into his house. He died. The house was left to his children. They put her out.

2. *Do any of your grown children live with you?* If at all possible, when someone is going to be married, we want to try to get all of the grown children to move out of the house. It is very difficult to adjust to a new marriage if there are other people living in the home with whom you have to adjust. If the grown children are going to be in the house when the new spouse moves in, the newcomer must be willing to understand clearly and accept that there will be some difficulty with all these people adjusting to one another.

3. *Do you have any insurance policies, and who is the beneficiary?* Also, find out the amount or value of any policies. Many times, these things are not discussed by older people when they get married and it can be very devastating, especially if the survivor has been counting on this. After a couple get married and years have passed, one spouse may discover that the other has left the children as the beneficiaries rather than the mate, who really has a need for the money. Sometimes the grown children don't even need the money, but the elderly surviving spouse in her sixties, seventies, or eighties really does.

4. *Do you have a will? Who is the beneficiary?* The other person should know about the will. The two are going to become one, and there should not be any secrets.

5. *Are you willing to include your new spouse in your will?* This must be discussed. I have seen situations in which a mate will never include the new wife or new husband in the will and never intended to do so.

6. *List your medical problems, if any.* Sometimes older people have medical problems, so they marry to have someone to take care of them. The new spouse needs to know about these problems.

BOOKS FOR FURTHER KNOWLEDGE AND USE IN FAMILY MINISTRY

Eyrich, Howard A. *Three to Get Ready: Premarital Counseling Manual.* Grand Rapids: Baker, 1991.
Wright, Norman H. *Before You Remarry.* Eugene: Harvest House, 1988.
_____. *The Premarital Counseling Handbook.* Chicago: Moody, 1992.

Part 3

TRAINING FAMILIES FINANCIALLY

Chapter 9

TRAINING FAMILIES HOW TO USE THEIR RESOURCES

Pastor Brown picks up the phone to hear Michele Clark frantically exclaim, "We're being put out on the street. We don't have any place to stay. I told James this was going to happen. I told him! I told him!" Then she begins to cry. Although this is not the first time during his pastorate that Pastor Brown has received a call such as this, he is still surprised that this family has this problem. These kinds of phone calls bring automatic stress into the life of a pastor because such crises are not always easy to resolve.

Michele had stopped working a year earlier to stay home to take care of her three young children. As a matter of fact, James, her husband, had insisted that his wife quit her job. He was proud of the fact that she no longer had to work. In the phone conversation, Michele revealed their rent was four months behind, and there were other bills unpaid. Pastor Brown closed the phone conversation by instructing Michele and James to come to his office so he could see what the church could do to help them.

However, Pastor Brown had a sinking feeling. He hoped what money the church would provide for this family would solve their problem permanently, but in the past, some families seem to expect the church to continue to bail them out indefinitely—for example, when their utilities are turned off or when money is needed for lawyers, usually to defend teenagers and young adults in trouble. The church's funds are limited, having other budgetary responsibilities, and it cannot afford too many family financial crises. Pastor Brown looked at Michele and James's giving records and discovered that before Michele quit her job, she gave more to the church than James. Now, she was giving nothing because she no longer earned an income. James consistently gave less each month since she had been at home, and the last three months, this family had given nothing to the church.

Pastor Brown began looking at the giving records of his other church members and discovered that it was a small minority who were doing most of the giving. The church needed its members to do better than this. Pastor Brown decided he would again preach on giving. Whenever he did, there was a slight increase in giving, but during his sermon presentations, the response of the congregation was not very encouraging. He knew that some people even resented his preaching about giving.

As he glanced through the giving record, he realized that a number of people in his congregation did not have good paying jobs. Some were unemployed. The experience of Pastor Brown is duplicated in many of our churches.

As a family training center, the church must help train its families financially. So often, our public schools fall short in preparing our children to earn an adequate income and teaching them how to manage it wisely. So often, Christians are angry with God concerning their financial suffering, in spite of the fact that Jesus said, "Therefore I tell you, do not worry about your life, what you will eat or drink; or about your body, what you will wear. Is not life more important than food, and the body more important than clothes? So do not worry, saying, 'What shall we eat?' or 'What shall we drink?' or 'What shall we wear?' For the pagans run after all these things, and your heavenly Father knows that you need them" (Matt. 6:25, 31–32). God has not promised to make every Christian rich, but He promises to meet our needs.

We need to help our people understand how the economic system operates concerning employment as well as occupational supply and demand. Education and training is still the name of the game in America. Education determines occupation. Occupation determines income. Wise stewardship or management of income determines resources for the family. We can express this in an equation:

Education + Occupation = Income + Wise Management = Resources for the Family

EDUCATION

Years ago, we worried about adults who had only a fifth- or sixth-grade education. Today, in some of our urban areas, there is a crisis of high school dropouts. Sometimes mothers agree with their sons who don't want to return to school for fear of bodily injury or death. We have to help not only high school dropouts but also many of our high school graduates who are functionally illiterate. The first step in addressing this problem is to encourage these adults whose self-esteem has been affected by a lack of education and development. I remember years ago, when we started our church's literacy program, the radical change in the personalities of some of our adult students who learned to read and write for the first time. They became more ambitious and began dreaming about their future occupational possibilities. One of the most touching things that happened in our literacy program was the letter writing of a sixty-five-year-old man to his eighty-five-year-old praying mother. She lived in another city, and he shared with her that God had answered her prayers, because not only did he now know Jesus Christ as his Lord and Savior, but he could also read and write.

Some towns and cities have evening public adult education classes that will enable an adult to earn a high school diploma. Also, there are state-certified high school diploma equivalency programs. Some churches have included such programs in their church ministry as a service to the community and their members.

Post-High School Training

We are living in a society that demands more than a high school diploma if we are going to have jobs where people can earn an adequate income to support a family. Post-high school training is a must. This training may include the following:

- Community college
- College
- Trade and vocational school
- Courses and seminars for paraprofessionals
- Apprenticeships (offered by unions, hospitals, etc.)
- Job retraining programs

Families will need counseling to help them finance adult education, to schedule the amount of time involved, and to realize family sacrifices needed to obtain adult education. Too often, good planning did not take place before the married person undertook the difficult task of working full time, going to school, finding time to study, and carrying out family responsibilities at the same time. Worse, some married people made the decision to further their education, independent of their spouse, not gaining their support, and the marriage ended in divorce.

Other Effects of Education on the Family

- There is a direct correlation between educational achievement and family income.
- Simply being able to read and write well is a benefit to the family.
- Education will aid husbands and wives in communication with each other.
- Knowing how to read will help in understanding the Bible better.
- An educated parent is better able to help the children learn school subjects.
- A greater educated African-American community will understand better how the American system functions, which will enable us to reap more benefits for our families.
- Better education will aid us in exposing white racism and better enable us to deal with this problem.

Adult Literacy Programs

I don't believe that any church should try to solve all family problems by starting a program or ministry for every ill that exists. I believe we should see what is already offered in our communities by agencies and other churches before we try to deveop programs ourselves. For instance, several churches near us have feeding programs for the poor. I see no reason for us to do the same. Instead, we have specialized in family counseling and training through our counseling center and Christian Research & Development Institute, which is open to the community and other churches. No matter how small or large a church is, it is limited in finances and personnel and cannot meet every need in the community.

Those local churches that have some illiterate members in need of help should do research to see what adult literacy programs already exist before embarking on such an endeavor. However, some public school boards and government agencies will train and supply materials for such programs in churches.

Use the Professionals and the Better-Educated to Help Raise the Living Standards of the Disadvantaged

One of the strengths of the black church is that it is not a church separated by class. Some American churches are homogeneous in their economic class makeup. The black church is heterogeneous in general, in that you may find a doctor, a laborer, an ex-prison inmate, an educator, a plumber, a social worker, a secretary, and a lawyer—all sitting in the same pew. In our church, we have taken advantage of this strength in many ways. One of them is that we try to enlist some of our professional people to aid the less advantaged in our congregation to achieve a better quality of life. We have discovered that there is adult peer pressure. We see this work in a positive way. We are an inner-city church. Many of our professionals or higher income people are the first of their generation in this category. They have the same background as the people we are trying to help. Some of them have overcome great odds to be a professional or to be in a higher income bracket. This inspires our disadvantaged people to realize that they too can leave poverty and have a better quality of life.

WORK ETHICS

Years ago, when we were a farm and industrial community, it was easier to teach morals, including work ethics. On the farm, the family worked together, played together, prayed together, and worshiped together. When African-Americans migrated from the South to the North, they came looking for jobs and a better way of life, and prayer and the Bible were still in the schools. In today's service economy and high-tech lifestyle, too many of our people are unprepared and unable to compete in the marketplace.

The drug trade is a major industry in most of our neighborhoods, and this draws some of our young people to criminal activity as users and illegal entrepreneurs. It has caused jails and prisons to be filled with the "cream of the crop" of our gifted, black young people. Some single mothers turn their heads as if they don't know where the money, which is providing more material comfort for the family, is coming from. Even some parents are involved in the drug trade. It is difficult to convince a child or teenager who is making over five hundred dollars a week as a lookout, or one thousand dollars a week as a seller, to stop taking part in the drug trade.

Earlier I talked about the importance of families being evangelized and converted. God brings order to a person's and a family's life. A supernatural transition takes place. The new convert is enlightened by God, the Holy Spirit. He has a new spiritual mind, and God is the center of his life. To convince a natural man to give up large sums of money selling drugs and begin sacrificing and learning a legal trade just because the drug trade is wrong is almost impossible. In offering Jesus Christ as Lord and Savior, we are offering him life that will make him whole. The drug trade is a dangerous rat race that can only offer material gain but not the deeper needs of the heart, such as love, peace of mind, joy, and many other blessings.

We were created to work. God has standards and instructions as to how we may acquire income. Only a born-again committed believer will submit to such directives. If we know that after conversion we see radical change in some people, shouldn't we also expect a radical change in how money is acquired? In some cases, we pastors have not made God's teachings on work ethics clear and plain on Sunday mornings. Here are a few of these principles:

1. Work is a gift of God to provide satisfaction, income, and possessions to enjoy (Eccles. 5:19; Titus 3:14).
2. Work will enable us to help others (Eph. 4:28).
3. We are to discover our God-given gifts, talents, and abilities (Exod. 31:3; Deut. 28:8).
4. Laziness is sin (Matt. 25:26; Heb. 6:12).
5. We cannot serve God and money (Luke 16:13).
6. Get training and education (Prov. 2:10; 9:9).
7. God encourages business ownership (Prov. 12:11).
8. A person in business must be helpful and fair (Ps. 112:5).
9. The Lord holds the employer accountable for how he or she treats employees (Col. 4:1).
10. God is the one who gives us success (Gen. 39:3).
11. When God causes His followers to prosper, He does not add sorrow to it (Prov. 10:22).
12. As employees, we are to submit to the authority of the boss (Col. 3:22).
13. As workers, we are to work with all our hearts for the Lord (Col. 3:23).
14. We are serving the Lord Christ when we are good workers (Col. 3:24).
15. God will bring judgment upon those who violate His work ethics (Col. 3:25).

UNEMPLOYMENT

If we are to "work as unto the Lord Christ" when we are employed, we are to look for a job as unto the Lord Christ when we are unemployed.

In other words, Christians who are unemployed should be full-time job seekers. A minimum of twenty hours of job searching activity every week is necessary until one finds a job. Being unemployed can be humiliating and debilitating for a person who really wants to work. A few months without finding a job can lead to discouragement, anger, and depression. It takes the faith of a Christian to not give up and give in. During times of unemployment, God still promises to provide (Ps. 34:10).

The unemployment check and the welfare check can be deceptive to some of the unemployed. Sometimes when a person loses a job and is receiving assistance, he or she decides not to seek a job right away and goes on an unemployment sabbatical. I know people who were offered jobs but turned them down because they felt they deserved a break and had earned the right to receive unemployment checks. This is not part of God's economic system. These checks are given to assist those who are unemployed, not to those who are turning down God-given opportunities. The person who waits to look for a job the week prior to his or her last check and does not find a job has a bad problem.

Job Search Instruments

Sometimes being unemployed will cause us to assess our marketable skills. Sometimes this can be a blessing. I remember when I was a young, married father with lots of bills. I was forced to search for a better-paying position as a mechanical-design engineer. I had been turned down for a raise by my then employer. However, as a young Christian attending Bible college, my faith in God was strong and I was in awe about all I was learning about God. I found a two-week-old newspaper want-ad section on a windowsill in a men's room. I saw a job I thought I might try for, called the company, and made an appointment to be interviewed in three days. After work that day, I went to the library to learn how to write a resumé and assess my skills. During the interview, it was clear that I was being interviewed by an experienced man who knew what he was looking for. The company had been trying to fill the position for three months and had been disappointed by two candidates. The interviewer continued to ask the question, "Can you really do all this?" throughout the interview. He finally said, "If you can do half of what you say you can do, I will give you the salary you are asking for now and give you another raise in ninety days." I received my second raise in ninety days.

That experience changed my life by helping me realize that God has given gifts to all of us and that by faith we should believe His word. A few years later, I was laid off and without a job for weeks. I went through the same process of assessing my skills, updating my resumé and going on job interviews. I turned down two jobs and accepted the third job—to my wife's relief.

Ways the Church Ministry Can Help the Unemployed

1. Help them to identify marketable job skills and abilities.
2. Help them with resumé writing.
3. Help them with a cover letter that will accompany the resumé.
4. Church members should inform the ministry that helps the unemployed of available jobs, especially in areas where the member can use his or her influence to help another sister or brother in Christ to gain employment. These jobs should be announced on Sunday mornings and placed on the church bulletin board. As a church, we have gone through recessions (depression in the black community) and kept most of our people employed by giving out information.
5. The church can network and share job information from church to church.
6. Teach the unemployed how to do personal networking.
7. Teach them how to put together a job search plan (where to look for jobs).
8. Let them know how to respond to newspaper ads.
9. Let them know how to press for a job interview.
10. Role play the job interview. Role playing builds confidence.
11. Create jobs as a church, if possible.
12. Help the jobless get job training.
13. Encourage them to attend community college, trade school, or college.

UNDEREMPLOYMENT

This is the category of a great number of our families—honest, hard-working people who are not bringing home enough money to adequately take care of their family. Sometimes, both the mother and father are employed and still are just making it. For a single working parent who rarely has anything, this is a continual nightmare. When both parents are working or a single parent is employed, this leaves too many children unattended for hours during the day. We sometimes call these children latch-key children. I believe this is a direct contributor to the rise in teenage pregnancy. The ideal is for the husband to make an adequate income while the wife stays home to raise the young children, especially from infancy until the children are in school all day. Ideally, even then, the mother should work only part-time to enable her to be home when the children (including teenagers) come home from school. I really believe that being a homemaker is a full-time job, giving the wife little choice as to whether she can also be employed outside of the home.

The church as a family training center can help prepare families to have such ideal lifestyles which will help us do a better job of raising our children.

Ways the Church Can Help the Underemployed

1. Help the underemployed to have hope that they can do better through encouragement, information, and counseling. Some people in this predicament don't believe they can do any better. Some are not exposed to information that would help them improve their lot.

   Tyrone was an underemployed married father who worked as a cook in a local restaurant. Tyrone regularly asked for raises, to no avail. Tyrone was encouraged by his pastor to go back to school and learn another trade or change jobs. He was also given information concerning the City of Philadelphia's testing and interviewing candidates to become firefighters. Tyrone chose the firefighter testing, was interviewed, and was accepted to attend the firefighters' training academy.

   Although Tyrone was a high school graduate, he was not prepared for the difficult pre-med type of class he was expected to pass. Tyrone's wife, Connie, was a college graduate who tutored, coached, tested, and retested her husband during his training in the academy. Her love, encouragement, and determination in helping her husband to be successful and her faith in God were amazing. When Tyrone would score low on a quiz or examination, he would lead his wife in prayer and double his efforts to succeed. This couple had no social life during the time Tyrone was in the academy. Tyrone's and Connie's extended families were very supportive and did some baby-sitting so they could study together.

   Tyrone graduated from the academy and today is a firefighter and home owner, and Connie is home with their children.

2. The church can help these people match their gifts, talents, and abilities with proper job choices. Volunteers who serve faithfully in their church sometimes develop marketable skills. For example, we have had volunteers who have consistently helped us in our office work and are now employed as clerical workers, secretaries, and word processors. Volunteers also develop other skills by being involved in their church ministry, such as

- Leadership development
- Interpersonal relationships
- Organizational skills
- Planning
- Financial budgeting
- Clerical skills
- Selling skills
- Counseling skills
- Ability to learn and stretch themselves
- Security
- Maintenance
- Social services
- Youth services

3. The church can receive and pass on long-term occupational forecasts and trends. This is not secret information. It is published in national and local magazines and in books that can be accessed at the library, but the average person does not have such information with which to plan. There are ambitious African-Americans who waste time and money in being trained in an obsolete occupation.

4. Train the underemployed how to ask for a raise. They are not asking for charity when they ask for a raise; it is a business transaction. Their labor is valuable. Being a good worker, growing in responsibilities and skills, being punctual, being dependable in attendance, being a good team player, and getting along with the boss and other workers is worth something. These workers should be taught how to handle both a positive and negative performance review.

5. Train them in how to plan for career advancement.

6. Help them to determine if they are in a dead-end job with no hope for advancement.

7. Help them to change an inadequate job for a better-paying job. Sometimes this can occur within the company where they are cur-

rently employed. Sometimes people do not have the confidence that they can do better. The church ministers by believing in its members, based on God's creation of His people. We must help these people grow in confidence.

Eddy worked as an unskilled factory laborer. He was fascinated by the men at his company who worked "upstairs" and wore dress shirts and ties. Over a period of time, Eddy talked with these men in dress shirts and learned what types of jobs they did. He became convinced that he could perform at least one of those jobs but was afraid to inquire about a chance to prove himself.

Eddy's pastor was discipling him, and Eddy had grown to trust him enough to tell him about his ambition to work "upstairs." Eddy had never shared this with any other person. Eddy's pastor enthusiastically endorsed the idea, and together they role played, showing Eddy the best way to ask for the job opportunity. This was all the boost that Eddy needed. He had a good record as a factory worker, which gained his boss's support for his advancement. Eddy now wears dress shirts and ties and works "upstairs."

Changing a job by going to another company is more difficult. *No one should quit a job without having another job.* Too many people quit jobs out of sheer emotion, which can compound troubles, such as

- Not being able to get a good reference from the job they quit
- Having a more difficult time getting a job because it is easier gaining employment if you are already working—that is how the system works. Employers have more confidence in people who are working than in those who are unemployed.
- No income
- Falling deeper into debt

8. Some people are underemployed because they do not have a trade or occupation. When you ask people what they do for a living, they sometimes give you such answers as, "I work for Johnson & Johnson," "I'm into computers," "I'm into chicken processing." They are probably laborers—lifting computer boxes in the shipping department or cleaning chickens at a food-processing plant—but they do not have a trade or occupation. Some of our people do not have the foggiest idea of how to get training and which field of training to select.

9. Some people who are working and not earning an adequate wage are self-employed. They are owners of failing businesses, but pride keeps

them hanging on while their families suffer. Many marriages are in trouble or have broken down in such situations. Most new businesses fail even with adequate preparation. However, too many of our people go into business without knowledge of the business, training, a business plan, sufficient capital, and with a wrong attitude toward the consumer.

The church can help by enabling our people to be exposed to proper information concerning owning a business.

BOOKS FOR FURTHER KNOWLEDGE AND USE IN FAMILY MINISTRY

Bolles, Nelson Richard. *What Color Is Your Parachute? A Practical Manual for Job-Hunters and Career Changers.* Berkeley: Ten Speed Press, 1995.

Duncan, Mike. *Reach Your Goals in Spite of the Old Boy Network: A Guide for African-American Employees.* Edgewood: M.E. Dungan, 1990.

Jones, Gordon, and Rosemary Jones. *Naturally Gifted.* Downers Grove: InterVarsity Press, 1993.

Larsen, Dale, and Sandy Larsen. (1993). *Patching Your Parachute: How You Can Beat Unemployment.* Dowers Grove: InterVarsity Press, 1993.

Perkins, John M. *Beyond Charity: The Call to Christian Community Development.* Grand Rapids: Baker, 1993.

Reed, Gregory J. *Economic Empowerment Through the Church.* Grand Rapids: Zondervan, 1994.

Rivera, Miquela. *The Minority Career Book.* Holbrook: Bob Adams, 1991.

Chapter 10

TRAINING FAMILIES TO BE GOOD STEWARDS

A steward, during biblical times, took charge of the food, clothing, children, money, and property for persons of distinction or wealth (1 Chron. 27:25). Joseph was a steward over Potiphar's household (Gen. 39:4–5).

I believe that God, as Creator and owner, has made all of us not only stewards of the proclamation of the Word, but also to be good stewards of all He has given us. A steward takes charge. In biblical times, a steward received all the cash, recorded the accounts, paid all bills, and made the investments. We must train families to be good stewards of what God has provided.

I have talked about how to acquire income for the family primarily by being employed. It has been estimated that 90 percent of the people in America are having financial problems. This does not mean that these people are poor, for this is an affluent nation, but it does mean that most Americans are not good managers of their income.

The overview of what we want to accomplish with families is illustrated in the family financial process flow chart, Figure 3, on page 145. God's financial system is different from the world's system. God's system is a stewardship system. God gives us resources to manage under His ownership.

COMMON FAMILY PROBLEMS CAUSED BY POOR STEWARDSHIP

Problems caused by poor stewardship are not only family problems but church problems as well because they are brought to the pastor for help.

Problem	Poor Stewardship and Suggested Solution
1. Laid off from a job, depressed, with no hope of getting another job.	*Total hope was placed in existing job.* The individual must realize that he or she is a God-given resource. This includes the following: a. A mind to think b. God-given talents, gifts, and abilities c. Knowledge d. Experience e. Influence f. The ability to be retrained
2. Lack of housing, losing place to stay, or not having food or clothing for children.	*Buying food and clothing, paying rent or mortgage were not a priority, although God provided the money (Matt. 6:31–33).* A budget must be made and adhered to.
3. Husband and wife fighting over spending money.	Financial planning, budgeting, spending, and allowance for each must be agreed upon.
4. God is not blessing a Christian family.	*Giving to God and His church is not a priority.* Giving is a part of worship. There are times when God will not give to us when we

will not give to Him. Giving should be part of the family budget.

5. Earning a good income but not able to pay bills or paying bills more than thirty days late.

Over-extended credit card use. No budget. Good money management is needed.

6. Cannot get a mortgage to purchase a home or a loan to purchase a refrigerator, etc.

Bad credit. A plan must be put together to repair credit.

7. Claims that relatives and church members will not help them financially.

They borrow from relatives and church members and do not repay them. They are sinning against people who love them and must be committed to paying those whom they owe.

8. Lost job—fired.

Poor relationships with other workers, continual lateness, absenteeism, insubordinate and unproductiveness (common among some young workers today). These people must be challenged by a biblical work ethic (Titus 3:14).

9. Lost job—racism.

An understanding of company policy for presenting grievances is useful, and knowledge of the law is helpful.

10. Lost job—layoff.

It has been recommended by financial advisors that we should save six months' salary for such emergencies. It is also good to have more than one occupation or turn a skill into an occupation.

11. Don't have money to bury a deceased loved one or pay hospital bills.

Lack of insurance. Families need to purchase insurance, especially when they are young. Also, pastors need to let congregations know the cost of dying (funerals).

12. Don't have an automobile to get to work.

This could be a result of poor planning. Since many jobs are no longer in the inner city, this can be critical. Car pooling is very inexpensive; a used car may be the answer.

13. Can't meet child-support payments, and the court threatens jail if not paid.

Child-support payments should be included as a budget item to be paid. Parents should not only be financially responsible for their children, but also relationally responsible for them.

14. Can't send a worthy child to college.

No long-range planning and savings. A scholarship search is in order or school loans. Beginning an education at a community college is an option.

15. Gambling, lotteries, playing the numbers, etc.

Very poor stewardship of money based on public knowledge of the odds of winning. This is not included in God's biblical financial system. We are not to live by chance but by God's will for our lives.

16. Drug and/or alcohol addiction.

The destruction of the family by substance abuse is frightening. The will to quit and counseling are needed.

The Family Financial Process

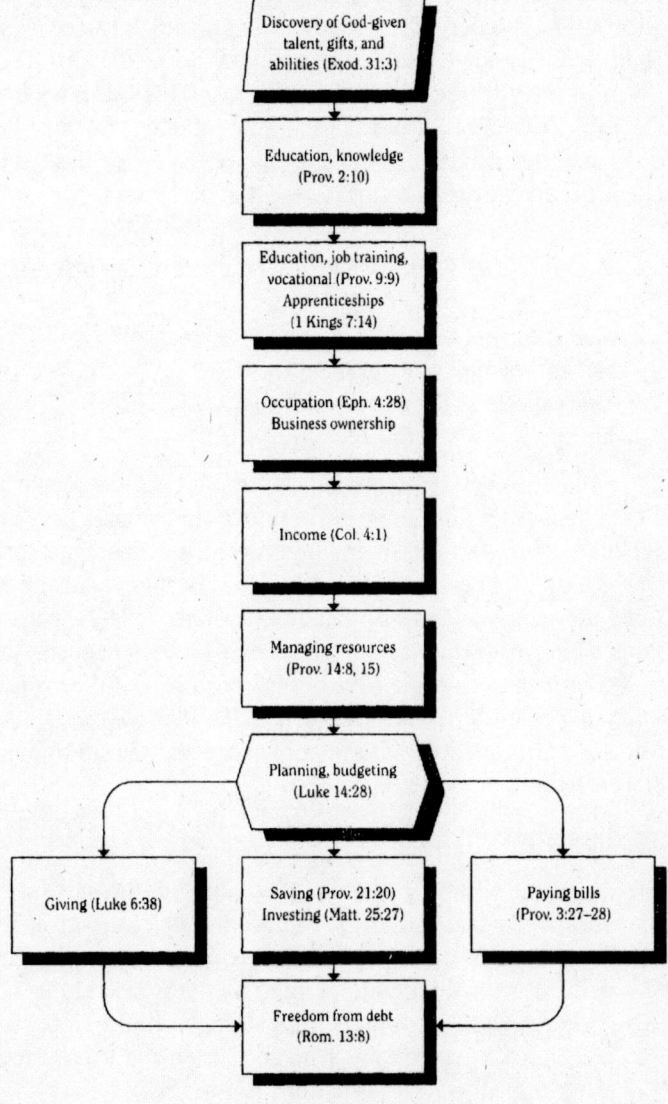

Figure 3

THE INDIVIDUAL CHRISTIAN AS A RESOURCE

Some people are born with many gifts and abilities, while others are perhaps less than average. We must help people to develop what they have and use it for the glory of God. God does not reward us based on our gifts or abilities, but on our faithfulness (Matt. 25:14–30; Luke 19:11–27). God has a plan for every believer's life (Ps. 139:16; Eph. 4:10). God is not prejudiced. He does not favor one group of people over another. We must herald the good news; we don't have to be the tail, we can be the head as believers (Deut. 28:13). We can be on top instead of at the bottom.

As a resource, we must remember the following:

1. God made us a resource by giving us gifts, talents, and abilities (Exod. 31:3).
2. God is against the exploitation of workers (Deut. 25:15). We should not allow employers to exploit us.
3. God expects us to be good workers (Col. 3:22–25).
4. Our labor is worth top dollar (Luke 10:7).

All of this will be of no avail if we cannot get our people individually to believe that each one is a resource. Individuals have been successful and prosperous—then, because of the economy or some other tragedy, they lost everything and had to start all over again. The only thing they started with was their abilities, knowledge, experience, and skills, which made them resourceful enough to become successful again.

Some of our people have never been successful because of fear, worry, low self-esteem and a lack of faith. Faith is powerful. It gets rid of fear and worry, and it builds self-confidence. We have to train people in biblical faith.

BIBLICAL FAITH

1. *Faith in God and His Word.* "How can a young man keep his way pure? By living according to your word. I seek you with all my heart; do not let me stray from your commands. I have hidden your word in my heart that I might not sin against you" (Ps. 119:9–11).
2. *Faith in what God can do through you.* "I am the vine; you are the branches. If a man remains in me and I in him, he will bear much fruit; apart from me you can do nothing" (John 15:5).
3. *Faith to believe in future success.* "Yet he did not waver through unbelief regarding the promise of God, but was strengthened in his

faith and gave glory to God, being fully persuaded that God had power to do what he had promised" (Rom. 4:20–21).

4. *Faith attitude.* We are what we think. Our thinking determines our attitude. "Now to him who is able to do immeasurably more than all we ask or imagine, according to his power that is at work within us" (Eph. 3:20).

5. *Faith eyesight.* To have a personal vision of success. God wanted Abraham to use his imagination to see success, by faith, before it actually happened. Abraham was to look at the land as if it already belonged to him, although other people already owned it. He was to see his future descendants numerically as the dust, stars, and sand.

> The LORD said to Abram after Lot had parted from him, "Lift up your eyes from where you are and look north and south, east and west. All the land that you see I will give to you and your offspring forever. I will make your offspring like the dust of the earth, so that if anyone could count the dust, then your offspring could be counted. Go, walk through the length and breadth of the land, for I am giving it to you." So Abram moved his tents and went to live near the great trees of Mamre at Hebron, where he built an altar to the LORD (Gen. 13:14–18).

> I will surely bless you and make your descendants as numerous as the stars in the sky and as the sand on the seashore. Your descendants will take possession of the cities of their enemies (Gen. 22:17).

6. *Faith to make a mid-course correction.* The ability to not lose your faith when things don't work out exactly as planned; instead correct the situation by adjusting the plans.

PLANNING

Planning is a biblical directive for wise people. A wise person looks ahead (Prov. 14:8). A fool will not plan ahead (v. 15). Planning may enable a person to give an inheritance to his children (Prov. 13:22).

Families will have fewer financial crises if we train them in short-term and long-term planning and if they are disciplined enough to practice the plan. We need to get families to think about what they would like to accomplish financially, with God's leading and help, as a family for this year, next year, and beyond.

The primary goal in family financial planning is to become debt free. Even after a family reaches this goal, circumstances beyond their control can cause new debts. Nevertheless, staying out of debt is a good objective for a family (Prov. 22:7).

Some Financial Wisdom Principles

1. Everything belongs to God, including us.

> For every animal of the forest is mine, and the cattle on a thousand hills. I know every bird in the mountains, and the creatures of the field are mine. If I were hungry I would not tell you, for the world is mine, and all that is in it (Ps. 50:10–12).

> Yours, O LORD, is the greatness and the power and the glory and the majesty and the splendor, for everything in heaven and earth is yours. Yours, O LORD, is the kingdom; you are exalted as head over all. Wealth and honor come from you; you are the ruler of all things. In your hands are strength and power to exalt and give strength to all. Now, our God, we give you thanks, and praise your glorious name (1 Chron. 29:11–14).

> Do you not know that your body is a temple of the Holy Spirit, who is in you, whom you have received from God? You are not your own; you were bought at a price. Therefore honor God with your body (1 Cor. 6:19–20).

   Submit to God's will for your life. Transfer ownership to Him.
2. The *love* of money brings evil (1 Tim. 6:10). Love God, people, and yourself, but use money and things.
3. Your life does not consist in the abundance of possessions (Luke 12:15).
4. Living in sin can stop prosperity (Prov. 28:13).
5. When God causes His followers to prosper, He does not add sorrow to it (Prov. 10:22).
6. God has pleasure in the well-being of those who serve Him (Ps. 35:27).
7. Follow God's "little-by-little principle" (Prov. 13:11). We should be patient as we

   • Earn a little more
   • Pay off a little more
   • Save a little more
   • Give a little more

8. Satisfaction in work is God's gift (Eccles. 2:24; 5:19).
9. Avoid co-signing for anyone.
   - It is poor judgment (Prov. 17:18).
   - It is a trap (Prov. 6:1–5).
   - It is even more foolish to co-sign for a person you do not know well (Prov. 11:15; 27:13).
   - You can lose your assets by co-signing (Prov. 20:16).

Some Considerations for Short- and Long-Range Financial Planning

1. Make giving to God and His church a priority. "Honor the LORD with your wealth, with the firstfruits of all your crops; then your barns will be filled to overflowing, and your vats will brim over with new wine" (Prov. 3:9–10).
2. The minimum that we should give to advance God's church is 10 percent of our gross income (the tithe, Mal. 3:10).
3. There should be adequate insurance protection. Insurance provides for the family in the event the principal family provider or providers are no longer able to work, or if they die. "If anyone does not provide for his relatives, and especially for his immediate family, he has denied the faith and is worse than an unbeliever" (1 Tim. 5:8).

   Insurance should provide for the following (if your existing assets will not furnish them):
   - Medical expenses
   - Dental expenses
   - Lost income produced by a principal family provider
   - Paying off (liquidating) family debts
   - Paying off (liquidating) mortgage on home
   - Funds for children's education (if you cannot save or invest for this)
   - Retirement income (if it is not done through investments); Social Security usually is not enough
   - Cost of funerals

4. Plan to provide for retirement above and beyond Social Security income.
5. Provide for six months of being unemployed. Layoffs and companies' downsizing, closing, or moving to distant places happens on a regular basis today.

6. Provide for children's college education.
7. Save and prepare for the future (Prov. 30:24–25). Save for

   - Emergencies
   - Depreciable items, such as a car, refrigerator, etc.
   - Future home
   - Education
   - Vacation
   - Furnishings
   - Funerals (when insurance is refused)

   Planned saving will reap benefits (Prov. 21:5).

8. Evaluate your present situation to see whether your present job or occupation enables you to reach your earning potential.
9. Evaluate whether you can improve your value in your present position or in the job market by attending college or vocational school or by taking courses.
10. Determine whether to rent or buy housing. Long-range planning is necessary for buying your first start-up home and toward finally moving into your dream home. Too many African-Americans have not been educated to this strategy.
11. Decide what investments to make and whom to make them with (Prov. 13:20; 20:18).
12. Using your experience, training, and capital, make plans for owning your own business.

GETTING STARTED TOWARD BEING A GOOD STEWARD

The goal is for a family to become debt free. Larry Burkett describes what it means to be in debt:

> Let me define a scriptural *debt*. Debt exists when any of the following conditions are true.
> — Payment is past due for money, goods, or services that are owed to other people.
> — The total value of unsecured liabilities exceeds total assets. In other words, if you had to cash out at any time, there would be a negative balance on your account.
> — Anxiety is produced over financial responsibility, and the family's basic needs are not being met because of past or present buying practices.[1]

1. Let God have His rightful ownership of everything that you own, including you. You must commit yourself to learning how God wants you to obtain and use money, then obey Him.
2. Determine your family income.

	Monthly Gross	Annual Gross	Five-Year Gross
Husband's Income $			
Wife's Income $			
_____ $			
_____ $			
_____ $			
TOTAL INCOME $			

The purpose for knowing the monthly income is to set up a budget. The purpose for knowing the annual income is budgeting, looking for waste, and cutting spending. The purpose for knowing the five-year income is long-range planning.

3. Determine debt.
   Use the "Determine Your Debt" sheet (see page 153).
4. Determine expenses.
   Use the "Monthly Family Expenditures" sheets (see pages 154 and 155).
5. Set up a budget (see sample budget on page 156).

> Suppose one of you wants to build a tower. Will he not first sit down and estimate the cost to see if he has enough money to complete it? For if he lays the foundation and is not able to finish it, everyone who sees it will ridicule him, saying, "This fellow began to build and was not able to finish." (Luke 14:28–30).

6. Develop your financial plan. "The wisdom of the prudent is to give thought to their ways, but the folly of fools is deception. A simple man believes anything, but a prudent man gives thought to his steps" (Prov. 14:8, 15).

   • Put your plan on paper. There is computer software that is also available.
   • Set dates to pay off each debt.

- Determine how much you will give back to God (tithes and offerings).
- Study some of the books as needed and use the resources suggested in this book.

7. Determine not to use credit unless it is a critical emergency, and strive to pay off credit card accounts in thirty days. Pay cash as you buy and save for future purchases (cf. Prov. 21:20).
8. Decide in what ways you can cut back on your spending and expenses.
9. Determine the amount you will save and hold in reserve monthly.

BOOKS FOR FURTHER KNOWLEDGE AND USE IN FAMILY MINISTRY

Burkett, Larry. *Your Finances in Changing Times.* Chicago: Moody, 1993.

_____. *The Financial Planning Workbook.* Chicago: Moody, 1990.

Eble, Diane. *Men in Search of Work and the Women Who Love Them.* Grand Rapids: Zondervan, 1994.

Richardson, Willie. *Thinking Right About Yourself.* Philadelphia: Christian Research & Development, 1984.

DETERMINE YOUR DEBT

Bills or Debt	Amount Owed	Monthly Payment	Annual Interest Rate	Annual Interest Cost	Date to be Paid Off

MONTHLY FAMILY EXPENDITURES

Fixed Expenditures:

Giving (Tithes and Offerings) $ _____

Transportation Cost to and from Job   _____

Savings   _____

Home Mortgage (Rent)   _____

Home Insurance   _____

Home Taxes   _____

Installment Payments   _____

Installment Payments   _____

Installment Payments   _____

Automobile Payments   _____

Automobile Payments   _____

Life Insurance   _____

Health Insurance   _____

Union Dues   _____

Credit Union   _____

_____   _____

_____   _____

_____   _____

_____   _____

_____   _____

Total Fixed Expenditures $ _____

MONTHLY FAMILY EXPENDITURES

Flexible Expenditures (controllable):

Home Repairs and Improvement	$ _____
Dry Cleaners	_____
Laundry	_____
Allowances	_____
Doctor	_____
Dentist	_____
Gifts (Birthday, Christmas)	_____
Clothing	_____
School Tuition	_____
School Books	_____
Magazines	_____
Baby Sitters	_____
Heating (Gas, Oil, Etc.)	_____
Electricity	_____
Water	_____
Gas (Gas Range, Water Heater)	_____
Telephone	_____
Car Gas and Oil	_____
Car Licenses, Registration, and Maintenance	_____
Music Lessons, Etc.	_____
Hairdresser, Barber	_____
_____	_____
_____	_____
_____	_____
Total Flexible Expenditures	$ _____

SAMPLE BUDGET

Annual Income: $24,000 (Before Taxes)
Monthly Income: $ 2,000 (Before Taxes)
Net Spendable Monthly Income
(After $500 in taxes): $ 1,500 (After Taxes)

Description	Monthly Budgeted Amount	When Due	Deposited Into Checking Account Weekly (Every Payday)
FIXED EXPENDITURES			
Giving Tithes	$200.00	Weekly	$ 47.00
Savings	25.00	Monthly	5.80
Rent	400.00	Monthly	92.30
Life Insurance	13.00	Every 3 Months (Due 21st of Jan., April, July and Oct.)	3.00
Sears	25.00	Monthly	5.75
Auto Payment	150.00	Monthly	34.65
Author Insurance	65.00	4 Payments a Year	15.00
Debt	40.00	Monthly	9.25
FLEXIBLE EXPENDITURES			
Utilities	150.00	Monthly	34.65
Telephone	30.00	Monthly	6.95
Clothing	25.00	Monthly	5.75
Recreation/Entertainment	10.85	Monthly	2.50
SUBTOTAL	1,133.85	**SUBTOTAL**	262.00
OTHER EXPENDITURES			
Auto Gasoline	80.00	Weekly	18.50
Grocery/Personal Items	250.00	Weekly	57.70
SUBTOTAL	330.00	**SUBTOTAL**	76.20
GRAND TOTAL	$1,463.85	**GRAND TOTAL**	$338.80

Part 4

TRAINING IN FAMILY RELATIONSHIPS

Chapter 11

TRAINING AND SUPPORTING SINGLE-PARENT FAMILIES

More than half of all families of African-Americans are single-parent families or substitute parents such as grandparents, aunts, and uncles. The growth of single-parent families must be curtailed if children are going to grow up in homes according to God's purpose for the family.

CAUSES OF THE INCREASE IN SINGLE-PARENT FAMILIES

Teenage pregnancy, divorce, and shacking up (or living together unmarried) are the major contributors to the increase of single-parent families. Alcohol and drug addiction are breaking up marriages and causing women to sell their bodies to get crack cocaine, resulting in fatherless and unknown-fathered children. Mothers and fathers are filling our prisons and jails at an alarming rate, leaving their children in the care of others or abandoning them. The homicide rate of African-American males is higher than that of any other group, and this deprives children of their fathers. The death rate of African-American males has caused African-American females to be the youngest widows in America.

There is a mistake made by two lovers in a moment of passion that brings an unplanned pregnancy. They don't love each other enough to marry—it was just sexual passion. One parent may be absent from the home because of marital separation or military duty. Sometimes husbands or wives don't like married life and walk away, deserting their family.

THE CHURCH'S SCRIPTURAL MANDATE

Certainly, some of the reasons for the increase of single-parent families is immorality and sin. I have spoken earlier concerning the need for evangelism, not only to satisfy the demands of God but also to have families consist of regenerated, born-again believers (John 3:3–7; Titus 3:5).

Simply being a Christian is not enough; there should be a commitment to live a holy and righteous life, walking in the Spirit (Gal. 5:24–25). Those who we believe to be close to God do sin (Rom. 7:14–20). The church is called to help save, deliver, restore, and forgive.

The people of God during biblical times were called by God to help widows and children who did not have fathers: "Learn to do right! Seek justice, encourage the oppressed. Defend the cause of the fatherless, plead the case of the widow" (Isa. 1:17). "Religion that God our Father accepts as pure and faultless is this: to look after orphans and widows in their distress and to keep oneself from being polluted by the world" (James 1:27).

God's people are told in these two verses to defend the cause of children who don't have fathers, to plead the case of the mother who is husbandless, and to look after this kind of family in their distress. The church must be the extended caring family—indeed, we are the family of God. We must minister to and support the special needs of the single-parent family. This includes a growing number of single-parent, male-headed homes and grandparents and other relatives who are substitute parents. One of the goals of ministering to these children is to guide them, as they grow up, toward establishing their own two-parent home.

FINANCIAL NEEDS

Single-parent, female-headed homes make up the largest segment of the poor among African-Americans. A woman who was middle class economically while married can find herself below the poverty line after a divorce, with no financial help from her ex-husband in the support of their children. A teenage parent can find herself buried on the public assistance rolls after having her second child without a husband because she is a high school dropout. The deep depression of a jilted spouse can cause an inability to earn a living or to make key decisions as the head of the family.

God called on His people to help provide for these kinds of families (Deut. 14:28–29). What can the church provide today?

1. *Encouragement.* Let such families know they are not alone. Whatever the church can do to help them, be willing.
2. *Biblical Counseling.* Depending on the family situation, there is a need for help with disappointment, unforgiveness, depression, parenting issues, insecurity, righteousness, hopelessness, guilt, money management, etc.
3. *Financial Assistance.* This enables the single parent to get education and training for a job. This can be in the form of monetary or informational assistance. It could be baby-sitting the children while the single parent attends school.
4. *Assisting the Single Parent as a Resource.* The following account illustrates how the church can help people discover unrecognized resources.

Some years ago a female single-parent came to me for counseling. Her major problem was that she was confused about God and her husband. She had tried to be a good Christian wife, but her husband left her anyway. She felt she had done the right things but God had not blessed her. Her husband told her one day he was tired of marriage and responsibility and that he would rather be single. Her unsaved husband left her sick in bed with an ongoing illness, alone with three young children. The rent and other bills were two months behind, and she was unemployed. I showed her how God had blessed her faithfulness. God healed her illness. Although she had no money and no job, God had taken care of her and her children by revealing to her that she was a resource. Within a few years, she became a court stenographer, all her bills were current, she was purchasing a home, all of her children were doing well in school, and she was a senior at college. She had missed seeing all of this because she focused on her disappointing marriage.

Within a few weeks of the counseling, her husband called her on the phone and asked if he could come home. She told him she would not consider it unless he went to marriage counseling, which he did. He had been living with another woman for two years, and she had been taking care of him. This woman had paid all the bills, although he had a full-time job. She did all the cooking and cleaning in the apartment where they lived. He contributed nothing.

I asked him what made him decide to return to his wife. He said the other woman said he would have to start paying part of the rent. His logic was, if he had to pay bills, he might as well be home with his family. I led him to Christ, and they were reconciled.

This deserted, sick single mother had come to realize that although she did not have money or a job and was in debt, she had the resources of God, her brains, and the abilities that she could use to raise her children and herself to a better quality of life. We as the church have to assist other single parents to realize and accomplish the same thing.

SPIRITUAL NEEDS

Single-parent families have the same spiritual needs as any other family, but because they are flying solo and dealing with some problems that two-parent families do not experience, there are some unique requirements.

1. *God's promises.* God defends the cause of such families (Deut. 10:18). God is an activist for such families (Deut. 22:22–24). He sustains the fatherless (Ps. 146:9).
2. *Let God be the other parent.* No woman can be a father. No father can be a mother. No aunt, uncle, or grandparent can be a birth parent. I hear single-parent mothers say again and again, "I'm trying to be the mother and father to my children." Such thinking is futile and an impossibility. Single parents must take the pressure off themselves and realize they can only be what God made them.

    Let God be a supernatural live-in parent. He is willing. "A father to the fatherless, a defender of widows, is God in his holy dwelling" (Ps. 68:5).

    Children should be led to Jesus Christ at an early age. Let God, the heavenly Father, meet the needs of these children. The children must be taught God's great love for them, His characteristics as their Father, and His awesome attributes.
3. Single and substitute parents must put their trust in God: "Leave your orphans; I will protect their lives. Your widows too can trust in me" (Jer. 49:11).

EMOTIONAL NEEDS

1. Single parents must not feel sorry for themselves because of their plight. Such self-indulgence can bring on depression, which distracts from child rearing, leading to more problems.
2. Single parents must realistically accept the circumstances they are in, with the goal of having the best life possible. Some single parents are angry, bitter, and angry with the world, in particular the opposite sex.
3. Single parents must not brainwash themselves into believing that having a spouse would solve all of their problems. Depending on the situation, getting married may make things worse.
4. The single parent must forgive the absent parent who played a part in bringing about these difficult conditions. If we do not forgive others, God will not forgive us (Matt. 6:14–15).
5. The single parent must not blame God. We all have free wills. Most single-parent predicaments come about because of choices made by the parent, not by God. Blaming God makes no sense, because we need His power in our lives.
6. The single parent should not try to turn the children against the absent parent. This is not mentally healthy for them.
7. Single parents must forgive themselves if it is their own fault they are single parents.
8. The single parent must combat loneliness by staying actively involved with extended families and the church, which is the spiritual family. Not only did God institute marriage to solve the problem of loneliness (Gen. 2:18), but He created the reproductive system of a woman so that everyone would be born and belong to a family (Gen. 4:1–2).

LEGAL NEEDS

Some Christians have problems going to court against another professing Christian or taking anybody to court because of 1 Corinthians 6:1–6. The church finds the single-parent family already in a broken situation. We are not dealing with a mother and father who are submitting to the authority of God and His Word, or they wouldn't be single parents to begin with. The exception to this is the person whose spouse is deceased. If the church can get the parties involved to sit down and agree, this is well and good. This is the ideal situation. However, as I stated in the beginning of this book, the church is usually brought into the picture after the fact. The church is brought in after a child is born out of wedlock, after a person has decided to marry the wrong person, after a husband and wife hate each other with a passion, after the couple have determined to get a divorce, after a spouse has deserted the family, and after unsaved people have done their damage.

In 1 Corinthians 6:1–6, these are believers with a civil dispute who are willing to submit to the authority of God and the authority of church leadership. As a pastor, I have been a part of helping families come to agreements they can live up to without going to court.

In Romans 13:1–5 we are told that the people who are in power to enforce the laws of the land are God's agents, to bring punishment on wrongdoers (v. 4). Anyone who brings children into the world and refuses to take care of them and support them is a wrongdoer and should be disciplined to do what is right.

The single parent should get legal advice in the following areas:

- Child support
- Child custody
- Visitation rights
- Wills and guardianship
- When the spouse has deserted
- When the spouse is living with someone else in an adulterous relationship and refuses to repent

TEENAGE PARENTS LIVING WITH PARENTS

1. *Forgiveness.* This type of single parenthood has its own unique problems. The church must teach and demonstrate forgiveness for all people who made a mistake or sinned and have repented. Parents should be willing to forgive their teenage or older children when they have children out of wedlock. There is a difference between forgiveness and permissiveness. Forgiveness expects repentance and a willingness to live a better life. Permissiveness condones continual sinful living, and there is no discipline and no expectation to be responsible before God.

It is wrong for parents to hate their unwed children and kick them out of the house at the news of a pregnancy. We are taught in the Bible that we should be merciful if we expect mercy from God (Matt. 5:7). Sometimes the parents are partly to blame because of a lack of accountability from their children and a lack of expressed love and affection. Some parents do not teach their children rules and standards for dating. Sometimes teenagers have too much unsupervised time without the presence of an adult.

In any case, the unborn child is going to be the grandchild to the unwed mother's or father's parent. This alone automatically involves the grandparents. It is not the fault of the unborn child that he or she is brought into this world under these circumstances. The child must have an opportunity to grow up in a loving environment in spite of the circumstances.

2. *Completing high school.* Parents should do all they can to help the teenage parent finish high school. As I stated earlier, education is the name of the game in America. Because teenage pregnancy is so common, some high schools have special programs for teenage mothers. If possible, parents should help their child to go beyond a high school education. It is a good investment. It will help teenage parents to have greater opportunities to support themselves and their child and to move out on their own.

3. *Adult responsibility and an adolescent mind.* This can wreak havoc in a family where there is more than one teenager or child. The teen parent has been forced into an adult world of parental responsibility and at the same time still thinks like an immature adolescent. Parents make a mistake when, as the grandparents, they take the full responsibility of taking care of and providing for the child. Parents should only assist their teenage son or daughter in carrying out the responsibilities of a new parent.

It is difficult for teenagers to attend high school, study, do homework, and take care of a child, but they must do it because it is their child. The hardships of being teenage parents should help them to mature and learn lessons that will stop them from having more children out of wedlock. In the case where both families of the teenage parents are Christians, they should cooperate and work together for the best future for their children and grandchildren. If the teenagers' parents are not Christians, this can be a problem in itself.

4. *Spiritual challenge.* After it is known that a teenager has been sexually active, the issue of salvation should be addressed. Some of our children who profess to be Christians at an early age and have been baptized may not be converted (Acts 3:19). Even if they are truly Christians, the responsibility of living the Christian life should be gone over with parents in a discipling setting, with the parents being the disciplers. To assume that teenage parents are Christians when

they are not is to be defeated by the Devil and have your own children lost to hell.

SINGLE PARENTS MUST BE ORGANIZED

1. *Use a schedule.* The single parent must make a weekly schedule, using a calendar in order to have a balanced life of work, responsibilities, play, church involvement, and relaxation.

   Many singles and substitute parents live lives of drudgery. They find themselves overworked, day in and day out laboring at hard, uninteresting tasks with no pleasure, no breaks, and no real vacations. As a matter of fact, they use vacations to do more for their children.

2. *Emergencies.* In case of emergencies, such as sick children at school who must be picked up and taken home, employed single parents must have a plan by which others will be able to help in such emergencies. If single parents have ongoing problems, such as the child's behavior that requires trips back and forth to school, the problem could cost them a job.

3. *Organization.* Children should be organized to help with household duties.

RELATIONSHIP WITH CHILDREN

1. Express love to your children. Many single parents have been successful in rearing wholesome, godly children. A parent's love was the motivating factor for the children. It is easy for you as a single parent to withdraw into yourself, seeking pleasure for yourself at the expense of your children. God loves us and expresses His love to us daily.

2. Discipline your children. There are enough problems being a single parent without having unruly children. They must obey you. There can be a problem with parents who have visitation rights and allow the children to do what they please or have whatever they want. You have one standard for the children and the absent parent has another. Children, being immature, may consider the parent who disciplines them as the bad parent and the permissive parent good. However, when the child is grown, he or she appreciates the discipline.

3. Boys should be taught their roles as males. Girls should be taught their roles as females. Role models for both boys and girls can be found at church. If the church has a good youth ministry, there is mentoring—whether or not it is called mentoring.

4. The family should eat meals together, but not in front of the television.

5. The family should attend church together. Sometimes teenage boys are reluctant to attend church because they are caught up in the sinful things of the world that all children, to a certain extent, are exposed to. Single parents should do all they can to help their boys and girls know Jesus Christ as their Lord and Savior.

6. Teach children the value of money. Some single parents do very well as wage earners and ruin their children. Children should not be given every material thing they ask for. They must learn that life will not give them everything they want.

7. Teenage parents should not feel they are a failure as parents when their children get into trouble, when the parents have done the best they can. The parents should not be defensive, attacking school teachers, church officials, and law enforcement people who bring the bad news. Sometimes this kind of attitude will prevent children from getting the help they need to turn their lives around before it is too late.

Get Help If Needed

The following are resources for assistance:

1. Relatives. Learn from Lois and Eunice (2 Tim. 3:14–16)
2. Friends
3. Church members
4. Other single parents
5. Christian schools. If possible, enroll your child in a Christian school
6. Agencies that specialize in the needs of children and single parents

Decision Making

1. Ask God for wisdom, and do not be led by emotions alone in decision making.
2. Develop a plan for dealing with problems and making decisions. *Write problems out* on paper. This alone can be very helpful in *seeing* solutions.
3. God has given some people in the body of Christ the gift of wisdom. Prayerfully ask God to lead you to them. These can be close friends, relatives, or your pastor.
4. Don't share with children those burdens that are beyond their maturity or ability to understand.

SINGLE-PARENT MINISTRY

1. *Workers*. The pastor and church must realize that single parents need the help of the church. The people who will make up the family ministry team are those who have a burden for single-parent families and some of the single parents themselves.
2. *Assessing needs*. A meeting should be held with the pastor, family ministry team, and some single parents to discuss the needs and problems of the single parents in the church. Later, when the ministry is up and running, the idea of serving single-parent families outside of the church can be considered. The church cannot solve all of the problems and needs of single parents, but the church ministries involved with these families can have some successes.
3. *Ministry objectives*. More than a decade ago when we completed steps one and two, I gave Sheila R. Staley, the first director of our Single Parent's Ministry, the assignment of coming up with a ministry strategy to address the problems of these families. The following are the partial results of her prayerful meditations and research, and these have blessed countless churches and single-parent families.

   • To establish within the church community a support system for single parents to guide them in the establishment and maintenance of a family, based on God's principles
   • To create a support cluster (small groups) of single-parent families for the purpose of edification and teaching (Rom. 12:10; 15:14; Gal. 6:2; 1 Thess. 5:11)
   • To establish two-parent support families to function as extended "adoptive families" for the purpose of edification according to Hebrews 10:24

4. *Ministry goals*. Establish for single parents and their children a foundation for living a balanced life based on five dimensions.

   • Spiritual: Living under the lordship of Jesus Christ, walking in the Spirit, being sanctified
   • Physical: Getting proper sleep, exercising, and having good, nutritional eating habits
   • Emotional: Developing right thinking, self-control, joy, and peace
   • Social: Having godly relationsips with the same sex, understanding Christian dating with the opposite sex, and enjoying social gatherings, concerts, plays, and trips

- Intellectual: Establishing life planning, family goals, educational goals, occupational goals, financial goals, and seeking vocational guidance

5. *Ministry Program.* Monthly workshop meetings. Instruction is given to single parents on such topics as the following:
   - Trusting God for a Spouse
   - Trusting God Concerning the Absent Parent
   - Resolving Bitterness
   - Handling Anger
   - Scheduling
   - Parenting as a Single Parent
   - Financial Planning
   - Legal Issues
   - Mothers Dealing With Male Children
   - Establishing Home Rules and Responsibilities
   - Health Issues
   - Community Resources

6. *Single-Parent Clusters.* Clusters are organized according to geographical location and personal preference. There should be no more than three families in a cluster. Clusters provide a vehicle for the single parent to establish relationships with other single-parent families to support one another in such areas as
   - God's principles for living
   - Transportation and travel
   - Baby-sitting
   - Recycling clothing, toys, children's furniture, etc.
   - Recreational and social activities
   - Child-rearing support
   - Fix-it skill-sharing, etc.
   - Children befriending each other

7. *Support Families.* These families consist of couples whose children are grown or who have no children. They desire to be an extended family to the single-parent family.
8. *Youth Ministry.* In cooperating with single parents, the youth ministry holds teenagers accountable to do their best in school and to honor and obey the parent.

Each single-parent family is different. Each family has different needs. Some families need more support and help from the church, others need less. One variable is the involvement of the natural extended family. The church should not take away from the families' responsibility if they are Christians and willing to help (1 Tim. 5:4). Economical and educational acquirement, employment, and alcohol and drug abuse are some of the other variables.

BOOKS FOR FURTHER KNOWLEDGE AND USE IN FAMILY MINISTRY

Bustanoby, André. *Single Parenting*. Grand Rapids: Zondervan, 1992.

Richmond, Gary. *Successful Single Parenting*. Eugene: Harvest House, 1990.

Staley, Sheila R. *Self-Counseling Workbook for Single Parents*. Philadelphia: Christian Research & Development, 1986.

Rekers, George Alan, and Judson J. Swihart. *Making up the Difference: Help for Single Parents With Teenagers*. Grand Rapids: Baker, 1984.

Whiteman, Thomas. *The Fresh Start Single Parenting Workbook*. Nashville: Thomas Nelson, 1993.

Chapter 12

TRAINING MARRIED COUPLES IN COMMITMENT

There are some very important commitments that married people must make, and these must become personal convictions. Christian couples must be committed to

1. God's will for marriage and family
2. The permanency of marriage
3. Loving each other with godly love
4. Forgiving each other

For too long some of us have assumed that just because two people are Christians, they automatically have a Christian marriage. Married couples must be trained in the biblical principles of marriage and family. There are no perfect people, so there are no perfect marriages. Therefore, there are going to be problems in marriages and families. Families must be trained in how to deal with problems. We must preach, teach, train, and counsel families so they may truly be Christian families.

GOD'S WILL FOR MARRIAGE AND FAMILY
God Instituted Marriage and Family (Gen. 2:18, 22–24; 4:1–2)

Today we hear some strange definitions of a family. We are told that an unmarried man and woman living together in fornication is a family.

When these same two people decide to live with some new "significant other," this also constitutes a family. A homosexual and a lesbian legally married to each other but having their sexual needs met by someone of the same sex is a family. Two lesbians or two homosexuals living together is a family. Two elderly people who are cohabiting yet will not marry for fear of losing their Social Security benefits is called a family. Lawlessness, ungodliness, and rebellion should not define family for the church of Jesus Christ.

God's Word tells us that God instituted marriage and the family, not man. Man instituted divorce and living together in an uncommitted relationship. God created male and female as husband and wife under His authority and in fellowship with Him. In other words, it takes three beings to complete a marriage—a husband, a wife, and God.

God also intended that there be children in a family, so He created the reproductive system. Couples have the choice of having children by childbirth or adoption, depending on God's will for each family (Mal. 2:15).

God's Purpose for Marriage Is Love and Companionship (Gen. 2:18; Mal. 2:14)

It has been said that companionship is the highest level of friendship. Married couples must be taught how to be friends. This friendship should grow in maturity to companionship and sweet fellowship in Jesus Christ (1 John 1:3).

God's Goal in Marriage Is Intimacy and Oneness (Gen. 2:24)

Couples need help in this area, but men in particular do. Couples must understand emotional intimacy, spiritual intimacy, and sexual intimacy empowered by God, the Holy Spirit. This can be very frustrating for husbands who don't have a clue as to what intimacy is, but it is a major need of a woman. A whole new world opens up to men when they learn and gain some competency in this area. God wants unity, not fighting (verbal or physical) between a husband and wife (Gal. 5:15).

Marriage Is a Lifelong Covenant with God That Should Be Broken Only by Death (Rom. 7:2)

Some people get married today only as a trial to see if their selfish desires can be satisfied; if not, they will get a divorce. God hates divorce (Mal. 2:13–16). The permanency of marriage must be heralded by the church. It must be publicized and disseminated among our single and married people.

When couples hold the permanency of marriage as a personal conviction, there is a greater motivation for working through marital problems.

The Marriage Should Reflect the Relationship of Christ and the Church (Eph. 5:25, 32)

Knowing this is extremely helpful for a husband in particular. The husband represents Christ in the marriage. The wife represents the church. Christ is a perfect model for a husband in how he relates to the church. All marriages should glorify Jesus Christ as Lord.

Christ Is the Way to a Successful Family (John 14:6)

It is useless to try to build a family without God (Ps. 127:1). A life without Christ is a family without Christ (Eph. 2:1–3, 12–13). Each family member must believe in Christ for salvation (Acts 16:30–31).

UNDERSTANDING WHAT LOVE IS AND HOW TO EXPRESS IT

It is disheartening to see a husband and wife who on their wedding day looked at each other with eyes of glowing love, and whose love has now degenerated into hate, bitterness, and intolerance. What happened to the love? Sometimes the couple themselves will give the answer to this question, "We fell out of love." Was God's intent when He established marriage to have it based on a frivolous love that is like a tree that climb—you can fall out of it?

Married couples must be taught about God's love. This is the foundational love that marriage must rest on. God's divine love—agape love—is the only kind of love that will take married life to the level of godliness that will glorify our Lord Jesus Christ. Other types of love are simply human and are very limited because they depend on how the person loved is being treated. Too many people can love their marriage partner only when they are being pleased. Human love is predominantly controlled by what we feel.

In contrast, God loves us even when we do not please Him. God's agape love is unconditional love. It is not an on-again, off-again commitment. Those who have received Jesus Christ as Lord and Savior have God's love in them:

> Dear friends, let us love one another, for love comes from God. Everyone who loves has been born of God and knows God. Whoever

does not love does not know God because God is love.... Dear friends, since God so loved us, we also ought to love one another. No one has ever seen God; but if we love one another, God lives in us and his love is made complete in us (1 John 4:7–8, 11–12).

This is one of the reasons that salvation is so important in marriage and family life. Only a saved person has the capacity and potential to practice love similar to the way God loves. Although all born-again Christians have God's love in them, they do not automatically love their mates as they should. They must understand what the Bible teaches concerning God's love in them and how to practice it.

Here are six things that married people need to know concerning the practice of God's divine love in the believer:

1. Love Must Be Practiced in Obedience to God

A new command I give you: Love one another. As I have loved you, so you must love one another. By this all men will know that you are my disciples, if you love one another (John 13:34–35).

Obeying God is submitting to the lordship of Christ. Those who claim to believe in Jesus Christ must obey His command to love others. He is not commanding us to *feel* love, but He commands us to practice loving others. Christians are called to love everybody.

I tell you who hear me: Love your enemies, do good to those who hate you, bless those who curse you, pray for those who mistreat you.... If you love those who love you, what credit is that to you? Even "sinners" love those who love them. And if you do good to those who are good to you, what credit is that to you? Even "sinners" do that.... But love your enemies, do good to them, and lend to them without expecting to get anything back. Then your reward will be great, and you will be sons of the Most High, because he is kind to the ungrateful and wicked. Be merciful, just as your Father is merciful (Luke 6:27–28, 32–33, 35–36).

If we were to wait until we had some good, loving feelings for our enemies, it would be impossible for us to love them. God commands us to love them in spite of what we feel. Not many Christians truly love their enemies or have even tried, because most have not understood that it is done with supernatural love—God's love—agape love.

When a marriage has deteriorated to the point that the couple or one of the partners has fallen out of love, they should be challenged to obey God's command to love one another, whether they are Christians or can be led to receive Christ as Lord. It should be clarified that the distinction between human, worldly love and God's love in the believer is that it is not driven by feelings but by love and obedience to Christ. This love is practiced by faith in God and His Word. If God says we can do it, we can. We can love by faith, trusting God that His commands are right and submitting to Him so that we can be empowered by the Holy Spirit to love this way.

There is so much emphasis on what the Holy Spirit does in a worship service—in preaching—but the church must help and teach Christian families to let the Holy Spirit have His way in their homes. When a couple says they don't love each other anymore, they must be challenged to repent and obey God. They must be filled with the Spirit (Eph. 5:18) and walk in the Spirit (Gal. 5:25). They can learn to love each other God's way—not the world's way or Hollywood's way. When they have fallen out of love, they no longer have feelings for each other. Then they become enemies. Yet there is hope for this couple. They must start loving each other as enemies. This is the lowest level of love, but it is commanded by God. "If your enemy is hungry, give him food to eat; if he is thirsty, give him water to drink" (Prov. 25:21). We love enemies by meeting their needs. An unloving couple must learn what their mate's needs are. Normally, when the relationship is this bad, a third person, as counselor, must assist in helping them to communicate and clarify what the needs are.

2. Love Is a Commitment to a Person

The Lord Jesus Christ demonstrates this by His commitment to us in our unsaved, ungodly condition.

> You see, at just the right time, when we were still powerless, Christ died for the ungodly. Very rarely will anyone die for a righteous man, though for a good man someone might possibly dare to die. But God demonstrates his own love for us in this: While we were still sinners, Christ died for us (Rom. 5:6–8).

Christ's level of commitment is shown by His love for ungodly people. Only divine love can motivate one to die for the ungodly. Ruth also demonstrates this type of love commitment toward her mother-in-law, Naomi (Ruth 1:16–17).

A love commitment motivated by the practice of agape love contributes to the permanency of marriage. Commitment is a matter of the will. One makes up one's mind to be committed. It is making a pledge to bind oneself to another. In this case, we are talking about binding to a spouse, through better or worse. It takes the person back to the commitment that was made formally on the wedding day.

When a husband reads in the Bible, "Husbands, love your wives, just as Christ loved the church and gave himself up for her" (Eph. 5:25), and says to God, "Yes Lord, I'll do it. I'll love my wife no matter what, no matter the condition, the circumstances, her mood, or her spiritual walk. Lord, I'll love her just as Christ loved the church. I will myself to do this." This is the marital agape love commitment.

3. Love Is Always Giving to the Person Loved

Again, God demonstrates this characteristic of His love:

For God so loved the world that he gave his one and only Son, that whoever believes in him shall not perish but have eternal life (John 3:16).

God gave Solomon wisdom and very great insight, and a breadth of understanding as measureless as the sand on the seashore (1 Kings 4:29).

You are awesome, O God, in your sanctuary; the God of Israel gives power and strength to his people. Praise be to God! (Ps. 68:35).

Praise the Lord, O my soul; all my inmost being, praise his holy name. Praise the Lord, O my soul, and forget not all his benefits—who forgives all your sins and heals all your diseases, who redeems your life from the pit and crowns you with love and compassion, who satisfies your desires with good things so that your youth is renewed like the eagle's (Ps. 103:1–5).

Love is always giving, but we human beings are so selfish. Pastors should be careful to emphasize the fact that love is giving to others. People can listen to a message on how Christians are to love one another and only hear how love should be applied to them. The message may be how to love others, but it is twisted by selfishness into, "How I should be loved." In counseling you can show a love passage in the Bible to a married couple, and the first response often will be, "He doesn't love me like that" or "She doesn't love me like that"—selfish ears listening with selfish hearts. How, then, should we love?

This is how we know what love is: Jesus Christ laid down his life for us. And we ought to lay down our lives for our brothers. If anyone has material possessions and sees his brother in need but has no pity on him, how can the love of God be in him? Dear children, let us not love with words or tongue but with actions and in truth (1 John 3:16–18).

- You must *give yourself* to your mate.
- You must *give* your mate the right to be *himself* or *herself*. *Give* your mate freedom to think differently and be different from you.
- *Give* and *share* material possessions.
- *Give* and make time for your mate.
- *Give* the benefit of the doubt to your mate.
- Always *give* your mate your best.

4. Love Must Be Expressed

People were bringing little children to Jesus to have him touch them, but the disciples rebuked them. When Jesus saw this, he was indignant. He said to them, "Let the little children come to me, and do not hinder them, for the kingdom of God belongs to such as these. I tell you the truth, anyone who will not receive the kingdom of God like a little child will never enter it." And he took the children in his arms, put his hands on them and blessed them (Mark 10:13–16).

It is obvious in the Gospels that Jesus loves children. In this passage He expresses love to the children by defending and blessing them. Children gravitated to Jesus on their own. They followed Him around. They were so underfoot that He picked them up and used them for object lessons as He taught adults.

It is not recorded in the Bible, but I believe that Jesus played with children; children will not follow you otherwise. He not only came into the world of adults but also into the world of children by expressing love to them.

Too many family members realize only after a loved one dies that they should have expressed more love to him or her. Some cases of bereavement are severe, not only because of loss but also because of guilt for not having expressed love adequately.

Love must be expressed by words

Some children have grown to adulthood and have never heard their parents tell them, "I love you." Many married people have never said or have stopped saying, "I love you." No one ever gets tired of hearing someone say "I love you," if it is said sincerely. If Jesus told His disciples who were around Him, "I love you," certainly married people and family members should say it daily.

Some husbands have protested, "She knows I love her without my saying it. I'm here. I pay the bills." If God says, "I love you," those who follow Him must do the same.

Married people should have their own love language. This is demonstrated in the Song of Songs.

> How beautiful you are, my darling! Oh, how beautiful! Your eyes are doves. How handsome you are, my lover! Oh, how charming! And our bed is verdant (Song 1:15–16).

> You have stolen my heart, my sister, my bride; you have stolen my heart with one glance of your eyes, with one jewel of your necklace. How delightful is your love, my sister, my bride! How much more pleasing is your love than wine, and the fragrance of your perfume than any spice! Your lips drop sweetness as the honeycomb, my bride; milk and honey are under your tongue. The fragrance of your garments is like that of Lebanon (Song 4:9–11).

Love words should include words of kindness, empathy, and affirmation of the other's worth. Love words should be expressed in attitudes of respect and deep devotion. Words are powerful and are not to be taken lightly in a marriage and family: "Let your conversation be always full of grace, seasoned with salt, so that you may know how to answer everyone" (Col. 4:6).

Love must be expressed by our deeds

If love words are not backed up by love deeds, they are worthless. Love should be expressed by deeds of affection. Warmth and affection have so much impact that "hug therapy" is being practiced in hospitals with crack-cocaine babies. These underdeveloped and drug-affected infants respond to the affection of these volunteers with medically positive results.

The problem with some married people who did not grow up with love and affection is that they are not motivated to be affectionate or, in most cases, don't know how to express themselves in this way. They must be open to learn and change. It is clear in the Song of Songs that the practical theme of this book in the Bible is the exercise of eros love between a husband and wife.

His left arm is under my head, and his right arm embraces me (2:6).

How beautiful you are and how pleasing, O love, with your delights! Your stature is like that of the palm, and your breasts like clusters of fruit. I said, "I will climb the palm tree; I will take hold of its fruit." May your breasts be like the clusters of the vine, the fragrance of your breath like apples, and your mouth like the best wine (7:6–9).

I have already discussed the fact that Jesus expressed love and affection to children, but He also expressed affection to or received affection from adults.

When a woman who had lived a sinful life in that town learned that Jesus was eating at the Pharisee's house, she brought an alabaster jar of perfume, and as she stood behind him at his feet weeping, she began to wet his feet with her tears. Then she wiped them with her hair, kissed them and poured perfume on them. . . . Then he turned toward the woman and said to Simon, "Do you see this woman? I came into your house. You did not give me any water for my feet, but she wet my feet with her tears and wiped them with her hair. You did not give me a kiss, but this woman, from the time I entered, has not stopped kissing my feet. You did not put oil on my head, but she has poured perfume on my feet. Therefore, I tell you, her many sins have been forgiven—for she loved much. But he who has been forgiven little loves little." Then Jesus said to her, "Your sins are forgiven" (Luke 7:37–38, 44–48).

Here is another example from Jesus' ministry:

Peter turned and saw that the disciple whom Jesus loved was following them. (This was the one who had leaned back against Jesus at the supper and had said, "Lord, who is going to betray you?") (John 21:20).

Expressing love and affection is to be like God, like Jesus Christ. "Whoever claims to live in him must walk as Jesus did" (1 John 2:6).

5. Love Is Shared Emotions

Rejoice with those who rejoice; mourn with those who mourn (Rom. 12:15).

For I wrote you out of great distress and anguish of heart and with many tears, not to grieve you but to let you know the depth of my love for you (2 Cor. 2:4).

One of the complaints of women is that men do not share their emotions. I believe this is generally true because of the world's macho image of what a man is, but it is not the biblical view of masculinity. Jesus is the perfect man and was not ashamed of displaying emotion (John 11:35).

One of the greatest releases and fulfillments is to have a friend to share your times of joy and sadness. Companionship is a husband and wife sharing the joys of the birth of their children, the delight of their child in a school or church program, the agony of losing a job (the family income), and the sorrow of the death of loving parents. It is in the spirit of Christ that such experiences stir our passions, being carried by life's waves of highs and lows; and through it all, a couple has grown and moved closer to God together.

Love is a shared emotion when a husband crosses over the masculine line to understand his wife's complexities as a woman and is rewarded by grasping some of the mysteries of femininity and by being motivated to know more about a woman, God's wonderful creation.

6. God's Love in the Believer Grows and Deepens

May the Lord make your love increase and overflow for each other and for everyone else, just as ours does for you (1 Thess. 3:12).

FORGIVENESS IN MARRIAGE

One of the reasons we love God is that He is a forgiving, merciful God. First John 1:9 is sometimes called the Christian's bar of soap because of its promises of forgiveness and cleansing. It is wonderful to have our guilt relieved as repentant believers, but what is also important is that this process enables us to be restored to fellowship with Christ. (1 John 1:5–10).

The same process is needed in marital and family relationships in order for a couple to remain in fellowship with each other. It is important that we practice forgiving our mates and other family members because there are no perfect people. If God has made provision for us to have continual fellowship with Him, who is perfect, by forgiving us, we certainly should follow His example in using the same process to keep marriage and families in fellowship.

Many marriages end in divorce because grace or forgiveness was not extended, practiced, or developed in marital relationships. God's Word challenges us as Christians to forgive. Certainly it must be a commitment of married people to forgive each other and model it for their children. "So watch yourselves. 'If your brother sins, rebuke him, and if he repents, forgive him. If he sins against you seven times in a day, and seven times comes back to you and says, "I repent," forgive him'" (Luke 17:3–4).

Rebuking is for getting issues on the table, not burying them in the heart in anger and bitterness. Sometimes married people offend or hurt each other unintentionally. Sometimes one mate assumes that the hurt was deliberate and does not talk about the issues, because the logic is, "If she [he] really loved me, it would not have happened." In these verses it is clear that we must be generous in our forgiveness.

The apostles' response in Luke 17:5 to Jesus' challenge to forgive is common today: "Increase our faith!" We Christians today, with our self-ishness and self-centeredness, will say we are spiritually inadequate to forgive someone seven times in the same day. We might say, "I could not get over being sinned against seven times in the same day, emotionally, to be able to forgive. I haven't grown that far yet." This is an emotional response that is common among Christians.

Jesus then gives the apostles a hypothetical situation about a servant who worked in a field all day plowing and tending sheep (Luke 17:7–10). Jesus points out that though the servant was tired, his duty would be to also prepare supper and wait on his master while he ate and drank. Jesus also pointed out that the master would not even say thanks because it is the servant's duty to obey him.

The granting of forgiveness cannot be dependent on how we feel but on our commitment to obey and do God's will. Forgiveness is forgiving a debt that is owed. The issue is not arguing if there is debt, hurt, pain, disappointment, or wrong done, but whether we will forgive the person for what was done or not done that has offended us. Forgiveness is a grace, the granting of unmerited favor to another. As we give this grace to another, God's grace will begin to work in our hearts to heal our pain and hurt. "Be kind and compassionate to one another, forgiving each other, just as in Christ God forgave you" (Eph. 4:32). "Bear with each other and forgive whatever grievances you may have against one another. Forgive as the Lord forgave you" (Col. 3:13).

If married people refuse to forgive each other, God will not forgive them:

> Forgive us our debts, as we also have forgiven our debtors. For if you forgive men when they sin against you, your heavenly Father will also forgive you. But if you do not forgive men their sins, your Father will not forgive your sins (Matt. 6:12, 14–15).

Married people deceive themselves when they harbor an unforgiving spirit and think they are still in fellowship with Christ. We cannot expect God to bless our lives when we are disobedient to Him. We must follow His example. God not only forgives us; He also forgets our sins.

> For I will forgive their wickedness and will remember their sins no more (Heb. 8:12).

> I, even I, am he who blots out your transgressions, for my own sake, and remembers your sins no more (Isa. 43:25).

> As far as the east is from the west, so far has he removed our transgressions from us (Ps. 103:12).

When married people forgive each other, they must not bring the offense up again verbally or dwell on it in their minds. When genuine forgiveness is practiced, the offense is forgotten as time goes on and as God's grace heals. In this way the marital relationship is building, growing, and maturing. Sometimes it is very difficult to forgive, but God demands that we forgive our mates.

Some offenses can be so shocking that trauma is experienced. Such offenses include adultery, incest by a stepparent, discovering that a mate is a drug addict, etc. At such times, it is difficult to think and get one's emotional bearings together. A short period of time can be allotted for emotional trauma, but forgiveness must follow.

The problem of forgiveness is not faith or spiritual growth, but obedience to our Master, God. We are not to forgive people because we feel like it. We forgive because our Lord and Master says so.

BOOKS FOR FURTHER KNOWLEDGE AND USE IN FAMILY MINISTRY

Coleman, Jim, and Sheila Coleman. *Friends for Life*. Dallas: Word, 1992.
Crabb, Larry. *The Marriage Builder*. Grand Rapids: Zondervan, 1982.
Liautaud, Marian V. *Swatting the Mosquitoes of Marriage*. Grand Rapids: Zondervan, 1994.

Chapter 13

TRAINING MARRIED MEN IN THEIR RESPONSIBILITIES AS HUSBANDS

MARRIAGE IS A RESPONSIBILITY

It should be clearly understood by every married person that marriage involves responsibility. It is your responsibility to meet the needs of your spouse for the rest of your life. These are God-given responsibilities that are spelled out in the Bible, God's Word. Of course, no mate can meet all of the needs in a person's life. Too often people who grow up in a bad family experience or those without parents expect marriage to make up for all past ill treatment. Pressure is placed on a spouse: "Make me happy; fulfill my miserable life." It is worse if these marital expectations are assumed, but never verbally expressed. Sometimes married people look to their spouse to be the parent they never had.

Only parents can meet children's needs. A mate cannot make up for an unfortunate family life. A spouse can only meet marital needs in a spouse's life, and no one does it perfectly. Only God can meet our deepest needs of love and fulfillment.

However, marriage can be a journey of love, friendship, partnership, and nuptial fulfillment.

THE LOVING LEADER

1. Husbands are to love their wives sacrificially, similar to the way Christ loves His church: "Husbands, love your wives, just as Christ loved the church and gave himself up for her" (Eph. 5:25).

This commandment for a husband characterizes his role as a loving leader. He is to be an active, lifelong lover. Every other responsibility flows out of this challenge. Jesus died for the church and sacrificed His life for our sins. He arose from the dead to justify us. He cares for us in His present priestly ministry, because He loves us.

Before He came to earth from eternity past, He willingly gave up His glory. He humbled Himself and took on the limitations of a human body. He was humiliated, persecuted, and abused because He loved us. He allowed wicked men to beat Him, spit on Him, and drive stakes through His hands and feet because He loved us. He subjected Himself to be crucified. Crucifixion was one of the most dishonorable ways for a criminal to be put to death, yet He had committed no crime. He suffered all this because He loved us.

Jesus forgives us and is merciful. He is patient with us. He extends His grace to us when we fail Him and let Him down. He prays for us and watches out for us because He loves us.

Every husband must love his wife in this way, as Christ loved the church. A husband must submit himself to the Lord Jesus Christ in order to do this. "Now I want you to realize that the head of every man is Christ" (1 Cor. 11:3). A man must be submissive and yielded to God the Holy Spirit and have a servant attitude to minister to his wife. A husband must depend on Christ to know how to meet the needs of his wife and express love to her. Christ created the woman, and He will give the open, teachable husband guidance (Col. 1:16).

After Christ, a man's wife is to be first in his life. "He who loves his wife loves himself" (Eph. 5:28). A husband must honor his wife and treat her as someone very special. She is special. She is his queen. Certainly, if a man believes he is the "king of his house," his wife has to be his queen. A husband should treat his wife as royalty.

Physical and emotional abuse have no place in a Christian marriage. "Husbands ought to love their wives as their own bodies. He who loves his wife loves himself. After all, no one ever hated his own body, but he feeds and cares for it, just as Christ does the church" (Eph. 5:28–29). A man is never justified in physically or emotionally abusing his wife.

A man's wife is his queen. He should use beautiful words when holding conversations with her, especially when other people are present. "Like a lily among thorns is my darling among the maidens" (Song 2:2). Continually praise and compliment your wife.

2. The husband is the head and leader of the home (Eph. 5:23; 1 Cor. 11:3). Pastors are instructed in their role as leader not to be "lording it over those entrusted to" them (1 Peter 5:3). The same is true of husbands. A woman should be following a loving leader, not a dictator or bully.

A husband shows his love by being a leader in his home. Some men like to think of themselves as "wearing the pants in the home," but that is all. We need Christian men who are active husbands and fathers, carrying out their responsibilies.

3. A husband is to be patient and understanding. "Husbands, in the same way be considerate as you live with your wives, and treat them with respect as the weaker partner and as heirs with you of the gracious gift of life, so that nothing will hinder your prayers" (1 Peter 3:7).

In relationships men and women are very different. Women tend to express more of what they feel than men do. Men tend to express what they think and mask their emotions. These differences can become frustrating to both people, especially men. Sometimes a husband may say, "I cannot understand women." The lack of understanding may be because he is trying to understand her as if he was trying to understand another male. She is a woman. Her thinking and emotions are from a woman's point of view, not a man's. God made her that way, and that's wonderful.

A husband must be patient and considerate, becoming a student, learning his wife. If a husband draws conclusions only from what the wife says, she will appear to be contradictory. But if he takes into account her words, emotions, moods, time of month, and actions, he will discover that there is a consistent pattern. He must be tolerant, not bitter (Col. 3:19). Husbands must nurture and care for their wives (Eph. 5:29).

"A wife of noble character who can find?" (Prov. 31:10). A man must realize that the blessing of having a wife is of great value. He is to tenderly care for her. We tenderly care for eggs. When we buy groceries, we always make it our business to know what bag the eggs are in. We carefully place that bag of groceries in our automobile, being sure it will not fall over and crack the eggs on our trip home.

Some of us don't care enough to know where our wives are. A husband should build his wife up, support her, and give her strength. He is to show her warmth and tenderness. He is to shelter, protect, and encourage her and minister to her needs as a husband. A husband is to cheer, comfort, and consider her a precious jewel.

CHAIRMAN OF THE PROBLEM DEPARTMENT

The husband is the chairman of the family problem department (Eph. 5:27). He is to help his wife with her problems. *Her* problems are *his* problems. I have heard men say, "That's her problem," or "She needs counseling, not me." If there is to be oneness, a man can never detach himself from his wife. He must learn how to relate when things are not going well for her.

1. A husband can help by talking with his wife.

Sometimes this solves her problem because he has been neglecting her.

2. A husband can help by listening to his wife, even if he is the problem.

A man must be disciplined enough not to be defensive if his wife is complaining about him. He must remember that he is the head of the home, and there is no higher-ranking person to turn to. Some men become angry when their wives turn to someone else with their marital or family problems, but it was he who closed the door when she tried to talk to him. I believe we as men sell ourselves short when it comes to what we can handle emotionally in a relationship with women, especially our wives. Think about this. Some of us have handled surviving on the streets or living in bad and dangerous neighborhoods, withstood the filthy profanities of our superiors in the military, endured Vietnam and Desert Storm, but lose it when confronted by a wife with PMS. Men have to be stronger than that.

3. A husband can be a sounding board.

Sometimes when a woman complains or communicates problems, she is merely processing her thoughts aloud and doesn't need "Mr. Fix-It" to jump in. She just needs her husband to be a sounding board. This is where patience and consideration are needed to distinguish between being a caring sounding board and a problem solver.

4. A husband can be ready to forgive.

If her problem came about because she broke God's order by not being submissive to her husband's leadership, she must be forgiven, not berated, but loved and extended grace.

5. A husband can correct lovingly.

If a husband must correct or tell his wife about her faults, he must do it lovingly, without anger or any negative emotion. If, in spite of his careful sensitivity to her feelings, she reacts in a negative way, make allowances for her, for it is difficult for her to have her hero discover her shortcomings.

6. A wise husband will listen to his wife in problem solving.

The wife is her husband's number-one advisor. When problems cannot be resolved within the family, wise men get outside help. God, the Holy Spirit, has given some believers the gift of wisdom. Outside help can come from one or another of these people, someone who has expertise in the problem area, or the pastor. Men should not allow sinful pride to stop them from getting outside help when needed.

7. A husband can express understanding.

Sometimes neither the husband nor anyone else can solve a wife's problem, but it means a lot to her to know that he wishes he could.

8. A man must turn to God first with all problems.

He should hear his wife's problems or family problems, then depend on God for guidance and direction.

PRIEST OF THE HOME

The husband is the priest of the home (Eph. 5:25–27). Before there were priests, prophets, or pastors, husbands led their families spiritually (Gen. 12:18). Although God has given us pastors, I don't think God has taken away a man's responsibility to give spiritual leadership to his wife and children. He is to lead by example as a follower of Christ. He is to help his wife grow spiritually and allow her to hold him accountable spiritually. In other words, when she questions his spiritual walk, he needs to have a submissive attitude. "Submit to one another out of reverence for Christ" (Eph. 5:21).

Wives should not have to beg and plead with their husbands to attend church or to be involved in the life of the church. A head of the home many years ago said, "Choose for yourselves this day whom you will serve. . . . But as for me and my household, we will serve the LORD" (Josh. 24:15).

USE OF AUTHORITY

A man must be careful how he uses his God-given authority as the head of the home (1 Cor. 11:3, Eph. 5:22).

Husbands and fathers must be taught that the authority which God gives a man is not to be used in any old way that he would like to use it, but must be governed by the will of God. Some men use their authority as a license of ownership of their wife and children. A woman is reduced to an emotional slave, and children are raised as mechanical, compliant puppets under the hands of a controlling tyrant. The pitiful thing about a family such as this is that the sons who have grown up hating their fathers for such treatment marry and become worse than their fathers.

I have also observed husbands slinking away from their responsibilities to lead because of the resistance of an unsubmissive wife. Some husbands and wives have reversed and perverted God's order for the home—the wife becoming the head of the house and the man becoming a passive follower.

The authority that God gives a husband is guided by the Scripture.

1. A husband's authority arrives through his service to his family.

> Jesus called them together and said, "You know that the rulers of the Gentiles lord it over them, and their high officials exercise authority over them. Not so with you. Instead, whoever wants to become great among you must be your servant, and whoever wants to be first must be your slave—just as the Son of Man did not come to be served, but to serve, and to give his life as a ransom for many" (Matt. 20:25–28).

Our men used to say to their sons and sons-in-law, "Take care of home first." Fathers used to hold their married sons accountable for their responsibility of caring for their families. However, some of us have followed the majority in society in self-indulgence and pleasure-seeking. With the number of female-headed, single-parent families growing, some young men don't have fathers to guide them as husbands.

Some of our fathers and grandfathers worked two full-time jobs to provide for their families. Many of our fathers and grandfathers have lost their lives protecting their families. A man must serve his family.

2. A husband's authority arrives through how he gives and expresses love to his family.

"So he got up and went to his father. But while he was still a long way off, his father saw him and was filled with compassion for him; he ran to his son, threw his arms around him and kissed him" (Luke 15:20). In the parable of the lost son, the son left home in rebellion and foolishness, a disappointment to his father. However, when this grown son came to his senses, he had freedom to return home, defeated and a failure, because of his father's love.

"So Jacob served seven years to get Rachel, but they seemed like only a few days to him because of his love for her" (Gen. 29:20). How many men today would work seven years to receive the hand of a woman? Jacob loved Rachel so much that it "seemed like only a few days to him." It is not likely that Rachel ever had to question if her husband loved her; he expressed it by his service.

3. A husband's authority arrives through being an example for his family.

Like the apostle Paul, he must be able to say, "Therefore I urge you to imitate me" (1 Cor. 4:16). A man must walk close to Christ, if he wants to be the kind of head of his home who will hear in glory, "Well done, good and faithful servant!" (Matt. 25:21).

4. A husband's authority arrives through his ability to stabilize his family.

If any of you lacks wisdom, he should ask God, who gives generously to all without finding fault, and it will be given to him. But when he asks, he must believe and not doubt, because he who doubts is like a wave of the sea, blown and tossed by the wind. That man should not think he will receive anything from the Lord; he is a double-minded man, unstable in all he does (James 1:5–8).

One of the things that women and children need is emotional security. When a husband is unstable, the family is always off balance. It is commonly seen in families when a husband is an alcoholic or a drug addict or when he refuses the responsibility of leadership.

A husband must be a man of wisdom and convictions. He is to be a loving leader, but he must be firm about the direction in which the family is going, led by God and His Word.

MANAGER OF THE HOME

A man must be a manager of his home. "He must manage his own family well and see that his children obey him with proper respect" (1 Tim. 3:4). A manager must have a vision for the direction in which he leads. A husband and his wife should dream and plan together for the future of their family, led by God, the Holy Spirit (Gal. 5:18). The manager sees that the plan is accomplished.

THE FAMILY PROVIDER

The husband is to be the family provider. "If anyone does not provide for his relatives, and especially for his immediate family, he has denied the faith and is worse than an unbeliever" (1 Tim. 5:8). The wife can help provide, but it is not her responsibility to provide for the family if she has a husband. "She makes linen garments and sells them, and supplies the merchants with sashes" (Prov. 31:24).

A woman's primary responsibility is to be home with her children. God created women to give birth to children, nurse, and nurture them. No relative or daycare center can meet the emotional needs of children as well as their mother can. Too many "latch-key children" are getting into trouble, experimenting with sex, alcohol, and drugs, and returning home from school with no adult supervision for hours.

It is critical that a man does everything he can to obtain a job that will support his family. This can be difficult to accomplish for a man who has no skills or vocation. It may mean that a man in his twenties, thirties, or forties or older must start all over again. He may have to return to school to learn a new occupation. Even after training he may have difficulty in obtaining employment, but he should not give up. If a man is going to get training in a new occupation, it is important for him to find out if there is a great need in the economy for such workers before he invests his time, effort, and money. He does not have to guess about such things or rely on his friends' opinions; this information is readily available.

In a racist, unfair society, it takes a tough, determined man who can persevere to accomplish gainful employment when he has a family and bills and is trying to work on an existing job or is unemployed. However, God is willing to help a man provide for his family. A man must seek the Lord. "The lions may grow weak and hungry, but those who seek the LORD lack no good thing" (Ps. 34:10).

Our Lord Jesus Christ has the authority and is willing to help men who live for him. "Therefore he is able to save completely those who come to God through him, because he always lives to intercede for them" (Heb. 7:25). "Then Jesus came to them and said, 'All authority in heaven and on earth has been given to me'" (Matt. 28:18). "'I am the Alpha and the Omega,' says the Lord God, 'who is, and who was, and who is to come, the Almighty'" (Rev. 1:8).

The Working Wife

If the wife must work to help her husband provide for the family, these things must be taken into consideration:

1. A woman should not work when she has preschool children. Some women refuse to quit their job when they start having children, although the family can live on the husband's income. They want to maintain their financial independence. Remember, God's will is oneness, not independence. Sometimes the husband and wife sacrifice their children's development for the materialism that two salaries provide.

2. A woman should not work unless her husband agrees. Sometimes it is a man's pride that stops him from agreeing that his wife should help by working, even though his income does not provide for family essentials, such as food, clothing, housing, and deliverance from financial bondage. Even if this is the case, a woman should not defy her husband to take a job. Some women have done this and now have a horrible relationship with their husband, or they have no husband at all because he left. Women who lose their husbands are in a worse financial condition than before. The family still has only one "breadwinner"—the wife, who cannot fully provide for them. Also, now she is a single parent.

Even if the husband does not abandon his family because his wife went to work against his will, there is bitterness. The husband will become more indifferent toward his wife. He may become preoccupied with outside interests or withdraw himself because of the affront to his manhood.

3. Mothers who have to help their husbands should have their working hours fit as closely as possible to the time that the children are in school. A mother should be able to see the children off to school and meet them at home in the afternoon. Sometimes this can be done only with a part-time job, but this may provide all the additional income the family needs.

4. If the husband agrees that his wife must work to help him provide, he should help equally or more with her home responsibilities. It is wrong for a man to come home from work and expect his wife to prepare his meals, take care of the children (including helping them with their

homework), do family laundry, clean the house, and be an energetic lover at ten o'clock at night.

It behooves a brother to perform as many of these domestic duties as possible to conserve his wife's energy for fun time. I have a friend who allows his wife to do little or nothing after she comes home from work. This brother always has a smile on his face and always rushes home with his wife after midweek Bible study and prayer meeting.

5. Sometimes a man cannot handle it if his wife has a better job or makes more money than he. Some feel defeated and less than a man. I know a wife who dreads getting a promotion or a raise because her husband will go into depression or be in a bad mood at hearing the good news.

With the problems of African-American males dropping out of school because of poor learning conditions, the high rate of male incarceration, the illegal drug industry in our communities, and the lack of post-high school education and training, many of our men are not prepared to compete in the job market.

African-American women are better educated than the men. There are more professional women than men. In our families, we encourage the girls more than boys for their security. It is common for parents to tell a son who is a junior in high school, "We don't have any money to send you to college. You will have to make it on your own." The same parents will tell their daughter, "We don't have the money to send you to college, but we will help you as much as we can." What causes the difference? I believe that because of the past history of our women being abused by men during times of slavery, we are more protective of our females in the workplace.

A man who has a bad attitude about his wife having a better job or having a higher income than his must change his attitude. He needs to give himself some credit for choosing such a gifted, talented woman. He needs to understand that money does not make the man but being godly does. A Christian woman finds security in a spiritual man. Also, in God's oneness, all income belongs to both of you.

SEXUALLY FAITHFUL

"A man who commits adultery lacks judgment; whoever does so destroys himself" (Prov. 6:32). God has called husbands to be sexually faithful to their wives. To be unfaithful to a wife is to be unfaithful to the Lord. We live in a day when men are bombarded with sexual temptation on television and in motion pictures, videos, music, and magazines. It is mind-boggling to see what is shown in a thirty-second television commercial or a magazine advertisement. The lyrics to music can be tanta-lizing, and the new sexually aggressive woman today thinks nothing of making sexual advances toward a man.

There is a shortage of available marriageable men, and some women will do anything to get a husband. We are living in such ungodly times that a man's being married will not deter some women's advances. Nevertheless, God's Word still instructs men:

> May your fountain be blessed, and may you rejoice in the wife of your youth. A loving doe, a graceful deer—may her breasts satisfy you always, may you ever be captivated by her love. Why be capti-vated, my son, by an adulteress? Why embrace the bosom of another man's wife? For a man's ways are in full view of the LORD, and he examines all his paths. The evil deeds of a wicked man ensnare him; the cords of his sin hold him fast. He will die for lack of discipline, led astray by his own great folly (Prov. 5:18–23).

Godly discipline must be exercised by the Christian man walking in the power of the Holy Spirit. The image of the macho man is that he does not turn down anything "offered to him on a silver platter." "If a woman is freely giving sex, why should I not enjoy myself?" Because to do so is wrong, sinful, and destructive to marriage and family. This kind of attitude is of the flesh and the ego, not of the Spirit of Christ. We Christian men must have a commitment to holiness and sanctification.

There are too many families that are dysfunctional because of sex-ual sins—a married man fathering a child in an adulterous relationship; a husband passing on to his wife a sexually transmitted disease; the "other woman" revealing herself to the wife either to get revenge on the hus-band because he will not leave his wife or to attempt to destroy the mar-riage so he will marry her; a child growing up not knowing his father because the mother will not reveal his identity in an attempt to protect her married lover; children being deprived of both parents through death because the husband brought AIDS home.

Sexual purity not only pleases God, but enables us to have better families.

THE FAMILY PROTECTOR

"When Abram heard that his relative had been taken captive, he called out the 318 trained men born in his household and went in pur-suit as far as Dan" (Gen. 14:14). A man, with God's help, is to protect and defend his family. A man needs to see that his home is as secure as possible from unwanted intruders. Neither he nor any member of the family should be driving an automobile without a driver's license or insurance or disobeying any traffic laws. Some men do not qualify for certain jobs because they do not have a valid driver's license or insurance.

The family should be protected from varmints such as mice, rats, cockroaches, etc. Broken door locks and windows should be repaired as soon as possible to ward off further problems.

The family should be protected from corruption as much as possible; we are exposed to more than enough by simply being in the world. Profanity must not be a part of family language, nor must it be allowed by guests or relatives who visit our homes. Health-destroying cigarettes and marijuana smoking should not be tolerated in a Christian home for the sake of family well-being and honoring God.

A man has to have faith and courage to maintain such home standards, and God is able to help him: "Be strong and courageous. Do not be afraid or terrified because of them, for the LORD your God goes with you; he will never leave you nor forsake you" (Deut. 31:6).

BOOKS FOR FURTHER KNOWLEDGE AND USE IN FAMILY MINISTRY

Cornwall, Robert, and Judson Cornwall. *Five Foundations for Marriage.* Lake Mary: Creation House, 1991.

MacArthur, John, Jr. *Different by Design.* Wheaton: Victor Books, 1994.

Sadiku, Matthew O. N. *Secrets of Successful Marriages.* Philadelphia: Covenant, 1991.

Chapter 14

TRAINING MARRIED WOMEN IN THEIR RESPONSIBILITIES AS WIVES

I am totally convinced that because of the ungodly and unbiblical positions and philosophy among unsaved women today, they are losing personal influence with men. I believe that women should receive equal pay for equal work, and they should not be discriminated against; however, I also believe that Satan is trying to obscure the fact that there are differences between men and women, thus tampering with God's creation. The Christian woman must filter out the corrupt philosophy of the world for the solid, unfailing Word of God.

With all of the problems we have as African-Americans in this society, our women cannot afford to buy into the positions of the majority of women. If our families are to survive, women must reject all but God and His Word. That will restore and build our families.

THE RESPECTFUL ENCOURAGER

The wife must respect her husband (Eph. 5:33).

Now I want you to realize that the head of every man is Christ, and the head of the woman is man, and the head of Christ is God (1 Cor. 11:3).

Wives, submit to your husbands as to the Lord. For the husband is the head of the wife as Christ is the head of the church, his body, of which he is the Savior. Now as the church submits to Christ, so also wives should submit to their husbands in everything (Eph. 5:22–24).

African-American men are generally not accepted as equals in our society. There is continual resistance to their having access to the opportunity structure—politically, economically, and socially. There is a tremendous amount of pressure on them just to survive. This is why you hear a brother say, "I'm just trying to make it." This is not only said by a minimum-wage earner but also by some of the fortunate men in corporate America.

There is very little sympathy for the African-American male's predicament, even among some of the sisters. He is blamed for every ill that we have in our community, from crime to the breakdown of the family, while the good he does is taken for granted, goes unnoticed, and is unheralded. Recently, we decided to give recognition to unsaved and unchurched men, as the Jews did for Cornelius in Acts 10. These were men who simply supported their families or who had taken on tackling some of the problems in our community, such as drug trafficking, misguided youth, and other problems. The names of these men were supplied by members of the church. The response was overwhelming. More than fifteen hundred people showed up for the Cornelius Award Night. Some of these men had never been given credit for the good they had done. Some of the men stood proudly to receive their certificate of recognition, men whose ages ranged from twenty to over seventy. Needless to say, some of the men received Jesus Christ as their Lord and Savior that night. For the next six months, however, men continued to return to our church, and accept Jesus Christ. Why did they return? We treated them with respect, and we encouraged them.

The wife can have this kind of impact on her husband for good, by showing respect and giving encouragement.

1. A wife is to respect her husband.

She should respect him in obedience to God. We do not respect people in authority because they deserve it, but because it is God's will. Children are instructed from God's Word to honor and respect their parents (Eph. 6:1–3). Christians are instructed to reverence governmental leaders in authority (Rom. 13:1–7). My wife points out to women, in her role as discipler, that most women respect and reverence their pastor (Heb. 13:7), but not their husbands.

A wife's respect for her husband is revealed in the way she talks to him and the tone of her voice. Respect is also revealed in her attitude toward her husband. Some wives regard their husband only when it is convenient, as Dr. Lloyd C. Blue points out, "to carry out the trash and zip up her zippers."

As I have stated earlier, there is never a justifiable reason for a man to abuse a woman, but some women do not help their own situation because of their blatant disrespect. When a woman places her hands on her hips when addressing her husband, no good thing is going to come out of her mouth. When a woman places a hand on one hip and points her finger at her husband, we're talking serious sin! It has been said, "No one can tell a man off like a sister." This has no place in a Christian home. Being filled with the Spirit should be evident not only in a church worship service but also in a wife's life with her husband.

The Bible tells us that Sarah obeyed Abraham and called him her master, a title of respect and reverence (1 Peter 3:5–6). What should wives call their husbands today? Maybe lord or master is outdated, but it should be something above "you insensitive dog." A woman should always try to use pleasant words and tones in speaking to her husband. He should be treated as a king (Prov. 12:4). If the wife is a queen, her husband is her king.

Respect is very important to a male. One of the reasons for the high homicide rate in "black on black crime" has to do with the lack of respect that lost, unsaved males have for one another. A gang war can start because of a lack of respect for territorial rights or being "dissed" in front of a woman. I have also been surprised to find among some of our well-known church leaders, white and African-American men, how important it is to them that they be addressed correctly—by their proper titles, no title at all (nondenominational pride), educational acknowledgment, size of congregation being pastored, etc. This, of course, isn't very spiritual; it is carnality, yet it is a reality.

2. A wife should submit to her husband's leadership as the head of the home.

Some women have trouble with submission to a husband. They fear they are going to become mindless slaves. Submission is a spiritual virtue of all Christians. Men as well as women are called to submission (Eph. 5:21). Submission means we cannot always have our way. Submission means we must yield to the wishes of someone else. Submission in a Christian marriage is presented in the context of two people who love each other. A husband submits to Jesus Christ and follows Christ's example of His submission to God (1 Cor. 11:3). A wise husband is a submissive leader, meaning he is open to his wife's opinion, suggestions, and advice as his God-given partner.

Submission in a marriage is also practical. No two people agree on everything. No two leaders lead in exactly the same way. No husband and wife think identically. There are deadlocks and times of impasse. I'm not referring to obstinacy and stubbornness, which are sins, but honest differences of opinion as to what should be done or what direction the family should pursue.

God has placed the burden of family responsibility on the husband. He is to love his wife sacrificially. He is worse than an unbeliever if he does not provide for his family (1 Tim. 5:8). Just as church leaders will give an account to God as to their faithfulness to their responsibility for the care of God's people, husbands likewise will give account for the leadership and care of their families. Wise counsel is given to church members as to how to help their leaders enjoy leading them: "Obey your leaders and submit to their authority. They keep watch over you as men who must give an account. Obey them so that their work will be a joy, not a burden, for that would be of no advantage to you" (Heb. 13:17).

We must remember that everyone whom God instructs us to submit to or obey benefits us in some way as they exercise their authority. Children benefit from the care, love, and guidance of good parents. Christians grow spiritually under godly leadership of pastors, elders, deacons, and other church leaders. Citizens benefit from a lack of anarchy when a government provides order, freedom, and peace. It is to the wife's benefit to submit to her husband. Many men have left home because of the difficulty of trying to lead a rebellious, unsubmissive wife because, under such conditions, the experience was not joyful but grievous.

3. It is detrimental to the family when roles have been reversed.

There is an example of role reversal in the marriage of Ahab and Jezebel. Although Ahab was in positions of leadership as a husband and the king of Israel, because of his ungodliness he followed the immoral leadership of his wife (1 Kings 16:30–31). One incident in particular that illustrates role reversal is the following:

Ahab offered to purchase a vineyard belonging to Naboth. Naboth refused his offer because the land was the inheritance of his ancestors. Ahab went home angry because he couldn't have his way, got into bed sulking, and refused to eat. Jezebel came home after a hard day at work—that of leading her worship temples of idolatry and sexual immorality—and found her husband in bed succumbing to his selfish desires and emotions. She asked him why he was sulking and not eating. He whined and complained to her that Naboth wouldn't sell him his vineyard (1 Kings 21:1–6). Her response to him was, "Is this how you act as king over Israel? Get up and eat! Cheer up. I'll get you the vineyard of Naboth the Jezreelite" (1 Kings 21:7). There are some negative consequences when a husband and wife reverse God's order of authority in the home.

- They are in sinful disobedience to God (1 Kings 21:20).
- The wife loses respect for her husband, whether she is conscious of it or not. Jezebel expressed this when she said, "Is this how you act as king over Israel?"
- When a man will not use his God-given authority, his wife will. Jezebel exercised the king's authority, "I'll get you the vineyard of Naboth the Jezreelite."
- Such a man cannot meet his wife's emotional needs as a husband because he relates to her as his mother. When she has a need for his masculinity, he is devoid of virility. Some women like running the show, but at the same time they are dissatisfied with their relationship to their husbands and don't have a clue as to what is wrong.

4. A woman can be both submissive and assertive.

That a person can be both submissive and assertive at the same time is demonstrated by David in his relationship with King Saul. Saul was jealous of David and insecure within himself and sought to take David's life. David had to flee for his life, but during this time he was committed to Saul in that he forbade his men to harm the king, and he continued to submit to him and serve him (1 Sam. 24:6–7). However, David demonstrated assertiveness in holding Saul accountable for his unfair and ungodly behavior:

> Then David went out of the cave and called out to Saul, "My lord the king!" When Saul looked behind him, David bowed down and prostrated himself with his face to the ground. He said to Saul, "Why do you listen when men say, 'David is bent on harming you?' This day you have seen with your own eyes how the LORD delivered you into my hands in the cave. Some urged me to kill you, but I spared you; I said, 'I will not lift my hand against my master, because he is the

LORD's anointed.' See, my father, look at this piece of your robe in my hand! I cut off the corner of your robe but did not kill you. Now understand and recognize that I am not guilty of wrongdoing or rebellion. I have not wronged you, but you are hunting me down to take my life. May the LORD judge between you and me. And may the LORD avenge the wrongs you have done to me, but my hand will not touch you" (1 Sam. 24:8–12). When David finished saying this, Saul asked, "Is that your voice, David my son?" And he wept aloud. "You are more righteous than I," he said. "You have treated me well, but I have treated you badly" (vv. 16–17).

A man is not always right in his judgment or his spirituality. As the leader, he needs his wife to hold him accountable as his friend, lover, and spiritual sister. Nevertheless, a wife must do this in a respectful and submissive way.

5. A wife must support and encourage her husband as a leader (Titus 2:5).

Being a leader of anything is not easy. Most men have not been trained in how to be a husband, a father, and the leader in the home in accordance with the Scriptures, nor have we seen an abundance of such leadership modeled. Also, some men are only recent converts and most of us are still learning how to please God and meet the needs of a wife. We need help from our wives. The primary reason God created a woman was to be a man's helper: "The LORD God said, 'It is not good for the man to be alone. I will make a helper suitable for him'" (Gen. 2:18).

How can a wife help her husband as a leader?

- Don't sit in judgment on his leadership.
- Don't question, either verbally or by attitude, every decision he makes. Such action does not assure confidence in a man's self-reliance.
- Don't be critical of his leadership when he is putting forth an effort, by making comments about the quantity or the quality of his work: "He's not doing enough," or "That's not the way I would do it."

The truth of the matter is that some men learn they are supposed to lead and try to lead the family, but after years of the wife's being in that role, she seems to qualify as a better leader than he because she has had more experience and he is a rookie. In this case, a woman's critical, judgmental attitude can kill her husband's desire to lead his family.

6. A wife should not offer unsolicited advice or give her husband orders.

Men and women are different in how they communicate. Men generally will not give each other unsolicited advice even if they know one is having problems. The most another man will say is, "I'm praying for you, brother." Men ask for advice only when they can't figure a problem out for themselves. At that point, most men will ask for help. The exception to this is a fool (Prov. 18:2).

In a good marital relationship, a wife can make suggestions. Remember, to suggest is to offer for *consideration,* so a wife should not get all bent out of shape if her husband does not follow her suggestion. A wise man will count his wife a valued adviser.

7. A wife should not perform her husband's responsibilities.

Because some men procrastinate or are just plain lazy, some wives do their work. Even when men do not procrastinate and are not lazy, some wives are impatient and decide, "I'll do it myself." Some men will let them do it.

Some years ago a wife decided she would shame her husband into performing his duties more expeditiously. She took upon herself the task of painting the exterior of their home in the blazing heat of the summer, although her husband said he would do it on a cooler day. Instead of feeling ashamed, he was irritated and angry with his wife for showing him up in front of their neighbors. She had a stroke and a heart attack. Now she can barely walk, let alone climb a ladder. Wisdom says she should have left the task in the hands of her husband.

8. A wife should get help if her husband is a poor leader or refuses to lead.

In such a case a wife should go before the Lord in prayer. God is more concerned than we are that husbands submit to His order. Too often wives talk to others before they talk to God. I'm not talking about lightweight prayer. I'm talking about what James calls the "powerful and effective" prayer of a righteous person.

After this kind of prayer, perhaps God will lead the wife to a man whom her husband respects and who he knows has his best interest in mind, such as a father, a brother, some other relative, a friend, or his pastor.

9. A wife should support her husband when he disciplines the children.

If a mother will not allow her husband to regulate behavior (discipline) when children are young, she may lose control of them when they become teenagers. By this time the husband may have withdrawn from this fatherly duty (Heb. 12:7) because of wanting to be at peace with his wife. At this point, a mother gives up because the teenage children are too much for her. She then calls her husband back in to be the "high executioner." "After all," she protests, "the children are also your responsibility."

This is the reason why in some homes there is a proud middle-aged father having fistfights with his six-foot, 200 pound teenage son, trying to maintain the fact that he is still the head of his house.

10. A wife should not use sexual intercourse to manipulate her husband's leadership.

Using sex to manipulate a husband's leadership is pure foolishness on a woman's part. First of all, it is sinful because a wife's body belongs to her husband as a gift of love from God. "The husband should fulfill his marital duty to his wife, and likewise the wife to her husband. The wife's body does not belong to her alone but also to her husband. In the same way, the husband's body does not belong to him alone but also to his wife" (1 Cor. 7:3–4).

Second, in the day in which we live, if the wife will not meet her husband's sexual needs, there are female predators who will jump at the opportunity to try to steal a husband by sex. The wife is not the only female who believes a man can be manipulated through sex. Sometimes the woman you have to watch out for is the carnal woman sitting on the same pew with you on Sunday.

Third, some men can adjust and do without sexual intercourse altogether. As long as they can still excercise their authority as the head of their homes, they are willing to give up their "birthright" to submit to the manipulation of a misguided wife. Also, these men love God and will not commit adultery. Countless times, I have asked women in counseling when they complain their husband has stopped having sex, "Who stopped first?" Usually, but not all the time, I get a sheepish, "I stopped first."

11. A wife should affirm her husband as her leader.

A wife should let her husband know in detail what he is doing right as a husband and father. He should be complimented for his accomplishments, such as

- Financially supporting the family
- Being a dutiful father
- Being a loving spouse
- Being a handy repairman
- Having good decision-making skills
- Being willing to involve his wife in the decision-making process
- Being willing to help others
- Growing spiritually
- Loving God
- Doing service in the church
- Making sacrifices for his wife
- Being sensitive to his wife's emotions
- Being patient

"Pleasant words are a honeycomb, sweet to the soul and healing to the bones" (Prov. 16:24).

A wife should be her husband's cheerleader. She should rally behind her man, back him up, and help him to be successful or give him hope for success. She should be in his corner, cheering him on for the big score. She should encourage him when he is ready to give up and quit; tell him, "You can do it, baby." Rally behind your husband when he has failed as a leader; tell him, "I'm still with you. Nobody is perfect."

Remember that African-American males are at war in this society, if only to try to obtain an education, reach their occupational potential, and provide for their families. When a man comes home, worn out and emotionally ragged, his wife ought to give him a hero's welcome.

THE WIFE AS HOMEMAKER

I am convinced that being a homemaker is a full-time job. Ask any man who had to stay home from work just a few days to take care of a sick wife and the children. Being a good housekeeper is becoming a dying art. It is indeed an art, which takes skill. Whatever happened to "spring cleaning"? Spring arrives every year. Cleaning got misplaced someplace.

Have you noticed that more children and adults suffer from allergies nowadays? Could one of the reasons be that we are simply suffering from dust?

There is confusion today as to whose responsibility it is to be the homemaker. It is difficult to find time or energy to perform such tasks when the husband and wife both have full-time jobs to make ends meet. The wife is the foreman of this detail (Prov. 31:27).

> The wise woman builds her house, but with her own hands the foolish one tears hers down (Prov. 14:1).

> Then they can train the younger women to love their husbands and children, to be self-controlled and pure, to be busy at home, to be kind, and to be subject to their husbands, so that no one will malign the word of God (Titus 2:4–5).

> So I counsel younger widows to marry, to have children, to manage their homes and to give the enemy no opportunity for slander (1 Tim. 5:14).

As I stated earlier, a woman who is helping her husband support the family should not be expected to perform housekeeping duties alone. I also think that even if a woman is a full-time homemaker, love says her husband looks for ways to give his wife breaks from what is sometimes drudgery.

1. A wife is responsible to provide food for the family.

"She gets up while it is still dark; she provides food for her family and portions for her servant girls" (Prov. 31:15).

The wife should purchase the food and cook the food. Some mothers have trained their children not to eat a wholesome breakfast by not cooking one. At best, these children eat a bowl of cold cereal and milk. At worst, they eat junk food. The mother shamelessly says, "My children will not eat breakfast if I fix it." Educators and nutritionists agree that children learn better when they start the day with a wholesome breakfast. If a woman is not a good cook, she should learn from a woman who cooks well.

2. A wife should be a good shopper.

I have learned over the years that shopping is one of the delights for most women. However, this also takes skill.

- A woman should not be an impulsive buyer.
- She should find ways to save money.
- She should plan ahead.
- She should use a shopping list.

"She is like the merchant ships, bringing her food from afar.... She considers a field and buys it; out of her earnings she plants a vineyard....

She sees that her trading is profitable, and her lamp does not go out at night" (Prov. 31:14–18).

3. A wife is responsible for the maintenance of family clothes.

"In her hand she holds the distaff and grasps the spindle with her fingers. . . . When it snows, she has no fear for her household" (Prov. 31:19–21).

Some people wastefully discard clothes because a button has been lost or a zipper is broken.

4. A wife takes care of her furnishings and appliances with her husband's assistance.

"She makes coverings for her bed; she is clothed in fine linen and purple" (Prov. 31:22).

5. Even if a wife is employed, her home has a high priority.

"She makes linen garments and sells them, and supplies the merchants with sashes. . . . She watches over the affairs of her household and does not eat the bread of idleness" (Prov. 31:24, 27).

BOOKS FOR FURTHER KNOWLEDGE AND USE IN FAMILY MINISTRY

Grunlan, Stephen A. *Marriage and the Family: A Christian Perspective.* Grand Rapids: Zondervan, 1984.

Jack, Wayne. *Strengthening Your Marriage.* Phillipsburg: Presbyterian and Reformed, 1977.

Wilson, B. P. *Liberated Through Submission.* Eugene: Harvest House, 1992.

Chapter 15

TRAINING MARRIED COUPLES IN COMMUNICATION AND UNDERSTANDING

We must help couples and families comprehend the difficulty and complexity of communication, understanding, and problem solving. One of the quickest ways to be defeated in these matters is to take for granted that they are simple. There are many variables to being successful which we will look at in this chapter. We must walk in and be controlled by the Holy Spirit. Christianity must be consciously practiced at home or Satan will try to destroy the family in these areas. We Christians have a tendency to ignore the negative biblical truths in the Scriptures, such as suffering, and instead hold on to the great promises of God. We need both. God has given us both to strengthen us to deal with the harsh realities of life on earth. In this chapter, we will look at negatives along with the positives that will give families understanding and help them discover what to avoid to gain success and contribute to their progress.

COMMUNICATION

H. Norman Wright states,

Misunderstanding occurs because there are six ways your message can come through.
1. What you mean to say.
2. What you actually say.
3. What the other person hears.

4. What the other person thinks he hears.

5. What the other person says about what you said.

6. What you think the other person said about what you said."[1]

Communication is complicated; good communication, however, is essential for a successful marriage and family living. Disagreements, conflicts, and misunderstandings are inevitable in family life, but verbal and physical fighting is not necessary. The rise of domestic violence can be directly attributed to relational frustration, communication breakdown, and a feeling of futility.

SELFISHNESS

Selfishness and its first cousin, self-centeredness, are destroyers of marriage relationships and are major roadblocks to communication. Selfishness is a trait of our sinful human nature. Basically, we are all selfish at times, and we need to be aware of this. Some people deny their obvious selfishness in marital relationships, but this is foolish if we want God to bless our homes. To be selfish is to be concerned chiefly or only with oneself. To be self-centered is to be engrossed in oneself, seeing things only from one's solitary point of view. We can deceive ourselves into thinking we are not selfish by the good we do for others. Paul reminds us, "If I give all I possess to the poor and surrender my body to the flames, but have not love, I gain nothing" (1 Cor. 13:3). Selfishness says, "That's your problem"; but God's Word says, "Carry each other's burdens, and in this way you will fulfill the law of Christ" (Gal. 6:2). Selfishness says, "You have a spiritual problem, and it is ruining our marriage," but God's Word says, "We who are strong ought to bear with the failings of the weak and not to please ourselves. Each of us should please his neighbor for his good, to build him up" (Rom. 15:1–2). The characteristics of selfishness in marriage can be summed up in 2 Timothy 3:2–5:

> People will be lovers of themselves, lovers of money, boastful, proud, abusive, disobedient to their parents, ungrateful, unholy, without love, unforgiving, slanderous, without self-control, brutal, not lovers of the good, treacherous, rash, conceited, lovers of pleasure rather than lovers of God—having a form of godliness but denying its power. Have nothing to do with them.

Growing in Christ is important to family development. Spiritual maturity means to be more like Christ. The antidote to selfishness is the selflessness and humility of Christ.

Do nothing out of selfish ambition or vain conceit, but in humility consider others better than yourselves. Each of you should look not only to your own interests, but also to the interests of others. Your attitude should be the same as that of Christ Jesus: Who, being in very nature God, did not consider equality with God something to be grasped, but made himself nothing, taking the very nature of a servant, being made in human likeness (Phil. 2:3–7).

SOME REASONS WHY COMMUNICATION MAY BE POOR IN MARRIAGE

1. Poor Communication Before Marriage

Some people do not realize the importance of communication until after they are married. There was such an interest in getting married that the lack of communication went unnoticed or was downplayed. Perhaps the courtship was too short and the couple really didn't know each other. Weaknesses that were ignored before marriage now are major problems. Perhaps before marriage, the relationship was dominated by sinful sexual involvement that was interpreted as love, but after marriage has led to mistrust and guilt. Perhaps unresolved conflict before marriage has grown to hostility, strife, and continual clashes. Premarital counseling helps to avoid some of the above.

2. Role Confusion

God presents distinct roles of a husband and wife in the Scriptures. Having knowledge and commitment to the responsibility of these roles goes a long way in clarifying communication and promoting harmony. The world has no clear directions for marital roles.

3. A Lack of Self-Acceptance

Sometimes the problem is not communication with the mate but with a person not accepting him or herself. Sometimes when people do not discover and appreciate who they are in Christ, they transfer their negative thoughts to others.

4. Self-Righteousness

Although there is a problem of being unequally yoked when a believer is married to an unbeliever, sometimes an aggravating factor is the self-righteousness of the believer. The believing mate is encouraged and instructed to be aware that his or her behavior and treatment may make the difference in the salvation of the unbelieving mate and lead to a life of joy together in the Lord (1 Peter 3:1–7).

5. Not Knowledgeable of Communication Skills

I think all of us can improve as we study a book, take a class, or are counseled in what relational communication is and how to improve our skills.

DISHONEST COMMUNICATION

We are told in God's Word that God wants us to grow up in Christ, to become mature, "speaking the truth in love" (Eph. 4:13–16). In order to have good marital and family communications, we must have love and honesty. However, there are ways that we practice dishonest communications.

1. Wanting Only to Be Complimented

There are people who refuse any correction by their family members. This is foolish because these are the ones who love and know us better than others and perhaps will help us when outsiders are not committed enough to us to do so. As a matter of fact, one of the responsibilities of church leaders is to use Scripture to rebuke, correct, and train us in righteousness, and this is motivated by love and commitment to the family of God (2 Tim. 3:16).

2. Exaggerating Problems

Married people should never use such terms as "You always . . . ," "I always . . . ," "You never . . . ," "I never. . . ." The minute you use such terms, the Devil will remind the other mate of the exception. Sometimes, because of our emotions, we believe what we are saying, but we are guilty of unintentional lying.

3. Making Comparisons When Confronted

Instead of being open and honest, facing up to faults, some married people, when corrected or confronted, respond, "You are guilty of the same thing or worse." This confuses the issues.

4. Always Having to Be Right

Very rarely will people say they are perfect, but there are those who communicate as if they are. They expect their mate to always agree with them, and they interpret disagreement as a lack of love and support.

5. Speaking for the Other Person

The conversation goes something like this: "You really made me look like a fool tonight; I wouldn't do that to you. Why did you do it? I know what you're going to say. You don't know what I'm talking about. I'm not accepting that this time. No matter what I said tonight or what subject was on the floor, you disagreed with me in front of our friends. What is the reason you always do this to me? I know what you're going to say. I can tell by the expression on your face. I don't buy it. I know why you do it. You don't love me." Instead of a dialogue, we have a monologue.

Sometimes a mate will speak for the other in the presence of other people. "John, I hear you have a new job. How is it?" asks Robert. John's wife, Kathy, replies, "He has a great job, and he is doing fine." Robert looks directly at John and continues, "How does your new position compare with the old one?" John opens his mouth to speak, but Kathy is faster. "The pay is much better, and he gets more benefits." Robert and John give up.

6. Deciding the Other's Motives

We are warned in Matthew 7:1–2 about judging others. Married people are guilty of doing this to each other too often. Statements such as "You meant to hurt me," "You did it because you don't love me," "You really don't care about me," "All you care about is yourself" are all judgmental. It is better to ask the reason for an action or lack of action, or ask someone to repeat what he or she said, than to judge someone's heart or mind. Only God can read minds and hearts.

7. Pretending Not to Hear

There are many ways this dishonest tactic is used—pretending not to hear, pretending to be asleep when the mate is speaking, hiding hurts behind a smile, not wanting the mate to know you are hurt because of pride, saying there is nothing bothering you when this is not true, and refusing to admit there is a problem when one exists.

8. Lying

Lying has to be the most destructive flaw in dishonest communication. It not only breaks down trust in what is being said, but it also breaks down trust in the liar. Love, oneness, and communication must be built on trust. This is one of the reasons I believe we should work on developing friendship in marriage. Best friends tell each other the truth. Also, friends can handle the truth.

9. Justifying Faults

Using rationalization, excuses, or blame-shifting to justify our faults and sin can be a destructive discourager to a spouse. This is very prideful and foolish. It is foolish because none of us is perfect. That is why we need a Savior. We all have a sin nature that we will have until the day we die. The people who live in our house know this as a fact. We grow in the "grace and knowledge of Christ." The first step in growing is to admit we have a problem, fault, weakness, sin—or else God cannot help us to change.

10. Becoming a Dishonest Peace-Keeper

Although the Lord has called us to be peacemakers, there is such a thing as dishonest peace. Most people do not like experiencing arguments, anger, resentment, hard feelings, and tension. Some married people will say or do anything just to keep peace in the home, giving in sometimes to a mate who is wrong, selfish, and carnal. The peacemaker's needs are not being met, and there is no real communication going on. The bully of the twosome is shocked to hear one day that the peacemaker is getting a divorce or is leaving.

11. Hinting

Even when there is seemingly direct communication, there can be misunderstanding. There are people who either hint, insinuate, or imply without making clear what they are trying to communicate. Plus, some married people think longevity should give one the ability to read minds.

12. Attacking When Guilty

Another way of communicating in a dishonest way when one is guilty is to attack your mate, finding fault in the mate so as to cover a wrongdoing.

BASICS OF GOOD COMMUNICATION

Spirituality is the foundation for good communication in a Christian home. Not only do we need salvation, but we must also live in obedience to God's Word and submit to God, the Holy Spirit. Instead of an atmosphere of selfishness and insensitivity, there should be the loving, compassionate spirit of Christ. If we are truly Christians, it should be apparent that Christ is in us. The husband's, the wife's, and the children's attitudes should reveal the nature of Christ or the fruit of the Spirit. Spiritual growth must be a priority for the family, led by the husband and father or the single-parent female.

Be Committed to Communicating

Married people and families must accept the fact that communicating can be complicated and emotionally hard work. There must be a commitment to talking things out as opposed to giving up and repressing feelings and problems. Face problems with God's help.

Talk to God First

Whenever there is a marital or family problem, always talk to God about it first. Ask for guidance and help. Above all else, we must ask for the power and ability to conduct ourselves as Christians as we attempt to deal with problems or issues.

Tolerate Disagreement

Accepting people and allowing them to disagree with us is a sign of maturity. No two people think alike. It's been said that "two heads are better than one." Good communication is open communication. Disagreement does not necessarily mean that one person is wrong and the other person is right, or one position is inferior to the other. It can simply be a different point of view.

Talk to Each Other

Talking should be done calmly and lovingly. Remember that the two primary members of the family started out as lovers. Talk should be direct and constructive. There are different reasons for talking: to deal with a problem, exchange information, express love, to hold someone accountable, seek advice, make family decisions, express concern for the person loved, and experience Christian fellowship and companionship.

Listen

Sometimes we think that communication is merely talking and therefore fail to develop our listening skills. Being married is an intimate relationship and is therefore emotional. Sometimes even as our mate or another family member speaks, we are not listening to what that person is saying, even though we are silent; we are thinking about what we are going to say next.

Listening means we need to hear what is being said. We must be focused and not distracted by anything else. Listening is hearing not only sentences and paragraphs, but also how words are being used and understanding the meaning of what a person is saying. There is more than one definition for some words in the dictionary, and sometimes we use words based on our definition, which may differ from that of the person we are talking to. Listening is also picking up on feelings and the needs in a person's life. The ability to do this determines our sensitivity to others.

Use Nonverbal Communication

"Who winks with his eye, signals with his feet and motions with his fingers, who plots evil with deceit in his heart—he always stirs up dissension" (Prov. 6:13–14).

Not all communication is transmitted by talking and listening. There are nonverbal communications that are transmitted by observation and by touch.

A smile can communicate more than one thing. A smile with teeth unexposed could indicate that a person is thinking about something humorous. A smile that exposes the upper teeth is usually a warm greeting. A broad smile, exposing upper and lower teeth, usually is connected with laughter. A smirk smile (mouth drawn into an arch) could mean contempt or mockery.

It is common for a spouse to ask his or her mate, "What's wrong?" The spouse's reply may be, "Nothing is wrong." The concerned mate pursues the issue and says, "I know there is something wrong; I see it on your face." Then, there is the rebuff, "Leave me alone; nothing is wrong!"

Ignorance of the fact that we communicate nonverbally can hinder communication and understanding. In the case above, the spouse who wanted to be left alone did not realize that the nonverbal message was the opposite of what was being said. Walking slowly into the house, head and shoulders lowered forward, arms hanging loosely, conveys dejection, depression, despondency, sadness, gloom, and low spirits. We do communicate nonverbally.

Think and Concentrate

Do not simply respond or react in a conversation, but think before you speak (Prov. 15:28). We are to be quick to listen and slow to speak

(James 1:19). There are times when wisdom dictates that we remain quiet (Prov. 11:12; 18:13).

Be Truthful

It is impossible to communicate with a liar, and it is disheartening and confusing to try to do so. Lying breaks down trust. Trust is an important component of love, which is the anchor that stabilizes marriage. Believing in the character and the spirituality of a person increases the growth and the development of the relationship. Telling your spouse the truth is a loving thing to do (Eph. 4:15). Telling the truth is not always a good experience, but it always has God's support. In the long run, it is the right thing to do. Clear communication must be built and understood on facts, not fabrications.

Caution must be used sometimes in when and how truth is revealed. In speaking the truth we must try to be sensitive and tactful.

Ask Questions

Understanding what another person is trying to say or the message he or she would like for us to receive is not always easy. Sometimes, rather than to respond, we need to ask questions for clarification. Ask such questions as, "Can you repeat that?" "Can you rephrase that?" "Is this what you mean?" "Give me an example."

Use Soft and Gentle Words

Soft or gentle words turn away anger, and harsh words stir up anger (Prov. 15:1). Words can bring healing in relationships (v. 4). Using God-given wisdom in communication also heals.

Solve Problems, Don't Place Blame

If our communication is to be constructive, then we want to concentrate on solving marriage and family problems, rather than placing blame. We must get beyond fault-finding to resolve the problem.

Admit Wrongs

To stay in fellowship with Christ, we must confess our sins to Him. If we do not, fellowship is broken. We must agree with God; He is right, and we are wrong (1 John 1:9).

Married people must do the same for each other. Mates must admit when they have behaved wrongly, said the wrong thing, or had a wrong attitude. They must ask for forgiveness and apologize for their sinfulness. The only thing that will stop us from doing this is pride, which is another sin. I believe that when we admit our wrongs, it gives our spouse hope for change and growth in the relationship. Forgiveness must be asked for and granted.

Always Forgive

Since all of us are in the flesh, all of us are selfish sometimes. We should be humble enough to forgive others, especially those in our family. It is devastating when one person asks another person for forgiveness and is refused. Unforgiveness cripples a marriage and impedes communication. Remember, the ability to forgive is another indication of spiritual maturity.

Try to Make Up As Soon As Possible

"'In your anger do not sin': Do not let the sun go down while you are still angry, and do not give the devil a foothold" (Eph. 4:26–27).

We should keep all family and marriage issues current. We don't want the issues to smolder and burn inwardly, then burst into blazing flames of anger. This gives the Devil the opportunity to cause more trouble and evil. The husband should give leadership to see that current issues are placed on the table to be resolved. The goal is reconciliation and a deeper relationship. Don't let problems build up; make up.

Build Each Other Up

A portion of communications between married people should be for the sole purpose of edification—to affirm the other's worth, to express appreciation.

Say "I Love You" Every Day

Every day, married people should say, "I love you." No one ever gets tired of hearing this if it is backed up with loving behavior and attitude. Jesus told men He loved them (John 14:21). It is Christlike to tell your spouse and other family members you love them.

Some Don'ts for Good Communication

1. Don't raise your voice or argue.
2. Don't bring up past sins or mistakes.
3. Don't call each other unkind names.

4. Don't use profanity in communication.
5. Don't feel sorry for yourself.
6. Don't dominate the conversation.
7. Don't lose your temper.
8. Don't both talk at the same time.
9. Don't discuss your mate's faults with others unless you have already discussed it with your spouse, and the person, such as your pastor, receiving the information is going to help both of you.
10. Don't have Christians praying about your mate's faults in a public prayer meeting.
11. Don't try to win an argument, but try to get understanding to resolve issues.
12. Don't use sarcasm.
13. Don't lose control of your emotions and start yelling, crying, or fighting.
14. Don't keep score of the wrongs of your mate.
15. Don't engage in physical violence.
16. Don't rub it in when your mate apologizes.
17. Don't nag or needle your mate.
18. Don't suppress your anger; rather, solve the problem that causes the irritation.
19. Don't become discouraged over conflict and refuse to talk.
20. Don't be mean and revengeful to your mate.

GAINING UNDERSTANDING

> Blessed is the man who finds wisdom, the man who gains understanding, for she is more profitable than silver and yields better returns than gold. She is more precious than rubies; nothing you desire can compare with her. Long life is in her right hand; in her left hand are riches and honor. Her ways are pleasant ways, and all her paths are peace. She is a tree of life to those who embrace her; those who lay hold of her will be blessed (Prov. 3:13–18).

Married people should look at learning to understand and communicate as an interesting and fulfilling lifelong adventure. Only God has instant understanding, because He is omniscient. I am going to give some key areas of learning and personal research in order that one may acquire and grow in understanding of a mate. Certainly, time itself will be an asset in getting better understanding. Married people must spend time together praying, planning, playing, problem solving, and worshiping and serving God. Time together gives experience in understanding how you think and feel as individuals and how you think and function together. Not only has God laid out a plan for the individual, but He has a purpose for individual families. Experiences in life can be good or bad. They can be exhilarating or tragic. In any case, God does not leave the individual, a couple, or a family alone to face life's ups and downs.

THE UNIQUENESS OF YOUR SPOUSE

As we observe snowflakes on a black cloth, we see that no two flakes are alike. So it is with God's creation of human beings—no two are the same. Married people would save themselves some unnecessary grief by accepting the fact that everyone is unique. If we didn't realize that before marriage, we certainly discover it after marriage. We cannot change grown people. We must love and accept the uniqueness of God's creation. The beauty of snowflakes is unquestioned—so is the uniqueness of people.

We must commit to being lifelong students—learning about our mate, as there is continual change because of spiritual growth, emotional maturity, the aging process, and the impact of life's experiences.

Although we will examine some of the trails that will give us insight into our mates, we must always keep in mind that no matter what we learn from the knowledge of family background, there are differences between men and women, personality and temperament differences, life cycles, and the emotional phases of a woman, we must still ask God for understanding of our mate as an individual.

Family Background

We are all products of the family God allowed us to be born into. There are some unique family characteristics that can be detected in some families. It is important that we be aware of the home life of our life partners. We have been greatly influenced—for better or for worse—by our home environment and how we were reared.

If you have a spouse who is not very affectionate and has problems expressing love, it could be that family members were distant and indifferent toward one another. If a wife is having problems sexually, perhaps she grew up being taught only the negative and sinful aspects of sex, or she may have been raped or sexually abused. If a married couple are having financial problems because one is a spendthrift and the other is obsessed with money and materialism, family background may give a clue as to why these people behave as they do.

If there is a conflict between a wife and her mother-in-law as to the time and continued involvement of the son-husband in his responsibilities toward them, it could be that as a boy he and his mother were physically and emotionally abused by his father, until he and his mother ran away for their survival, and then there followed a divorce. As a boy, he promises his mother he will always take care of her and never let anything happen to her because of the guilt, pain, and helplessness he experienced when they lived with his abusive father. For years, he has played the role of a surrogate husband in the area of duty, responsibility, and psychological support for his mother. His mother, in turn, dedicated her life to rearing her son, refusing any relationship with a man for fear that if she got married, her son might experience further abuse from a stepfather.

Differences Between Men and Women

"So God created man in his own image, in the image of God he created him; male and female he created them" (Gen. 1:27).

It is fruitful and worthwhile to train married and single people in the differences between men and women, especially when there are antifamily philosophies that deny the fact of differences or try to obscure them. Having some understanding of this subject will enhance our knowledge of our mates.

Men relate to women in communicating and problem solving as if the women were men. Men expect women to think and react the way they would in these situations; women expect men to feel and behave like women in relationships. Because of these differences and others, both men and women can have impossible expectations of the other. We can become demanding, resentful, judgmental, and intolerant.

If a man tells a woman, "I will be there at seven o'clock to take you to dinner," he means seven o'clock; he gave his word. When the woman agreed and said, "I'll be ready at seven," she means taking everything into consideration. If she lays her outfit out at six-thirty and discovers she does not like the combinations or something does not fit, time is not important any more. What is important is her appearance. Men find it very difficult to link their emotions with their verbal communication, whereas women have a natural ability to accomplish this.

Men are solution-oriented. Women are problem-oriented. Men are "Mr. Fix-Its." If something is broken, we want to fix it. When a woman asks a man what he thinks of their relationship, he is at a loss for words. She didn't say it was broken. To him, if it is not broken, there is no reason to discuss it.

When a woman says, "We have to talk," her husband is usually apprehensive. He is nervous, for the differences between men and women are so great that he believes if he engages in conversation, she will take him on a journey into space to a faraway, unknown planet in another galaxy, and she is the only one familiar with this strange world and the strange language spoken there. He knows this is true. He has been on the trip before.

Personality and Temperament Differences

I remember reading in 1968 the original version of Tim LaHaye's book *The Spirit-Controlled Temperament*. I was astounded that the book could come so close to describing my personality. Tim LaHaye has revised and expanded the book, and over a million copies have been sold. He also offers a temperament analysis.[2] There are also the Taylor Johnson Test, the Myers-Briggs Type Indicator, and others.

Books and analyses on the subject of personality and temperament are great references for married people to help them zero in on a better understanding of the strengths and weaknesses of the type of person they are married to, but this does not remove the responsibility of knowing the unique individual.

The emotional phases of a woman in relationship to the female reproductive system are very important in marital understanding. The husband and wife need to understand the emotional effects of the monthly cycle, premenstrual syndrome, postpartum depression, tubal ligation, hysterectomy, perimenopause, and menopause. Over the thirty years I have been pastoring and counseling, it is clear that ignorance in these areas can be devastating to a marital relationship.

BEING FRIENDS

In addressing single Christians, I have spoken of the importance of friendship. I believe that good relationships don't just happen because we are Christians, but, with God's help, we must develop them. The ideal is that before a couple is married, they are first friends, then they move into a courtship that leads to engagement, and then they enter marriage, which leads to companionship. Companionship is the highest level of friendship; however, the relational evolving I described above is new and has not caught on as being a Christian alternative to the world's dating and courtship.

Therefore, Christian couples must consciously develop friendship skills with the idea of becoming best friends. There are some great advantages to this. Best friends can talk about anything and everything, including matters in which they disagree. Best friends are loyal to each other. Best friends are supportive, no matter what may come or what the circumstances are. Best friends forgive each other and readily forget offenses. Best friends love each other and share life's blessings together.

When Christian couples become best friends in marriage, they spend time sharing, praying, playing, and problem solving together. They are continually loving and affirming one another.

BOOKS FOR FURTHER KNOWLEDGE AND USE IN FAMILY MINISTRY

Carter, Les. *The Push-Pull Marriage.* Grand Rapids: Baker, 1983.

Chapman, Gary. *The Five Love Languages.* Chicago: Northfield, 1992.

Crabb, Larry. *Men and Women.* Grand Rapids: Zondervan, 1993.

Gray, John. *Men Are From Mars, Women Are From Venus.* New York: Harper Collins, 1992.

Harvey, Willard. *His Needs Her Needs.* Old Tappan: Fleming H. Revell, 1986.

Hybels, Bill, and Lynne Hybels. *Fit to Be Tied.* Grand Rapids: Zondervan, 1991.

Lush, Jean. *Emotional Phases of a Woman's Life.* Old Tappan: Fleming H. Revell, 1987.

Meier, Paul, and Richard Meier. *Family Foundations.* Grand Rapids: Baker, 1981.

Minirth, Frank, and Mary Alice Meier; Brian and Deborah Newman; Robert and Susan Hemfelt. *Passages of Marriage.* Nashville: Thomas Nelson, 1991.

Osborne, Cecil G. *The Art of Understanding Your Mate.* Grand Rapids: Zondervan, 1970.

Penner, Clifford, and Joyce Penner. *The Gift of Sex.* Waco: Word, 1981.

Smalley, Gary. *Hidden Keys of a Loving Lasting Marriage.* Grand Rapids: Zondervan, 1988.

Chapter 16

TRAINING MARRIED COUPLES IN PROBLEM SOLVING

PROBLEM SOLVING

It is when we have problems, difficulties, troubles, or crises in the marriage or the family that some of us as Christians forget our faith, who we are, and to whom we belong. As believers in the Lord Jesus Christ, we are told, "His divine power has given us everything we need for life and godliness through our knowledge of him who called us by his own glory and goodness" (2 Peter 1:3).

Since God has already given us "everything we need for life and godliness" and because "in all things God works for the good of those who love him" (Rom. 8:28), we as married people are never left alone to deal with problems without Christ. Remember, it takes three people to have a Christian marriage—the husband, the wife, and the Lord Jesus Christ. We must focus on Christ immediately when we face problems as individuals and as married couples.

The way some of us practice our Christianity is that Jesus shows up at the church house but not at our house. We must practice the presence of Christ during a crisis. Because some of us have not made a habit of recognizing God's presence at home during problems, we handle problems the way unsaved people deal with their difficulties. Such situations give us, as parents, opportunities to model for our children how we include Christ in our lives.

The church, in developing its family ministry, must be an assistant or an extended family to couples and families going through troubles. Couples need to understand in advance the impact of life cycles on their lives, such as having and taking care of an infant. There is a period after the new mother leaves the hospital that the doctor tells her to abstain from sexual intimacy with her husband. Along with this break in intimacy and the broken rest that new parents experience because of feedings and taking care of the baby, some husbands feel abandoned and lonely.

Couples also need to be aware of the challenges of parenting adolescents who sometimes are manipulators and may exploit parents' disagreements concerning child rearing. They need to be aware of the "empty nest" syndrome that affects some marriages.

They need education and spiritual support when the family has lost some or all of the family income through the loss of a job or some debilitating illness. They need to understand and be understanding of the unique pressures of being a woman or a man—being a working mother or being a father who works two jobs to support his family with no opportunity to spend quality time with his wife and children.

During times of problems and trouble, married people need to be reminded of the initial marriage vows they agreed to, their commitment to stand together through "better or worse" situations, through good times and bad, until death separates them. The practice should be that a married couple will unite more fully with Christ and each other during times of transition, difficulty, or crisis.

ROADBLOCKS TO IDENTIFYING PROBLEMS

You cannot solve problems that you cannot identify as problems. However, when we do not practice the presence of Christ in our families, which would enable us to experience God's peace, grace, and joy during troubles, negative emotions dominate and hinder us in communicating and understanding the problems and block us from finding a solution.

Problem ⟶ Practice the Presence of Christ ⟶ Solution

Problem ⟶ Blocked by Negative Emotions | No Solution

The following are a number of common roadblocks to identifying problems:

1. Lack of Adaptability and Flexibility

Some married people are stubborn and rigid. Earlier I spoke of a single's mentality versus a married person's mentality. When you are single, you don't have to change, but when you are married and God is causing you to grow as a couple into oneness, you have to change; you have to be adaptable and flexible. People are marrying later in life these days. Sometimes men and women do not find suitable mates until they are relatively old. Some of these people are set in their ways.

When we submit to God, the Holy Spirit, we can change. We can change our lifestyle to include our mate. We can submit to our mate's will for love's sake.

2. Lack of Empathy

One of the most painful things a woman can hear her husband say is, "You have the problem, not me. You need the counseling." Such a man is ignorant, with no empathy. When we submit to the Holy Spirit, we can use our hearts and our minds to put ourselves in someone else's place. We must work at imagining what it is like to be in the place of our mate or other family members, especially our children. Too many couples are insensitive to what their children go through when the parents have a verbal or physical fight.

3. Inability to Work Through Problems

Some people do not have the skills, ability, or courage to face up to and work through problems. Some people, as singles, did not know how to work through problems, and being married has only made things worse. In this chapter, I hope to give some basic insight into how to work through problems.

4. Lack of Emotional Stability

For various reasons, some adults' emotional maturity has been crippled. Perhaps they had domineering parents who did everything for them and wouldn't let them grow up, or they simply were never taught the responsibility to handle life issues. Some people refuse to grow up. They pretend life is a lark. They do not want to accept the realities of living.

When we have faith in God and His word, we can face all of life's problems.

5. Inability to Give and Receive Love

People who have trouble receiving love usually grew up in families that did not express love. Even when such people have Christian relationships and are receiving and experiencing agape love—unconditional love—from a believer, they are not comfortable and mentally do not believe that those who love them are sincere. Living with such suspicion does not enable them to give love in return.

A person with this kind of problem must study the Scriptures and understand and accept God's love for them in Jesus Christ:

> I pray that out of his glorious riches he may strengthen you with power through his Spirit in your inner being, so that Christ may dwell in your hearts through faith. And I pray that you, being rooted and established in love, may have power, together with all the saints, to grasp how wide and long and high and deep is the love of Christ, and to know this love that surpasses knowledge—that you may be filled to the measure of all the fullness of God (Eph. 3:16–19).

6. Self-Centeredness

Some of us are so self-centered that we cannot see another person's point of view, whether it is our spouse or any of our children. My wife and I went out to dinner with a couple many years ago, and it was obvious to us that the husband was a self-centered, dominating man. Among other things, when the husband decided what he wanted to eat, he laid his menu on the table. He asked his wife what she was going to have. She responded with delight as to what she was going to order. His response was, "No, no, you don't want that," and took the menu out of her hand. When the waiter came to receive our orders, the husband ordered what he thought she should have. His insensitivity made me feel uncomfortable, but later when the food arrived and his wife ate only a few forkfuls, leaving the rest, I found it sadly amusing. What she wanted to order cost half as much as what he ordered for her, but he had to pay for the food she didn't eat.

When we submit to Christ and let God, the Holy Spirit, take control of our lives, we become Christ-centered rather than self-centered. That is exactly what this husband eventually did. A few weeks later, this couple came in for marital counseling. Today, not only is this man a loving and sensitive husband, but he is also helping other men to be Christ-centered husbands.

7. Having Bad Attitudes

Having an attitude of anger or bitterness and an unforgiving spirit can block solutions to marital and family problems. Having an attitude of indifference, coldness, callousness, alienation, or detachment will close off problem-solving ability.

No matter how bad the situation, we cannot allow ourselves to degenerate into such unspiritual and un-Christian attitudes. Along with the self-destructiveness of this frame of mind, we lose the joy of our salvation, break fellowship with Christ, and are not submitting to the Holy Spirit.

8. Being Selfish

The selfish person looks out only for his or her own interests rather than those of the spouse or children. This is exhibited in the way we spend—one of the common areas of family and marital problems. Whatever we want, we buy, without consideration for the family as a whole. When we don't get what we want out of the marriage, we are unhappy, regardless of whether or not it is God's will. Again, Christ is left out.

A Christ-centered person is an unselfish person.

9. Poor Communication

Speaking in generalities, putting several issues on the table at the same time, and not staying on the subject are examples of poor communication.

10. Lack of Motivation

Sometimes people are overwhelmed by the number of problems they have, the duration of the problems, and the complexity of the problems. Some people have been depleted of their strength, living with problems. At this point, a person needs outside help. Sometimes we are too close to our own problems. We need a fresh perspective.

There is always hope because there is always God. "Why are you downcast, O my soul? Why so disturbed within me? Put your hope in God, for I will yet praise him, my Savior and my God" (Ps. 43:5). "For everything that was written in the past was written to teach us, so that through endurance and the encouragement of the Scriptures we might have hope" (Rom. 15:4).

COMMON PROBLEM AREAS

There can be all kinds of problems. I am still amazed, after thirty years of ministry and striving to help families, to hear problems I couldn't have imagined were possible. Here are some general guidelines about the direction to travel toward solutions.

1. Communication Problems

Communication between a husband and wife is foundational to the health of a marriage and the family. When there is a breakdown in communication we would like first of all for the people involved to be calm, so we can see what the issues are. Sometimes the relationship is so bad that negative emotions run high. Nothing can be accomplished unless there is enough calmness so that each individual can express what the issues are.

Using paper and pen, have each person take notes as the other person speaks with no interruptions. Patience must be exercised, because when people are upset, they tend to talk a long time, emotionally, and in generalities.

Some people are not good communicators, so couples need instructions in developing skills of listening, self-expression, processing what is being said, understanding the other person's point of view, and respecting their differences.

Sometimes there is fear and intimidation in expressing oneself. It may be fear of a verbal or physical fight. It may be embarrassment when there is a counselor or a family-life team worker involved. We have experienced the foolishness of people coming to our counseling center for help and then, after a few sessions, agreeing between themselves to limit the information given. Usually the husband has made some promise to do better, threatened to quit counseling, or do bodily harm. It is impossible to help people when we do not know the truth of their problems.

Sometimes we cannot help people with their communication problems unless we also work on their other problems at the same time.

2. Relational Problems

In relational problems between husband and wife or other family members, there will be such issues as deficiencies in love, sensitivity, caring, support, intimacy, and respect. An outgrowth of these root problems can be disappointment, discouragement, hurt, anger, and depression.

The resolution is realizing God's love for each person and making the commitment to love God by obeying Him in forgiving and loving one another and working through the problems.

3. Sexual Problems

Again, there can be many different reasons for problems in this area. There can be psychological reasons such as a consistent routine in sexual relations that becomes boring to one partner. It could be emotional, such as a husband's severely hurting his wife's feelings without asking for forgiveness or apologizing. It could be physical because of an illness, medical difficulties, or the side effects of some medication. It could be the lack of romance in the husband. Such problems can be resolved through open communication, sexual education, counseling, or consultation with the family physician.

4. Spiritual Problems

This is the most neglected area by couples when they are having marriage or family problems. It is clear that if the couple do not know the Lord, they are still living in darkness, following the ways of the world, gratifying the cravings of their sinful nature and following its desires and thoughts, doing Satan's bidding.

When a professing Christian is not submitting to the Holy Spirit, disregards the teachings of the holy Scriptures, and is far from demonstrating a Christlike spirit, there will be marital and family difficulties.

There needs to be repentance and the acceptance of Jesus Christ as Lord and Savior by the nonbeliever as well as repentance and submission to the lordship of Christ by the believer.

5. Financial Problems

Most financial problems stem from a lack of personal financial management. Being trained in financial management and being held accountable will resolve these problems.

Sometimes the problem is a lack of adequate funds to support an individual or family. In this case, we help a person to examine the resource possibilities and other available aid.

6. Children's Problems

Usually children's problems involve behavior problems and failures in schoolwork. One of the reasons for behavior problems can be that the child is not a Christian and needs to be led to Christ. It could be that the child is acting out because of parental neglect and a lack of love. There can be emotional trauma because of the parents' bad marriage or a divorce. Immorality of parents can have a bearing on the conduct of their children. Parenting training may be needed.

Failure in schoolwork could be caused by any number of things. The key here is the parents' interaction with teachers and school officials. In order to determine the cause of the failure, we should consider the quality of the teaching, the size of the class, and the amount of direct help being received from the teacher. The child's study habits should be examined along with his or her eyes. The child may need to be tested for a learning disability. If there is a learning disability, a parent does not need to be ashamed or go into denial but remember that children with such hindrances do learn and grow up to be responsibly employed people. Also, God loves these children and will care for them.

Sometimes the child is in the wrong school or in an educational program that is not suited to him or her. Different kinds of aptitude tests can determine this, along with the natural gifts and abilities God has given. A wrong school could be a school in which there are discipline problems that hinder students who really want to learn. A wrong educational program could be home schooling by parents who have basic education deficiencies themselves. It could be racism practiced by a teacher or by school officials.

7. In-law Problems

In-law problems can be some of the most difficult problems to completely resolve. We can help a couple learn how to not allow in-laws to interfere with their relationship, but if the in-laws don't like from day one the person their son, daughter, brother, or sister married, they may refuse to accept that person. There isn't a lot that can be done about it.

One of the techniques used in building relationships with in-laws is to spend time with them so you can get to know them and they can become acquainted with you. Love can cover a multitude of sins.

Past or Present Relationship

Sometimes a husband or a wife will have a friend who has been a friend long before he or she met and married the present spouse. For whatever reason, the spouse does not like the friend or feels insecure because this person is a member of the opposite sex. It may be that the relationship developed after marriage. Some married people take this position: "This is my friend, and it has nothing to do with you. You have a problem that you need to resolve in your life." The problem with this attitude is that it does not correspond with God's goal of oneness in a marriage. If there is a choice that must be made between a spouse and a friend, in accordance with our marriage vows of commitment to our spouse and the level of significance God gives to the marriage relationship, the friendship must be broken rather than risk breaking a marriage through divorce. Some men, in particular, seem not to take these situations as seriously as they should, unless it is the wife who has the friend.

An even more difficult situation to deal with is parents of children from a previous relationship who want a close friendship. Sometimes we sin or make a mistake and spend the rest of our lives paying for it. Whether it involves having children out of wedlock or children from a previous marriage, there can be major problems with a person from a previous relationship. Sometimes taking legal action can help but at other times, with the grace of God, a person has to live with unpleasantness.

PROBLEM SOLVING

The goal of a strong Christ-centered family is to face up to problems and crises and to deal with difficulties using the power of God in a positive and constructive way. With God's help, adversity can strengthen a family and draw its members closer together. When we attempt to resolve problems, there can be a few different outcomes:

1. The problem is resolved.
2. It turns out that it is not really a problem.
3. It cannot be resolved at this time.
4. It cannot be resolved by us, and the conclusion of the matter is out of our hands.
5. It cannot be resolved at all, and by God's grace, we must live with it.
6. It can be resolved only by God.

HOW TO PRESENT A PROBLEM TO YOUR SPOUSE
1. Pray

It is wise to turn to God in prayer when trouble and problems arise. It can save us from wasting time and energy, worrying, taking the wrong action, and saying the wrong thing. God has a way of calming us in a time of trouble, giving us quiet confidence that everything will be all right.

2. Write out the Problem

This is a difficult thing to do when we are emotionally upset, but it is the second thing we must do to quiet our spirit. One of the things we ask counselees to do when they come to our counseling center for help is to answer this question on paper: "What is the problem or problems?" Surprisingly, a few people, after writing out the problem, decide they don't have a problem or find the answer to their troubles when they read what they have written. This exercise can be a means for God to talk to us.

Writing out the problem will also clarify the issues for us and can be used by the counselee as notes in presenting a problem to the spouse.

3. Look for a Solution

In presenting a problem it is always better to be able to offer a solution or options that may lead to a solution. To do this will take thinking, meditation, a sensitivity to God's Spirit, and experience in problem solving.

4. Examine Yourself

After thinking it through, do you find that you are being overly sensitive? Is it worth talking about to your mate? Are you expecting too much from an imperfect spouse? Sometimes we discover the problem is within ourselves, and, after talking to God, we discover that we do not have to bother our mate.

5. Plan a Good Time to Talk

When we have a valid problem to present to our spouse, we must choose a good time to talk. It is not wise to present problems before a meal when people are hungry and their energy level is down. Nor is it wise to talk about problems after 10 P.M. It is the end of the day, and at that time most of us are tired. Circumstances may dictate, however, that this is the only time available to talk. If so, both parties must be very careful to walk in the Spirit and take their tired conditions into consideration if things don't go well.

6. Present Problems Clearly and in Detail

In presenting a problem, we must try not to condemn or accuse. Although it may be your mate's fault, the most important thing is to resolve the problem, neither placing blame nor desiring to win an argument. Simply complaining is not necessarily the way to get your point across. It is better to present the problem calmly, clearly, and in detail.

7. Allow Your Mate Time to Think About the Problem

After the problem has been presented, if your mate is willing to respond immediately, fine. He or she may need time, however, to think about what you have shared. Perhaps you have been thinking about the issues for days, weeks, even months, but the problem is new to your spouse. Your mate may have been unaware that you considered something a problem.

8. Continue Conversations over a Period of Time

The more emotional or complex the problems are, the less likely it is that everything can be resolved in one or two discussions. Time for thinking, processing, praying, researching, and investigating must be allowed between discussions. Discussions on heavy issues should be no longer than sixty minutes. Follow-up discussions should be agreed upon and scheduled.

9. Don't Argue

If the discussion gets very emotional and an argument starts, postpone the discussion, but don't give up.

PROBLEM SOLVING TOGETHER

"Love is as strong as death. . . . Many waters cannot quench love; rivers cannot wash it away" (Song 8:6–7).

A commitment to solving problems together can strengthen and deepen oneness.

1. Invite God into the Problem-Solving Process

James says, "You do not have, because you do not ask God" (James 4:2). One of the benefits of being Christians is that God would like to be involved in our lives for our own good. But we have a free will. God must be deliberately included; God must be invited to participate in our problem solving. There are some problems that only God can solve. If we exclude God, we exclude a critical resource.

God loves us and cares for us beyond our comprehension. His love for us is unending and eternal. It is futile to tackle problems without Him.

When couples face problems, they should remind each other that God loves them. They should pray together, inviting God to lead and guide them and resolve problems with and for them, or give them grace to bear them. Couples also need to remind each other that they were married because they loved each other, even if they are having relational problems. "Love is as strong as death," so, combined with God's love, they can face and deal with all problems.

There should be a commitment to act like Christians, maintaining the spirit of Christ while working through problems.

2. Identify the Problems

One of the hindrances to solving problems is not communicating clearly and understandably. Speaking in emotional generalities is not helpful. We need to be specific. What? How? When? It is also good to request, "Give me an example."

Sometimes the issues are so emotional that it is better to write each other a letter, expressing yourself as to what the problems are. After reading the letter or letters, if both of you want to use this method, before coming together, make notes to use as a means of being clear.

Another technique to use when there are relational problems that have negative emotions we want to defuse, is to privately and individually use what I call My Love Inventory, as shown on page 233. After the individual or couple have completed the love inventory, they should come together for discussion, understanding, repentance, forgiveness, and reconciliation.

Jay E. Adams has what he calls the Family Conference Table. This technique has proven to be invaluable in obtaining data from counselees in order to help them, but it is also a good tool for training couples and family members in how to communicate better and work through problems. The couple agrees to meet for one hour, three to five times during the next seven days to work on their problems. The purpose of the first family conferences is to gather information concerning the problems in the marriage and family, or where they think they are going wrong in the marriage. The husband is in charge. The wife or the husband can be the secretary, recording the information that comes out of the conference. It depends on who writes better notes. The meeting must be opened in prayer and closed in prayer. Although the meeting should be for one hour, if the couple find they are not accomplishing very much after a half hour, they should close the meeting and try again the next day.

They will use a sheet of paper, $8^{1}/_{2}''$x11$''$ and draw a vertical line down the center. At the top of the left side, write the husband's name. The wife's name goes on the right side. The husband tells first how he has failed or needs to improve as a husband. This is recorded on his side of the paper. When he is finished, his wife draws a line under his list and helps him by adding to the list what he may have forgotten or is not aware of. On the right side of the paper the wife lists her failures or ways she can improve. Again, when she has completed her list, her husband may help her by drawing a line under her list and adding other items, as shown on page 234. In these first meetings, the goal is not to solve the problems but to clarify what they are. In subsequent meetings, the couple will work on resolving issues.

3. Deal With Problems According to Priority

When problems are many and complex, they can be overwhelming. When the many problems in the church of Corinth were reported to the apostle Paul, he did not become overwhelmed. He simply dealt with each issue and concern one by one. In chapters 1 through 4 he deals with the party spirit and divisions in the church. In chapter 5 he challenges the Corinthians to practice church discipline to rid the church of immoral-

List the good points of your spouse (children, brother, sister, father, mother, etc.).	List the bad points or issues that are causing problems with your spouse.	List your wrong reactions and attitudes to your spouse's bad points and problems.	Read 1 Corinthians 13:4–7 (modern translation). In practicing love toward your spouse, how should you respond?
1. My husband is a good provider.	1. He yells at me when he gets angry.	1. I become angry and refuse to talk, or I yell back at him.	1. Although I get angry, I should not stop talking to him, or I should not yell at him.
2. He is a Christian and attends church faithfully.	2. He is not understanding.	2. I become discouraged and depressed.	2. I should not feel sorry for myself because my husband is not perfect.
3. He is very intelligent.	3. He is tired and grumpy.	3.	3. I should balance the checkbook so he would not have a reason to yell.
4. He is a good father.	4.	4.	4.

Husband	Wife
1. Sarcasm—every now and then.	1. Sometimes uses profanity when upset and angry.
2. Stubborn behavior.	2. Depressed often.
3. Drives without insurance and loans out car.	3. Does not like husband's appearance.
4. Usually interested sexually at inappropriate times.	4. Constantly feels lonely.
5. Tells lies.	5. Does not feel dependent upon husband; never trusts him.
6. Has clothes all over the house, dirty socks under the bed, on counter, in rec room, middle of the floor, etc., anywhere he takes them off.	6. Difficulty in being affectionate anymore, since being rejected so long, so often.
7. Does not bathe regularly or keep hair clean and combed.	7. Feels bad about having to be the responsible leader—financially, physically, and emotionally, because he has left it for me to be responsible.
8. Wears dirty clothes.	8. Have to say what's on my mind in front of children—only time available.
9. Does not eat regularly or with family.	9. Resent my husband and regard him as a burden.
10. Last out of bed, but will not make it.	10. Makes me angry—you make use of the word "lie" very often.
11. Agrees upon one thing, but does another.	
12. Does not remember marriage date.	
13. Does not put things back after using.	
14. Puts tools on refrigerator, counter, all over.	

ity. In chapter 6 the issue is lawsuits among Christians. In chapter 7 he handles marital and single-adult problems. In chapter 8 he takes on the challenge of food sacrificed to idols, and so on.

So as not to be overwhelmed by problems, we must trust God, no matter what. We must itemize and prioritize our problems. We cannot tackle all our problems at once. The couple must seek God's wisdom to determine what is a priority and start working on those items that will begin to bring about peace, security, or reconciliation. Often, as we begin to tackle the top priorities on our list, God begins to move with us, and some of the lesser priorities seem to be resolved, as we achieve victory over the greater problems.

4. Work Through Problems

In working through problems, the following questions are helpful:

- What is the problem?
- What caused the problem?
- How can the problem be resolved?
- How can we prevent the problem from recurring?
- If we fail again, what will we do?
- What can we learn from this problem?
- If the problem cannot be solved, how will we live with it?

List all possible solutions to a problem. Use imagination and discussion to consider the consequences of each solution. Sometimes what we think is a solution may cause a brand new, unnecessary problem. Choose the best solution.

5. Get Outside Help If Needed

If you and your mate are bogged down in your discussions and can't resolve the problem, get help. Do not allow sinful pride to stop you from using other resources that God has provided to bless your marriage. Both of you should agree to ask a trusted friend, a relative, or your pastor if one of them is willing to assist you. Many couples never take this step because of pride, and their marriage continues on a downward spiral, then ends in divorce.

6. Set an Action Plan and Accountability

Although some people know how to resolve their problems, they do not necessarily do what is required to follow through to completion.

Those who are having financial problems because of poor management may know they should make and follow a personal budget. They know they should adhere to the budget and the financial plan in order to be delivered from economic bondage but, for whatever reason, they do not.

When God has led us, guided us, and answered our prayers by giving us solutions for problem solving and we do not submit or obey, this is sin. A plan of action should be written, and we should perform accordingly. Husbands and wives should submit to each other at this point. They should hold each other accountable or have a friend, relative, or pastor do so.

BOOKS FOR FURTHER KNOWLEDGE AND USE IN FAMILY MINISTRY

Carter, Les. *Broken Vows*. Nashville: Thomas Nelson, 1991.

Courtright, John, and Sid Rogers. *Your Wife Was Sexually Abused*. Grand Rapids: Zondervan, 1994.

Frank, Don, and Jan Frank. *When Victims Marry*. Nashville: Thomas Nelson, 1990.

Hanson, Freya Ottem, and Terje C. Hausken. *Mediation for Troubled Marriages: Establishing a Ministry for Conflict Resolution*. Minneapolis: Augsburg, 1989.

McManus, Michael J. *Marriage Savers*. Rev. ed. Grand Rapids: Zondervan, 1995.

Mayhall, Jack, and Carole Mayhall. *Opposites Attract Attack*. Colorado Springs: NavPress, 1990.

Moorehead, Bob. *Before You Throw in the Towel*. Dallas: Word, 1992.

Splinter, John P. *The Complete Divorce Recovery Handbook*. Grand Rapids: Zondervan, 1992.

Chapter 17

TRAINING PARENTS AND CHILDREN

TRAINING PARENTS

As it is with being married, raising children is complex, challenging, and difficult. We are to rear the children that God has given us in such a way that we can return them to God for His use and glory. With so many evil influences present today, I believe it takes parents, the church, and the school working together as a team to get the job done. However, the major responsibility is still with the parents.

It is important for children in single-parent families that their extended families and the church, serving as an extended family, play an active role in their nurturing and support to offset not having a father or mother.

SURVIVAL AND LIFE-AND-DEATH CONCERNS

Trying to raise children in our drug-infested, crime-polluted, violence-prone cities and towns without a vigilant, protective parental eye on our children is sheer foolishness. These are not the days when parents can be caught up in their own personal pursuits of following a career, earning a dollar, seeking pleasure, or finding a mate, while neglecting to get into the world of their children. For our children to survive, be safe, and enjoy a long life, parents and churches must take the following objectives seriously.

Keeping Our Children Alive

Recently, I was watching a television news program that featured parents who keep their children in the house, behind barred windows, and doors with security locks, for their safety. These parents were criticized by sociologists and child psychologists because it is thought they are depriving their children of social development by not allowing them to play outside with other children their age. It also was disclosed during the program that this was a neighborhood where gunfire was heard so often that even the patrolling police were used to hearing it and ignored it. There were constant drive-by shootings. The murder rate was so high that insurance companies stopped writing life-insurance policies for teenage and young adult males. The critics of these parents didn't live in the neighborhood.

Because of the drug culture, anger, violence, despair, and poverty, millions of our families live in such environments. In order to protect their children, it should be a goal of parents to move out of such neighborhoods. Economically, this is not always possible. In the same television program, it was shown that some of the parents escorted their children to and from school or saw that they were escorted. In regard to keeping children at home to protect them, depriving them of social development, church youth ministries can help by programming activities to meet this need. Surely parents should do whatever they can to save their children's lives.

Keeping Our Children Off Drugs

In order to keep our children off drugs, parents need to be aware of their availability, especially marijuana and crack cocaine . We must be on the alert for adult drug users who may be in our families, who may sometimes be careless in their irresponsible state. Not only should parents be educated as to the symptoms of drug use, but they should also educate their children about the dangers of drug use.

Keeping Our Children Out of Jail

Keeping our children out of the drug culture will help keep our children out of jail and prison. Parents must also be vigilant and involved with their children's friends, even guiding them in the selection of friends. Again, the church can help by creating a Christian youth community. Parents should get to know the parents of their children's friends. A family I know became very alarmed when their eight-year-old child's teacher was concerned about the graphic sexual knowledge the child revealed in a health class—a knowledge far beyond his age. These Christian parents were baffled as to how their child could have such information. With further investigation, they discovered it came from one of their neighbors. They had taken their neighbor's eight-year-old son to Vacation Bible school that summer, and he professed to receiving Christ. These Christian parents had allowed their son to frequently visit the home of his newfound Christian friend. But that friend's family watched X-rated movies as a pastime and also used illegal drugs. Parents need to know the parents of their children's friends.

Not all the people in jail are guilty of a crime. I believe the majority need to be there, but not all. Some are in jail because of ignorance of the law, violation of their constitutional rights, poverty, or not being able to obtain suitable legal counsel. Certainly, like people in any other vocation, there are good law-enforcement officers and bad law-enforcement officers. Sometimes the African-American community is the dumping ground for undisciplined police officers with problems.

Our children must be reared to respect and submit to law-enforcement officers (Rom. 13:1). However, they must also be taught to protect themselves from bad or racist police, sheriffs, etc. Before a law enforcement person pulls a weapon, young people should make sure their hands are in plain view. In spite of the fact that they may be shocked and confused if a police officer pulls a weapon on them, they should raise their hands slowly and submit silently. If the officer orders them to speak on the street, after being taken to jail, or even in their own home, under no circumstances should they confess to a crime they did not commit, no matter how afraid they become.

When a child, a teenager, or a young adult has been arrested, whether guilty or not, legal representation should be obtained right away. The young person should have a lawyer at the preliminary hearing, during the trial, and at the sentencing. If possible, bail should be paid to get our children out of jail. Failure to raise bail can be a great disadvantage. A defendant can be kept six months, eight months, or more before the trial under the same conditions as convicted prisoners. Usually an overworked lawyer with a large case load is appointed by the court. There are restrictions on the time that the lawyer can meet with the defendant. As part of our family ministry, we give our congregation a list of criminal attorneys. Parents should hold their children accountable as to where they are at all times and monitor the time it takes to travel from one place to another. Children and teenagers are not fully developed, mature adults and need parental supervision.

Keeping Our Children from Having Children

Children are to be taught right from wrong by parents, and the parents must model what they teach. It should not be assumed that children will automatically do what is right. Remember, children have a sinful nature, the same as adults. Children must be led to Christ at an early age and be discipled by their parents. While growing up, parents must try to protect their children from worldly corruption. It has been said that it is not good for Christians to shelter their children from the evil realities of the world, but that they should let them face these realities in preparation for living in the world. After observing Christian families the last thirty years, I have seen more damage done because of a lack of protection from corruption than harm from being innocent. For young and older adults, there is no value in learning the evil in this world.

Parents should censor television programming, movies, reading materials, and music for objectionable, immoral, and anti-God information or values. Again, it is important that parents monitor the friendships of their children. "Do not be misled: 'Bad company corrupts good character'" (1 Cor. 15:33).

Parents must teach their children early about sexuality. What you teach is determined by the age of the child. There is much Christian material on the subject that is suited for children's needs. Children should not have to learn about sexuality from school and corrupt children. Instead, they should grow up knowing that this is a subject they can freely discuss with Mom and Dad.

As parents teach their own children about sexuality, they also teach God's purpose of creation, the roles of and differences between male and female, the values and morality of godliness, and the use of the body God gave them. For parents who are reluctant to talk to their children about sexuality, I have suggested that they give their children a book to read on the subject, graded for their age. After the child or adolescent finishes reading the book, the parent then discusses the subject based on the child's questions or questions asked by the parent, to discern what the child has learned.

Parents must have guidelines for their children's spending the night at their friends' homes or having friends spend the night with them. There must be written guidelines for dating and rules for entertaining friends. For example, teenagers should not be left alone, unsupervised. This does not mean they should not have any privacy with their friends, but they should not be secure in believing that an adult will not walk into the room any minute.

Working parents whose children get home before they do in the afternoon must have another trusted adult to monitor their children.

Above everything else, children who receive Jesus Christ as Lord and Savior can live a godly Christian life if taught, discipled, and supervised.

Keeping Our Children in School

In some of our communities, there are alarmingly high rates of children, boys in particular, dropping out of school. Education has been the vehicle for many to rise out of poverty. It is a proven fact that, in general, over the long haul, people with a high school education are better wage earners than those who have not graduated from high school. Those who have a college education or post-high school vocational training are greater wage earners than high school graduates.

Parents have to establish a pattern of involvement in the education process of their children rather than totally depending on and trusting a school system to educate their children. Parents must read books on child development in order to know what to expect at any given age. Some children have learning disabilities that call for special educational measures. However, when parents are told their child has a learning disability, they should get a second professional opinion because some children have been diagnosed wrongly based on cultural differences between the black child and the white educator.

Parents must hold their children accountable to attend school and do their schoolwork, for the Bible states, "Folly is bound up in the heart of a child" (Prov. 22:15). We cannot expect children to fully understand the importance of education. Parents should know what subjects or classes their children are taking and work with the teachers, knowing what their child must do to succeed.

Learning to read must be a priority, because lack of reading skills affects all other subjects that are taught. Parents need to be vigilant in knowing if the children are staying on their grade level in reading. Children are merciless in making fun of other children who don't read well.

Many children who have behavioral troubles in school are also struggling with their reading. Also, not reading well can be a demotivator for a child.

Some children drop out of school because they fear bodily harm or death. They have been intimidated by a violent bully or an urban gang. Sometimes these issues can be settled when the parent brings the situation to the school official's attention. However, this does not always work, so it may mean transferring the student to another school or the family moving out of the neighborhood or the city.

PARENTAL TRAINING

For the church to assist families, there should be parent training classes in the following areas:

- Child development
- Loving and understanding children
- How to lead children to Christ
- Christian parenting
- Disciplining children
- How to help children with their school work
- Raising spiritually strong children

RIGHT AND WRONG ATTITUDES TOWARD CHILDREN
Wrong Attitudes

We are living in a day when there is a general negative attitude toward children. We are encouraged not to give birth to children. Abortion is considered the choice of the mother to thwart God's reproduction process, while unmarried people living together (cohabitating) is glorified as a right. There used to be a time when if a wife conceived, there was joy when she told her husband. Too often today, when she finds out she is pregnant, she is disappointed, and when she breaks the news to her spouse, they both go into depression.

Parents take actions without considering the effect these actions may have on their children. One of the most devastating of these is divorce. Children are at a disadvantage because they are not old enough to make their feelings known clearly and forcefully. No child normally votes for the dissolution of his parents' marriage. As a matter of fact, some children falsely believe they are somehow responsible for their parents' breakup.

Because of parents' pursuit of money, pleasure, and careers, some children are neglected relationally by their fathers and mothers.

Christian parents sometimes are not much different than nonbelievers in their attitudes toward children. For instance, some nonbelievers have reasons for having only one or two children, or no children at all. They say children are too much trouble; they will interfere with career goals; raising them costs too much money, so they cannot afford them; and they must own a home first, etc. When we surveyed young married Christian couples and asked them about their child-bearing plans, their answers were identical to the answers of nonbelievers. The Christians, though, make it sound spiritual. They say they are inadequate to raise children, so it could not be God's will for them to have children. They believe it is God's will that they be established in their career or pursue their education first, all the way up to a doctorate degree. They cannot afford children, or they want to be able to purchase a home first in God's will.

Right Attitudes

Every Sunday school child knows that the Lord loves children. If we are to be godly, we are to have the same attitude that God has toward children.

Children are a blessing from God.

Adam lay with his wife Eve, and she became pregnant and gave birth to Cain. She said, "With the help of the LORD I have brought forth a man" (Gen. 4:1).

"May God Almighty bless you and make you fruitful and increase your numbers until you become a community of peoples" (Gen. 28:3).

"I will bless her and will surely give you a son by her. I will bless her so that she will be the mother of nations; kings of peoples will come from her" (Gen. 17:16).

Children bring joy and happiness to a home.

Sons are a heritage from the LORD, children a reward from him. Like arrows in the hands of a warrior are sons born in one's youth. Blessed is the man whose quiver is full of them (Ps. 127:3–5).

Children are a physical expression of love between a husband and wife.

So Boaz took Ruth and she became his wife . . . and the LORD enabled her to conceive, and she gave birth to a son (Ruth 4:13).

God cares for children.

> A father to the fatherless, a defender of widows, is God in his holy dwelling (Ps. 68:5).

> Because I rescued the poor who cried for help, and the fatherless who had none to assist him (Job 29:12).

Children are to worship God with their parents.

> There, by the Ahava Canal, I proclaimed a fast, so that we might humble ourselves before our God and ask him for a safe journey for us and our children, with all our possessions (Ezra 8:21).

> And on that day they offered great sacrifices, rejoicing because God had given them great joy. The women and children also rejoiced. The sound of rejoicing in Jerusalem could be heard far away (Neh. 12:43).

When we champion the cause of children, we champion God's cause. In recent times, state and federal governments have become callous concerning the welfare of poor children. Parents, the church, and all Christians must stand and take care of our children.

PARENTAL COMMITMENT TO MEETING NEEDS OF CHILDREN

Time

Parental commitment is needed for the well-being of our children. There must be a commitment of time. Children should not grow up in our homes without parents taking the time to get into their world.

Parental Influence

More than once, surveys and studies have proved that parents have the greatest influence on children for good or bad. I remember the first time I was reading the Bible through as a new Christian. I was astounded that God would instruct Israel to kill all Canaanites as they possessed the land, including women and children. I felt that surely the children should be spared because of their innocence. However, after thirty-two years of being in the ministry and leading in obeying the Great Commission to help others into the kingdom of Christ, I understand better why God commanded Israel to destroy the children. In reaching out to a lost world, we have found unbelievable wickedness in families. Children in such families learn wickedness, and I believe deep-rooted wickedness is passed on at birth from the soul of the parents. Except for the grace of

God, none of these children from perverted and wicked families would come to a saving knowledge of God.

On the other hand, the Bible says of King Asa, "Asa did what was right in the eyes of the LORD, as his father David had done" (1 Kings 15:11). Although David was Asa's great-great- grandfather, he left a godly legacy that impacted Asa's life. Parents must recognize the influence and impact they have on their children's lives. Parents are natural role models for their children. Parents should be models of success. Parents must rise to their highest God-given potential as examples for their children. But it is equally important that parents model how to handle failure with the help of God. We speak of discipleship ministries in church, but parents should be leading their children to Christ and conscientiously discipling them spiritually.

Parents should involve children in the family decision-making and problem-solving processes. For example, when children are very young, a husband and wife will decide where to have a family vacation, selecting at least two choices they agree on. The parents give the two choices to the children to make the final decision as to where the family will spend their vacation. Parents should ask for their children's prayers when parents have to make decisions or when problems arise. Parents should explain to children the thinking that brought them to a decision or the resolution of a problem. Also, the children should be told about parents' human limitations that sometimes make putting the problem entirely into the hands of God the best decision. The families should celebrate together in praise of God when He has given victory, supplied a need, or in other ways answered prayer.

As my good friend John Perkins of Harambee Ministries says, "Let's create some memories." Some of us can think back to our childhood and remember some warm, loving, or fun experiences in our family's lives. Parents must take time and plan to make some memories.

Physical Needs
Food

Children must grow up learning good, healthy eating habits in light of studies that have proven that what we eat makes a difference—from developing obesity to cancer. Food must be nutritious or children will not develop proper mental or physical health. Parents must study the subject; nutrition is too important to guess about. The church could invite nutrition and health experts in to lecture on the subject as part of the church's family ministry.

Health Care

Some parents neglect the health care of their children because they think they cannot afford a doctor, are not able to take time off from work, or refuse to wait in long lines at a clinic. Years later, some parents regret this kind of thinking when it is discovered that the child has a severe health problem that, if discovered and treated earlier, could have been avoided or corrected. Now the parent suffers from guilt. A lack of health care can affect children psychologically. Teachers have told parents that their children have a learning deficiency, when the real problem may be a sight or hearing deficiency—not a brain deficiency.

Clothing

Clothing should be clean and in proper repair. Clothes don't have to be expensive, but the children must not be ashamed of what they have to wear. Children must be taught that parents cannot afford everything children want. They should also see the lack of wisdom in keeping up with the latest fads that are driven by a lost, materialistic world.

Shelter

I have already spoken of trying to provide housing in a relatively safe neighborhood, if possible. The home itself should be comfortable and clean. Children should not have to battle with cockroaches, mice, or rats. In old and decaying housing, this is not always easy. Sometimes the landlord must be challenged, and cooperation of neighbors in an apartment building or row home is required. A child should not be ashamed to bring a friend home.

The home should be safe. An alarming number of children are killed in the home each year through parental neglect, carelessness, and accidents. Loose railings, broken steps, dilapidated chairs, and toys that are made defective should be taken care of by parents.

Recreation

Play and recreation are a must for the physical growth and development of a child. Some parents demand that their children be still and stop wiggling, when God put the wiggle in them. Parents need to be educated as to what is best for their child at any given age.

Emotional and Intellectual Needs

Freedom from Fear of Rejection

The emotional needs of a child are crucial. Children are God's precious gifts to parents and should be treated accordingly. Children are to be loved and freely given the opportunity to express love without fear of rejection. Many a naturally affectionate child's spirit has been broken by an insensitive parent. Help children through emotional let-downs.

A Sense of Worth

If everything that God created is good (Gen. 1:31) and we are "fearfully and wonderfully made" (Ps. 139:14), then it should be expected that parents accept their children as persons of worth. All children have some God-given purpose. Parents must help them through school education and parental education to discover their God-given natural gifts, talents, and abilities. In addition to this, after children receive Christ as Lord and Savior, they are given spiritual gifts by God, the Holy Spirit, that must be discovered and used. Parents must encourage and motivate children toward achievement. Learn each child's temperament and personality. Love each child as an individual.

A Growing Interdependence

Parenting should help a child to progress from dependence to independence and interdependence. Children should be aided in having a high self-esteem because God created them, and they should be helped in discovering who they are in the will of God. Children should be respected as people by parents and not publicly embarrassed in front of their friends or anyone else.

Early Education in the Home

Intellectually, children need to learn by seeing, hearing, touching, smelling, and tasting. Opportunities to explore and discover should be given. There should be faith in their ability to learn from both parents and teachers. The child's first and continuing education is at home. Educators believe that the first five years of a child's life are crucial to his or her development. It is believed that 50 percent of a child's character and personality is developed by the age of three, 75 percent by the age of five. This is why it is so important for mothers to be home with their children, if possible.

Support Outside the Home

As I wrote earlier about parents' involvement in the educational process of their children, it is very important that parents visit the school and talk with teachers concerning the child's progress. Teachers are encouraged by the parents' interest and concern for their child. Fathers should lead in this area. Some white teachers, in particular, assume that our children have no fathers. We must dispel this myth by having Christian fathers getting involved in the education of their children, whether or not they are married to the children's mothers. African-American males should serve on school boards and teacher-parent associations, not only for the good of their own children, but also for other children, that they may see more male leaders active in the community.

Reinforcement of Achievement

A good report card should be rewarded. When a child has a poor report card, the parents should talk with the child and the teacher. If the child is trying but needs more help in understanding the subjects, get help; perhaps the parent needs to help more or get a tutor. If the child has poor study habits or is plain lazy, this should be corrected before it is too late. Children must be encouraged to develop a love for reading.

The Discipline of Sleep

Children should get enough sleep. They cannot be fresh and alert for school if they are allowed to stay up late into the night watching television, playing video games, or listening to music.

Spiritual Needs

The greatest act that parents can do for their children is to lead them to a saving knowledge of Christ and to walk in the Spirit before them as they are growing up. I am not talking about being a perfect parent, but a righteous one. Children should be taught about God as early as possible. My mother taught me how to pray to God when she taught me how to talk as a child. I grew up talking to God.

Not all Christian instruction and worship should be left up to the church. Fathers who are leaders of the home or single-parent mothers should lead in instructing their families about God.

These commandments that I give you today are to be upon your hearts. Impress them on your children. Talk about them when you sit at home and when you walk along the road, when you lie down and when you get up. Tie them as symbols on your hands and bind them on your foreheads. Write them on the doorframes of your houses and on your gates (Deut. 6:6–9).

Mothers are to teach their children about God:

I have been reminded of your sincere faith, which first lived in your grandmother Lois and in your mother Eunice and, I am persuaded, now lives in you also (2 Tim. 1:5).

But as for you, continue in what you have learned and have become convinced of, because you know those from whom you learned it, and how from infancy you have known the holy Scriptures, which are able to make you wise for salvation through faith in Christ Jesus (2 Tim. 3:14–15).

Children's understanding of God and spiritual things should be monitored and challenged from time to time. It should not be assumed that because children came to Christ at an early age and were baptized that they will automatically grow into spiritual maturity without parents ministering to them. Although children can be saved, they are still developing physically, emotionally, and intellectually and are limited in what they can understand about the responsibilities of being a Christian. It is a good practice that at each birthday after children receive Christ as their personal Savior that parents talk with them about what salvation is and what it means to live the Christian life.

The Need to Express Love to and Receive Love from Children

To accept and love a child is to accept and love Christ:

"Therefore, whoever humbles himself like this child is the greatest in the kingdom of heaven. And whoever welcomes a little child like this in my name welcomes me. . . . See that you do not look down on one of these little ones. For I tell you that their angels in heaven always see the face of my Father in heaven" (Matt. 18:4–5, 10).

A father should start spending time with his children from their birth. He should feed them, bathe and clothe them, and change diapers. Although women are better at nurturing, men also, as fathers, have a responsibility to nurture. Children can sense warmth and love, even as infants. Teenage daughters need their fathers just as much as sons do.

Both parents should play with their children and enter their world. Parents should watch their children's favorite television programs with them sometimes. Learn how the professional on television relates with your child.

Spend personal one-on-one time with each child. Don't have a favorite child. Favoritism can cause sisters and brothers to hate each other (see Gen. 37:3–28). Don't compare children with each other. Partiality shows immaturity on the parent's part.

Celebrating Birthdays

The day that a person is born is significant. God, in His wisdom and providence, has a will and purpose for each person's life. Celebrating a child's birthday and making a "big deal" out of it is very important to building a child's self-esteem in Christ. On birthdays, children should be reminded that God has a plan and mission for their lives and that God will reveal His will for them through His Word and His Spirit as they grow up.

A birthday party is one of the ways to celebrate, but it is not the only way. The day can be made special by less expensive celebrations.

Have a special birthday family dinner at home. The birthday child gets to choose the dinner menu, because it is her birthday. Before the meal, candles are lit on a birthday cake. The family sings "Happy Birthday." The honoree blows out the candles. Dad leads the family prayer of thanksgiving to God for placing the honoree in the family and gives thanks for positive characteristics and known God-given gifts, talents, and abilities in the child. Once we had candles on a sweet potato pie, at the honoree's request. By the way, parents should be open to eat whatever the child wants for dinner. This can be interesting, challenging, and amusing.

A variation of the above is the honoree's being allowed to choose a restaurant for the family birthday dinner. Again, parents must be open to eating something they would not normally eat for dinner.

Sisters and brothers should be taught to memorize family members' birth dates and give birthday cards and gifts. A gift can be made, be saved for, or be something used that belongs to another family member that the honoree would love to have. This also fosters sacrifice and goodwill among sisters and brothers.

The Need for Discipline

"Train a child in the way he should go, and when he is old he will not turn from it" (Prov. 22:6).

To discipline a child is to train a child. Christian psychologist Henry Brant calls discipline "helping children." There are two extremes that some parents practice concerning child discipline: being permissive or being too rigid, strict, and unfair. These extremes hinder children's development toward adulthood and distort their understanding of the fatherhood of God. For example, the writer to the Hebrews used human parenting as an illustration to clarify God's parenting of His children by raising a question, "For what son is not disciplined by his father?" (Heb. 12:7). He continues, answering his own question: "Moreover, we have all had human fathers who disciplined us and we respected them for it. How much more should we submit to the Father of our spirits and live!" (Heb. 12:9). In light of widespread divorce, separation, single-parent families, parents who are addicted to drugs, and irresponsible parents, we cannot assume that there is loving and godly parental discipline in our homes.

OUR OBJECTIVE AS PARENTS IS TO TRAIN OUR CHILDREN

To train is to (1) mold character, (2) direct performance, (3) make one responsible for self and others, and (4) develop the person.

Training is more than telling children what to do. Children cannot train themselves. Parents must spend time knowing each child in order to build specific characteristics in the lives of their children. Parents should study the Bible as a family textbook on what character ought to be, modeling Christ above anyone else.

Parents should pray to God, asking for wisdom and guidance in training their children, even before they are born:

> Then Manoah prayed to the LORD: "O Lord, I beg you, let the man of God you sent to us come again to teach us how to bring up the boy who is to be born." So Manoah asked him, "When your words are fulfilled, what is to be the rule for the boy's life and work?" The woman gave birth to a boy and named him Samson. He grew and the LORD blessed him (Judg. 13:8, 12, 24).

Goals for Child Training

"And the boy Samuel continued to grow in stature and in favor with the LORD and with men" (1 Sam. 2:26). Here are some of the goals parents should have for training children.

1. To lead your children to accept Jesus Christ as their Lord and Savior.
2. To help your children to become self-reliant by giving them responsibilities and patiently seeing that they carry them out, even if it means doing a chore over and over.
3. To help them to depend on God as their heavenly Father.

4. To build in them self-acceptance and confidence in what God has placed inside them as Christians.
5. To help them mature as adults and not remain children in adult bodies. ("When I was a child, I talked like a child, I thought like a child, I reasoned like a child. When I became a man, I put childish ways behind me" [1 Cor. 13:11].)
6. To help them develop relational skills with family members and other people.
7. To encourage them to be dedicated and loyal to their family.
8. To develop a Christian work ethic in your children. ("For even when we were with you, we gave you this rule: 'If a man will not work, he shall not eat.' We hear that some among you are idle. They are not busy; they are busybodies. Such people we command and urge in the Lord Jesus Christ to settle down and earn the bread they eat" [2 Thess. 3:10–12].)
9. To be strong in the Lord and stand up to the negatives and challenges of people and life.
10. To instill in children the desire to achieve, accomplish, and do the best they can according to their God-given abilities.
11. To show them their responsibility to care for and assist their parents in old age. ("Listen to your father, who gave you life, and do not despise your mother when she is old" [Prov. 23:22].)
12. To teach them to respect authority, whether it is that of parents, school teachers, Sunday school teachers, pastors, police officers, or other leaders.

Instruction of Children

Discipline should be consistent, loving, and fair. Discipline begins with instructing children in an atmosphere of love and patience. Many parents expect certain conduct from their children but have not taken the time to teach and instruct children as to what behavior they expect from them.

A mother is talking on the phone while watching her toddler explore his world. The phone conversation seizes her full attention, and she loses track of the baby's location. She finishes her phone conversation and becomes alarmed because of the absence of the tot. She searches for him and finds him three feet from the cooking stove with all burners at work, plus a ham baking in the oven. The little guy is headed for the pretty lights, the steam whizzing from the pots, and the chorus of strange sounds coming from the stove. In horror, the mother screams, "Reggie! Reggie!" She scares the baby; he stops where he is and begins to cry.

During the following weeks as little Reggie attempts to investigate the kitchen, his mother hinders his exploration with spine-chilling screams and with slaps on his hands and legs when she thinks he might be heading for the stove. Reggie might be a baby, but he is not stupid. He can't figure out the reason for his mother's hostile behavior, but it has something to do with the kitchen. Every time he goes into the kitchen, she gets crazy, so he reasons it is not safe to go into the kitchen or he will be tortured.

Mom is baffled when she has to drag Reggie into the kitchen, kicking and screaming, when she wants to feed him. Before she can remove the tray from Reggie's high chair, he runs out of the kitchen. She runs him down, tackles him, and with great determination gets him into the chair. Reggie screams and yells in terror.

It would have been a lot simpler if Mom, instead of being emotional, yelling, screaming, and slapping him on his hands and legs, had with patience and loving kindness communicated with Reggie specifically what it was she did not want him to do.

It gets worse with parents of teenagers. Authoritarian parents command, "Do what I say. Don't give me any lip. Do what I say," with no civil conversations explaining reasons for their commands. Permissive parents are ridiculous. When the teenager is acting like the brat he is, the parent says, "I raised him in church. I don't know why he doesn't treat me like the nice kids at church who behave with their parents."

One of the great highlights in the Bible is in the book of Proverbs, where a father is instructing and advising his sons.

> "Listen, my sons, to a father's instruction; pay attention and gain understanding. I give you sound learning, so do not forsake my teaching" (Prov. 4:1–2).

> "Listen, my son, to your father's instruction and do not forsake your mother's teaching" (Prov. 1:8).

Children are instructed by their parents' example. Children are imitators of their parents, whether the behavior is negative or positive. Parents must be an example of what they want from their children. The truth being taught must be modeled and illustrated in the lives of Mom and Dad.

"As for you, if you walk before me in integrity of heart and upright-
ness, as David your father did, and do all I command and observe my
decrees and laws" (1 Kings 9:4).

He did what was right in the eyes of the LORD, just as his father
Amaziah had done (2 Chron. 26:4).

He did evil in the eyes of the LORD, because he walked in the ways of
his father and mother and in the ways of Jeroboam son of Nebat,
who caused Israel to sin (1 Kings 22:52).

A Code of Behavior

Children, obey your parents in everything, for this pleases the Lord
(Col. 3:20).

"Honor your father and your mother, so that you may live long in
the land the LORD your God is giving you" (Exod. 20:12).

Children must obey and honor their parents. Children must be
taught and know what they may and may not do. They must know what
is acceptable behavior and what is unacceptable. Husbands and wives
must work the code of behavior out together. Since the mother generally
spends more time with the children, the husband must listen to and
highly value her opinion and counsel.

Parents should settle their differences of opinion in private. Children should not be allowed to exploit the disagreement between parents
by playing one against the other. If the mother and father cannot work
out an agreement concerning child discipline, behavior expectations, or
a rule, the wife should submit to the husband as the head of the house
unless he is advocating sin or criminal child abuse.

If parents change the rules, inform the children about the change
and the reason why. I remember coming home from work to find my wife
perplexed and feeling a little guilty. Earlier that day, my oldest teenage
son brought to her attention that his younger brother had more freedom
to play and move about in the neighborhood than he did at the same age.
Neither I nor my wife had realized that we had become less protective of
our second son than our first, so the rules had changed.

I openly explained to my oldest teenage son that when he was born,
no instruction manual was given to us when we brought him home from
the hospital. Being the first child, he was our guinea pig. All we knew was
that God gave us a beautiful child, and we were determined to love and
take care of him. We didn't know how to be parents. We learned by trial

and error. I reminded my son that we always asked our children to pray for us, as parents, that God would give us wisdom. My son laughed and thought it amusing that he didn't come with an instruction manual.

Letting the children know when rules change is not done to get the children's approval, but to be fair to them and to prevent them from being confused. In my experience as a pastor and director of an urban biblical counseling center, consistency in parents' managing of their children is a major issue in the family.

Spiritual Correction

"The rod of correction imparts wisdom, but a child left to himself disgraces his mother" (Prov. 29:15).

When children have done wrong or need correction, spanking or punishment should not be our first thought. That is not how God, our Father, deals with us. The Bible should be regularly used as a training resource for part of correction. Children should learn not only what the parents' standards are but also God's standards. Parents must realize that we cannot always be with our children, especially teenagers, and teenagers must know they are under not only parental authority but also the authority of a heavenly Father who is omnipresent. Christian children must grow up with a consciousness of God's presence with them for protection and fellowship.

Letting children know that parenting is governed by the will of God and under the authority of His word will aid them in the realization that they are also being parented by God.

Rather than spanking a child, perhaps parents should give a warning, or a reminder may be sufficient. It is also important that when a child gets into trouble with his parents, he has an opportunity to express himself.

Sometimes even when the child is dead wrong and deserves the worst, mercy and grace should be a parental option. Children must grow up experiencing and understanding how our heavenly Father parents. Again, the Bible should be open for instruction in what mercy and grace are.

We must not discipline children when we are infuriated or when there is a question as to whether we are in control of our anger. Don't threaten children, saying such things as, "I'm going to break your neck." "I'm going to knock your head off." "I'm going to bust your behind." "I'm going to skin you alive." Always discipline with love.

> Fathers, do not exasperate your children; instead, bring them up in the training and instruction of the Lord (Eph. 6:4).

Don't punish children every time they tell the truth concerning something they have done wrong. Show some mercy. However, children must not think they can get away with lying to avoid discipline. To encourage a child not to lie, there should be one consequence for the offense and a different consequence for lying.

Encourage children when you know they have tried but failed. Don't discipline a child for mistakes or accidents. This means a parent must take the time to obtain all the facts relating to the incident or issue.

Taking away privileges is another method of discipling children. What is effective with one child will not be effective with another in the same family. Sending my daughter to her room would be a pleasure for her; she enjoys being alone. For my youngest son, that would be punishment; he is a people person. Parents should not punish children by preventing their participation in church activities where they serve God. Don't take away a privilege unless you mean it. For example, "You are not going to be allowed to ride your bike again for the rest of your life."

Physical Correction

> Do not withhold discipline from a child; if you punish him with the rod, he will not die. Punish him with the rod and save his soul from death (Prov. 23:13–14).

> The rod of correction imparts wisdom, but a child left to himself disgraces his mother (Prov. 29:15).

> Discipline your son, for in that there is hope; do not be a willing party to his death (Prov. 19:18).

> Folly is bound up in the heart of a child, but the rod of discipline will drive it far from him (Prov. 22:15).

In light of some of the new laws that have been passed by our lawmakers to ward off child abuse, we must be careful with our use of corporal punishment. There has been a need to enforce such laws because of the rise in child abuse. However, our lawmakers did not take into consideration a parent's loving use of corporal punishment (Prov. 13:24). Some parents have lost control of their children for fear of going to jail if they discipline them. God disciplines those He loves (Heb. 12:6–7).

> Before I was afflicted I went astray, but now I obey your word.... I know, O LORD, that your laws are righteous, and in faithfulness you have afflicted me (Ps. 119:67, 75).

The Bible speaks of the use of "the rod" in child discipline. Usually the rod was a reed taken from the river. The rod was a jointed, hollow stem of coarse grass, therefore, light in weight. It was not used for the purpose of harming children, but for training them. A parent should never hit a child in the face with their hands. Wire coat hangers, electrical cords, wire, heavy belts, sticks, or paddles should not be used as "the rod." Some parents use very light belts or wooden paint stirrers so as not to harm the child.

Parents should never reject their children after they discipline them. Children must learn that Mom and Dad reject unacceptable behavior, but love and accept them.

BEING CONSISTENT IN CHILD TRAINING AND DISCIPLINE

Two of the greatest problems in the home are lack of direction for children and the inconsistency of parents as to what they want and expect from their children. Parents should write guidelines on paper, explain them, and give each child a copy. The guidelines may vary according to the needs and age of each child.

Home Standards

God expects us to honor Him in our homes. Some of us even ask God to bless our homes. We should have standards and rules that will please God and us. For example:

1. No smoking allowed
2. No guests allowed upstairs in bedrooms
3. Children must let parents know where they are at all times

Code of Conduct

It should be made clear what is unacceptable behavior and what will be the results of such behavior. For example:

1. Willful disobedience. Result: use of rod.
2. Willful disrespect of parents. Result: use of rod.
3. Stealing. Result: use of rod.
4. Not cleaning room. Result: must clean basement.
5. Not washing dishes properly. Result: must be done over again.

Responsibilities

A responsibility list must be made for each child. For example:

1. Your room must be kept orderly during the week (beds made, clothes hung, etc.). It must be cleaned every Saturday.
2. You must take trash and garbage out every Monday evening.

Dating Rules

Examples:

1. No dates with strangers or unsaved people.
2. No sex before marriage.
3. All dates must meet parents before going out.
4. Curfew: 10:00 P.M. on weeknights and 12:00 A.M. on weekends.

School Obligations

Examples:

1. Get up early enough in the morning to get to school on time.
2. Have exemplary behavior in school.
3. Be sure to get all assignments from teachers and ask for clarification when you do not understand assignments.
4. Understand that in the classroom you are there to learn, not to play or entertain classmates.
5. Continue to improve in study skills.
6. Do all homework and assignments to the best of your ability in a timely fashion.
7. Your full-time job is to be a successful student.

Spiritual Development

Examples:

1. Sunday is the Lord's Day, so church is the highlight of the day.
2. You must spend time with God daily in prayer and Scripture reading.
3. Seek godly friendships.
4. Serve God in ministry and faithfully participate in the youth ministry.
5. Tell parents when you are having spiritual struggles or need to talk about living your faith.

GUIDANCE FOR LOVING AND DEVELOPING TEENAGERS
Pre-Adolescence and Early Adolescence

Pre-adolescence and early adolescence occur at approximately ten to fourteen years of age—marking the transition from childhood to adolescence. The following are some of the characteristics of young people during this period.

Physical Characteristics

1. Rapid and uneven physical growth, especially at ages twelve and thirteen
2. Self-consciousness about size; desire either to gain weight or lose it
3. Poor posture and tendency to be lazy
4. Voice change and inability to control it at times
5. Development of the sex glands
6. Awkwardness in movement
7. Failure to be neat, tidy, and organized
8. At earlier age, girls usually larger than boys

Mental and Emotional Characteristics

1. Fluctuating and changing moods, such as joy, sulkiness, moodiness, etc.; sometimes loss of emotional control
2. Ability to concentrate longer and a growing ability to deal with and solve complex problems
3. Acceptance of ideas only after testing and seeing proof of rightness
4. A great awareness of strengths and weaknesses
5. The desire to be an adult; feelings of superiority over younger sisters and brothers
6. Demand for justice and fair play for themselves and others
7. Participation in and acceptance by peer group (their age group) seen as *very* important
8. A great desire to belong to a group, gang, or team
9. A strong desire for companionship in peer group
10. Demand for independence
11. Tendency to be secretive
12. Some immaturity mentally or emotionally and little experience of life and adult responsibility

How You Can Help Your Teenagers Develop During This Period

1. Be loving and kind.
2. Obtain books and study the physical and emotional changes the teenagers are going through.

3. Explain and teach the teenagers about the changes that are taking place.
4. Be loving but firm in discipline or you will lose control of your teenagers.
5. Take time with your children and give guidance.
6. This period of change is a great time to lead teenagers to the Lord Jesus Christ.
7. Help them to accept themselves.
8. Educate your child about sexuality.
9. Learn as much as you can about your children's friends. Discourage bad relationships.
10. Encourage and help to build relationships that are good for your child.
11. Give recognition when your children make an effort to accomplish something.
12. Help children learn to make decisions for themselves.
13. Respect their need for privacy, but warn them that you will be checking their rooms from time to time.
14. Plan activities with them at home to which they can invite their friends.
15. Build good communication with them so they can feel free to come to you with their problems.
16. Keep before them the responsibility of living lives that are well pleasing to God.
17. Discipline for growth and obedience, not for revenge and humiliation.

Teenage Years and Early Adulthood

Teenage years and early adulthood occur at approximately fifteen to eighteen years of age and mark the transition from adolescence to adulthood.

Physical Characteristics

1. Growth slowing down, but physical changes still occurring
2. Sexually mature
3. Body movements becoming coordinated and graceful
4. Concern about having a good physical appearance

Mental and Emotional Characteristics

1. Desire for new experiences, experimentation
2. Desire for thrills and excitement, to be where the action is

3. A strong desire for independence and freedom without being ru prepared for responsibility
4. Approval of peer group more important than the approval of parents
5. Idealism and optimism; unawareness of and lack of concern for possible dangers ahead
6. Ignorance of life because of a lack of experience
7. A strong desire to be considered an adult
8. Evidence of concern about God's teachings and one's personal eternal future
9. Temptation to do wrong seen as fun and adventurous
10. Tendency to be very impulsive

How You Can Help Your Teenagers Develop During This Period

1. Give more freedom according to the teenagers' performance in handling the responsibility that goes along with the freedom.
2. Have clear rules and standards. Give more freedom according to the teenagers' obedience to you.
3. Treat them as much as possible as if they were adults.
4. Include them in family planning.
5. Respect and listen to their objections and opinions.
6. Never give up on your children. Depend on God to help you with them.
7. Give guidance, but also help them to have a sense of freedom.
8. Help them with occupational direction and preparation.
9. Give them opportunities to increase in knowledge.
10. Help them find alternatives to the "bad crowd."
11. Move to a better neighborhood if you have to.
12. Express continual love and concern for them.
13. Prepare them for the reality of competing in a white society.
14. Prepare them for marriage. Teach them everything about marriage.
15. Have them bring their friends home for supervised activities.
16. Encourage them to get involved in extracurricular activities.
17. Help plan their free time, such as after school and during vacations and holidays.
18. Help them to achieve in school, but don't hound them.
19. Be generous in your praise of them.
20. Make sure they have the *right* friends and *good* friends.
21. Lovingly and firmly discipline them when necessary.
22. Help them to be good readers.

23. Talk to them as adults.
24. Don't nag or constantly criticize them.
25. Don't constantly leave them home alone.
26. Set a time by which they must be home (a curfew).
27. Have a godly dress code, taking into consideration their views, but leaving the final decision up to you.
28. Be a Christian example.

BOOKS FOR FURTHER KNOWLEDGE AND USE IN FAMILY MINISTRY

Balswick, Judith, and Jack Balswick. *Raging Hormones: What to Do When You Suspect Your Teen May Be Sexually Active.* Grand Rapids: Zondervan, 1994.

Cook, Rosemarie S. *Parenting a Child With Special Needs.* Grand Rapids: Zondervan, 1992.

Dobson, James C. *Parenting Isn't for Cowards.* Dallas: Word, 1987.

Hale-Benson, Janice E. *Black Children: Their Roots, Culture, and Learning Styles.* Baltimore: Johns Hopkins, 1986.

Hutchinson, Earl Ofari. *Black Fatherhood.* Inglewood: Impac, 1992.

Johnson, Greg, and Mike Yorkey. *Daddy's Home: A Practical Guide for Maximizing the Most Important Hours of Your Day.* Wheaton: Tyndale, 1992.

Johnston, Jerry. *Inspire Your Kids to Greatness.* Grand Rapids: Zondervan, 1993.

Lewis, Paul. *The Five Key Habits for Smart Dads.* Grand Rapids: Zondervan, 1994.

Lynn, David. *Parent Ministry Talksheets: Creative Discussions to Get Parents and Teens Talking About Issues That Concern Them Most.* Grand Rapids: Zondervan, 1992.

Meier, Paul D., Donald E. Ratcliff, and Fredrick L. Rowe. *Child-Rearing and Personality Development.* Grand Rapids: Baker, 1993.

Stephenson, Lynda. *Give Us a Child.* Grand Rapids: Zondervan, 1992.

Strom, Kay Marshall, and Douglas R. Donnelly. *The Complete Adoption Handbook.* Grand Rapids: Zondervan, 1992.

White, Joe. *Faith Training: Raising Kids Who Love the Lord.* Colorado Springs: Focus on the Family, 1994.

CONCLUSION

In establishing or improving our ministry to families and making the church a family training center, we will lead the way in stopping the downward spiral of the family. I have learned from history that it does not take a lot of people to make an impact, but one person, or a few people with made-up minds, can bring about change. We need more pastors and churches that will step up and say, "We will lead," "We will try to make an impact on family life," "We will reach out and evangelize lost families who do not know Christ," "We will bring them into the family of God, to be loved and trained in the things of God."

No pastor or church can solve all family problems. No pastor or church can even understand the complexity of some negative traits in some families. Some families and single people in your own church to whom you offer help will not accept it. Nevertheless, the majority of people will not only accept help but will be grateful enough to join in the work of saving and building other families to the glory of God.

I believe that those of us who take up this challenge can collectively change the destructive trends of families—even nationally—by our effort to make an impact on family life.

RESOURCES FOR FAMILY MINISTRY

Appendix 1

AFRICAN-AMERICANS AS RESOURCES ON FAMILY ISSUES

Dr. E. K. Bailey
Concord Missionary Baptist Church
3410 South Polk Street
Dallas, TX 75224
(214) 372–4543
Biblical Role of Husbands and Wives

Rev. Sidney and Carolyn Beal
Director of Counseling
Concord Missionary Baptist Church
3410 South Polk Street
Dallas, TX 75224
(214) 372–4543
Couples' Workshops

Rev. Richard and Jane Berry
Southwest Christian Fellowship
P.O. Box 42229
Atlanta, GA 30311
(404) 753–4313
Marriage

Rev. Dr. Michael E. Haynes
Twelfth Baptist Church
160 Warren Street
Boston, MA 02119
(617) 442–7854
Education

Dr. Lee June
Office of the Provost
Michigan State University
432 Administration Building
East Lansing, MI 48824
(517) 432–1001
Marriage Relationships

Mrs. Shirley June
412 Strathmore Road
Lansing, MI 48910
(517) 372–2821
Parenting

Mike Lyles, M.D.
Psychiatrist, Atlanta Counseling
    Center
4574 Kettering Drive
Roswell, GA 30075
(404) 396–0232
Family Counseling

George McKinney, Ph.D., Bishop
Church of God in Christ
5848 Arboles
San Diego, CA 92120
(619) 262–2671
Marriage and Families

Derek McNeil, Ph.D. Candidate
Northwestern University
6121 Mozart
Chicago, IL 60659
(312) 764-1777
Marriage and Family

Rev. Alonzo Medley
F.R.E.E. (Forgiveness, Restoration,
    Embrace and Establish) Ministry
655 N. 16th Street
Philadelphia, PA 19130
(215) 763-1473
Drug Addiction

Anthony Moore
1100 Countyline
Building 13, Apartment 8
Kansas City, KS 66103
(913) 831-9315
Children and Education

Carolyn Parks, Ph.D., Professor
University of North Carolina,
    Chapel Hill
4818 Crockett Court
Raleigh, NC 27606
(919) 966-0246
Single Women, Mental Health

Allen Sheffield, B.A., Manager
Coopers & Lybrand Accounting
400 Renaissance Center
Detroit, MI 48243
(313) 446-7457
Men

Rev. Timothy Winters
Christian Growth Ministry
2161 Helix Street
Spring Valley, CA 91977
(619) 469-6355
Debt-Free Seminars

Rev. LeRoy Yates
Circle Y Ranch
2329 S. Kenneth Avenue
Chicago, IL 60643
(312) 762-5708
(312) 881-4700
Marriage and Women's Issues

Mrs. Beverly Yates
Chicagoland Christian Women's
    Conference
2329 S. Kenneth Avenue
Chicago, IL 60643
(312) 762-5708
(312) 881-4700
Marriage and Women's Issues

(Please call us at 1-800-5511-CRD if you would like to add someone to this list.)

Appendix 2

MINISTRIES AND ORGANIZATIONS AS RESOURCES FOR AFRICAN-AMERICAN FAMILIES

Dr. Hank Allen, Professor
University of Rochester
21 Serville Drive
Rochester, NY 14617
(716) 266–5901
Marriage and Family

Clifford and Audree Ashe
Victorious Christian Women
P.O. Box 90051
Harrisburg, PA 17109
(717) 541–8785
*Women's Ministry and Couples'
Retreat*

Gerald Austin, Director
Center for Urban Mission
P.O. Box 2482
Birmingham, AL 35201
(205) 252–8284
Children and Youth

Dr. Lloyd C. Blue
Church Growth Unlimited, Inc.
P.O. Box 188
Mendenhall, MS 39114
(601) 847–4394
Marriage Workshops

Dr. Donald Burwell, Director
Fathers Education Network, Inc.
1435 Brainard
Detroit, MI 48208
(313) 831–5838
Fathers and Men

Alton Chapman, Director
Inner City Ministries
P.O. Box 6265
Chattanooga, TN 37401
(615) 698–3178
Youth

Haman Cross, Jr.
Spoken Word Ministries
14161 Vaughn
Detroit, MI 48223
(313) 538–1180
*Sexuality Seminars, Singles'
Workshops, and Youth*

Robin Dickson, Staff
Christian Family Outreach
19200 Roseland #408
Euclid, OH 44117
(216) 623–8787 ext. 5103
Women

Dr. Tony Evans, President
Urban Alternative
1808 West Camp Wisdom Road
Dallas, TX 75232
(214) 943–3868
Marriage Enrichment

Sidney Flores, Staff
Youth & Parents Together
737 N. 17th Street
Philadelphia, PA 19123
(215) 236–7181
Children and Families

Melvin Holley, President
United Men's Conference
3910 Bayview Drive
Lansing, MI 48911
(517) 882–1293
Men

Verna Holley, President
United Women's Conference
3910 Bayview Drive
Lansing, MI 48911
(517) 882–1293
Women

Russell Knight, B.A., President
Chicago Urban Reconciliation
  Enterprise
8430 Escanaba
Chicago, IL 60617
(312) 374–4330
Youth

Millicent Lindo, M.S.W.
Executive Director
Westside Wholistic Family Services
4909 W. Division
Chicago, IL 60651
(312) 921–8777
Family Counseling

Dr. Crawford Loritts
Legacy
4651 Flat Shoals Road, Suite 1A
Union City, GA 30291
(404) 969–7278
Family Seminars

Michael McReynolds, B.A.
Executive Director
The Builders Group
102 Walnut Street
Chattanooga, TN 37403
(615) 265–9564
Men

Matthew Parker, President
Institute for Black Family
Development
16776 Southfield Road
Detroit, MI 48235
(810) 545–7776
Family Ministry Resources

Marion Spellman, President
Peniel Ministries
P.O. Box 250
Johnstown, PA 15907
(814) 536–2111
Substance Abuse Families

Sheila Staley, Executive Director
Resources for Better Families
4701 Lancaster Avenue
Philadelphia, PA 19131
(215) 877–6705
Family Ministry

Dr. Clarence Walker
Clarence Walker Ministries
Christian African-American Therapy
2471 N. 54th Street, Suite 231
Philadelphia, PA 19131
(215) 878–1258
Marriage Workshops and Seminars

Carolyn B. Wallace, Executive
  Director
International Youth Organization
703 South 12th Street
Newark, NJ 07103
(201) 621–1100
Youth

Appendix 3

OTHER RESOURCES

American Alliance for Health,
Physical Education, Recreation
and Dance
1900 Associate Drive
Reston, VA 22091
(703) 476-3400
Contact: Millie Puceio, Manager

American Association for Marriage
and Family Therapy
1100 17th Street NW, 10th Floor
Washington, DC 20036
(202) 452-0109
*Contact: Mark Gunsberg, Ph.D.,
Executive Director*

American Family Communiversity
5242 W. North Avenue
Chicago, IL 60639
(312) 637-3037
Contact: Les Kohut, Ed. and President

American Home Economics
Association
1555 King Street
Alexandria, VA 22314
(703) 704-4600
*Contact: Dr. Karl G. Weddler,
Interim Executive Director*

American Social Health Association
P.O. Box 13827
Research Triangle Park, NC 27709
(919) 361-8400
*Contact: Margaret Webb, Executive
Officer*

American Sociological Association
1722 N Street NW
Washington, DC 20036
(202) 833-3410
*Contact: William D'Antonio,
Executive Director*

Association for Childhood Education
International
Georgia Avenue, Suite 312
Wheaton, MD 20902
(301) 942-2443
*Contact: Gerald Odland, Executive
Director*

Child Reach
155 Plan Way, Dept. L024
Warwick, RI 02886
(401) 738-5600
Contact: Kenneth Phillips, President

Christian Family Movement
6th and Kellogg, Room 202
P.O. Box 272
Ames, IA 50016
(515) 232-7432
*Contact: Kay Aitchison, Executive
Director*

Christian Life Commission of the
Southern Baptist Convention
901 Commerce Street, Suite 550
Nashville, TN 37203
(615) 244-2495
*Contact: Richard Land, Executive
Director*

Consumers Union of United States
256 Washington Street
Mount Vernon, NY 10553
(914) 667–9400
Contact: Rhonda Karpotkin,
Executive Director

Family Service of America
11700 West Lake Park Drive
Milwaukee, WI 53224
(414) 359–1040
Contact: Geneva B. Johnson,
CEO and President

Maternity Center Association
48 E. 92nd Street
New York, NY 10128
(212) 369–7300
Contact: Ruth Lubric, General
Director

Mental Health Film Board
One Moose Hill Road
Guilford, CT 06437
(203) 453–3224
Contact: Alberta Jacoby, Executive
Director

Mental Health Material Center
P.O. Box 304
Bronxville, NY 10708
(914) 337–6596
Contact: Alex Sarejan, President

National Association of Public Child
Welfare Administration
810 First Street NE, Suite 500
Washington, DC 20002
(202) 682–0100
Contact: David Shaw, Program
Manager

National Congress of Parents and
Teachers
700 N. Rush Street
Chicago, IL 60611
(312) 787–0977
Contact: Pat Henry, President

National Council on Family Relation
3989 Central Avenue NE, Suite 550
Minneapolis, MN 55421
(612) 781–9331

National Mental Health Association
1021 Prince Street
Alexandria, VA 22314–2971
(703) 684–7722
Contact: John Horner, President

North America Council on Adoptable
Children
1821 University Avenue, Suite N–498
St. Paul, MN 55104
(612) 644–3036
Contact: Joe Kroll, Executive
Director

Parents Without Partners, Inc.
8807 Colesville Road
Silver Spring, MD 20910
(301) 588–9354

NOTES

CHAPTER 1: THE NEED OF SALVATION IN THE FAMILY
[1]Charles M. Sell, *Family Ministry*, 2d ed. (Grand Rapids: Zondervan, 1995), 75.

CHAPTER 4: HOW TO DEVELOP FAMILY MINISTRY IN THE CHURCH
[1]Jim Larson, *A Church Guide for Strengthening Families* (Minneapolis: Augsburg, 1984).
[2]Royce Money, *Ministering to Families: A Positive Plan of Action* (Wheaton: Victor, 1987).

CHAPTER 5: HOW TO EVANGELIZE FAMILIES
[1]Willie Richardson, *You Have Been Crowned With Glory and Honor* (Philadelphia: Christian Research & Development, 1994).

CHAPTER 10: TRAINING FAMILIES TO BE GOOD STEWARDS
[1]Larry Burkett, *Your Finances in Changing Times*, rev. ed. (Chicago: Moody, 1993), 64.

CHAPTER 15: TRAINING MARRIED COUPLES IN COMMUNICATION AND UNDERSTANDING
[1]H. Norman Wright, *Communication: Key to Your Marriage* (Glendale: Regal, 1974).
[2]*LaHaye Temperament Analysis*, Family Life Seminars, P.O. Box 2700, Washington, DC 20013–2700.